This concise and informative guide to the American war for independence begins with the origins of the break between the colonies and England, provides a profile of the colonists and the Continental Congress, and then follows the conduct of the war in all theaters.

There is a bird's-eye view of the principal military operations of the war, a chronological compendium of events in capsule form, a discussion of the major forces, a list of important personalities, and an extensive bibliography.

The result is a handy and convenient reference for everyone who has either a passing or a major interest in the Revolution. It is also a chart for further study of the complex ramifications—military, political and ethnic —of the most important single event of the eighteenth century.

R. ERNEST and TREVOR N. DUPUY are the authors of *The Encyclopedia of Military History,* which has been through three editions, *Compact History of the Civil War; Brave Men and Great Captains; Military Heritage of America* and, individually, more than two dozen other volumes.

An Outline History of the American Revolution

PEOPLE AND EVENTS OF THE AMERICAN REVOLUTION
(with Gay M. Hammerman)
THE BATTLE OF AUSTERLITZ
REVOLUTIONARY WAR LAND BATTLES
(with Gay M. Hammerman)
REVOLUTIONARY WAR NAVAL BATTLES
(with Grace P. Hayes)
MODERN LIBRARIES FOR MODERN COLLEGES
COLLEGE LIBRARIES IN FERMENT
MILITARY LIVES (12 volumes)
MILITARY HISTORY OF THE CHINESE CIVIL WAR
MILITARY HISTORY OF WORLD WAR I
MILITARY HISTORY OF WORLD WAR II
HOLIDAYS
CIVIL WAR NAVAL ACTIONS
CIVIL WAR LAND BATTLES
CAMPAIGNS OF THE FRENCH REVOLUTION AND OF NAPOLEON
FAITHFUL AND TRUE

An Outline History of the

American Revolution

COLONEL R. ERNEST DUPUY
and
COLONEL TREVOR N. DUPUY

A T. N. DUPUY ASSOCIATES BOOK

HARPER & ROW, PUBLISHERS
New York, Evanston, San Francisco, London

Maps 3, 5, 12, 14, 16, and 21 are from *The Military History of Revolutionary War Naval Battles* by T. N. Dupuy (Franklin Watts, Inc., 1970), and maps 9, 11, and 17 are from *The Military History of Revolutionary War Land Battles* by T. N. Dupuy (Franklin Watts, Inc., 1970). They are reprinted here by permission of the publisher. Maps 8 and 19 were drawn by Clifton Line.

FIRST EDITION

Designed by C. Linda Dingler

Library of Congress Cataloging in Publication Data
Dupuy, Richard Ernest, 1887–
    An outline history of the American Revolution.
    "A T. N. Dupuy Associates book."
    Bibliography: p.
    Includes index.
    1. United States—History—Revolution, 1775–1783—Campaigns and battles. I. Dupuy, Trevor Nevitt, 1916–joint author. II. Title.
E230.D815   973.3'3   73-1803
ISBN 0-06-011127-5

75 76 77 78 79 10 9 8 7 6 5 4 3 2 1

Some day in the future seven young Americans—grand-children of one of the authors and great-grandchildren of the other—must stand shoulder to shoulder with millions of other citizens of their generation to sustain the nation their forebears established two hundred years ago:

> *Christopher*
> *Trevor III*
> *David*
> *Stuart*
> *Deborah Jean*
> *Noelle*
> *Ashley Grace*

To them we dedicate this compendium.

Contents

Preface, xv

PART I. THE SETTING OF THE REVOLUTION, 1
    1. Background, 3
    2. The Colonists, 6
    3. The Continental Congress, 10

PART II. NARRATIVE SUMMARY OF THE WAR ON LAND AND SEA, 17
    4. Lexington and Concord, 19
    5. Bunker's Hill, 22
    6. The Siege of Boston, 25
    7. The Invasion of Canada, 29
    8. The Beginnings of the American Navy, 34
    9. The Bahamas Expedition, 36
   10. Sullivan's Island, 38
   11. The *Turtle* vs. Lord Howe, 42
   12. Long Island, 45
   13. Kips Bay and Harlem Heights, 52
   14. Valcour Island, 56
   15. Cruise of the *Reprisal,* 59
   16. White Plains, 61
   17. Fort Washington, 65
   18. Trenton, 69
   19. Princeton, 73

20.   The British Plans for 1777, 77
21.   Ticonderoga, 80
22.   Hubbardton, 83
23.   Oriskany and Fort Stanwix, 84
24.   Bennington, 89
25.   Brandywine, 92
26.   Freeman's Farm (First Saratoga), 97
27.   Philadelphia and Germantown, 102
28.   Bemis Heights (Second Saratoga), 107
29.   Cruise of the *Ranger,* 111
30.   Valley Forge and von Steuben, 117
31.   Monmouth Courthouse, 123
32.   Stalemate at Newport, 129
33.   George Rogers Clark and the West, 132
34.   Stony Point, 136
35.   Fiasco at Penobscot, 139
36.   Cruise of the *Bonhomme Richard,* 141
37.   Savannah, 147
38.   Charleston, 150
39.   Camden, 154
40.   The Treason of Benedict Arnold, 159
41.   King's Mountain, 162
42. The Cowpens, 164
43.   Guilford Courthouse, 169
44.   Preliminaries in Virginia, 175
45.   Battle of the Capes, 179
46.   Yorktown, 182

PART III. THE PARTICIPANTS, 187
47.   The Patriot Forces, 189
48.   The Foreign Volunteers, 197
49.   The British Army in North America, 199
50.   Britain's German Mercenaries, 205
51.   The Tories, 211
52.   The French Army in North America, 215
53.   The Navies, 218
54.   Women Camp Followers, 223

PART IV. THE REVOLUTION AS WORLD WAR, 231

PART V. SELECTED BIOGRAPHIES, 243

PART VI. CHRONOLOGY OF THE AMERICAN REVOLUTION, 297

Bibliography, 321

Index, 325

Maps

1.   The Revolutionary War, 18
2.   Bunker's Hill, 23
3.   Sullivan's Island, 39
4.   Long Island, 46
5.   Valcour Island, 57
6.   Trenton, 70
7.   Campaigns of 1777, 79
8.   Bennington, 88
9.   Brandywine, 93
10.   Saratoga, 98
11.   Germantown, 103
12.   *Ranger* and *Bonhomme Richard,* 112
13.   Monmouth, 124
14.   Newport, 130
15.   Stony Point, 137
16.   Flamborough Head, 146
17.   Camden, 155
18.   The Cowpens, 165
19.   Guilford Courthouse, 170
20.   Washington to Yorktown, 177
21.   Chesapeake Bay, 180
22.   Yorktown, 183

Preface

The objective of this book is to provide for both buff and serious student a *vade mecum* of the War of the American Revolution, which brought the United States into the world two hundred years ago.

The work presents a bird's-eye view of the principal military operations of the war. It includes in capsule form a chronological compendium of events, discusses the major activities and characteristics of the participating forces, lists important personalities, and provides a selected bibliography.

In other words, it is a handy and convenient reference for everyone who has either a passing or a major interest in the Revolution. It is also a chart for further study of the complex ramifications—military, political, and ethnic—of the most important single event of the eighteenth century.

R. ERNEST DUPUY

Dunn Loring, Va.   TREVOR N. DUPUY

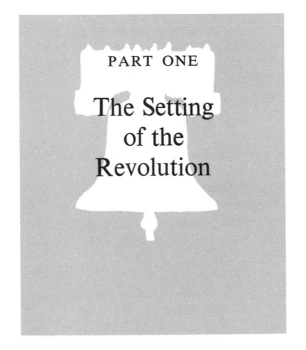

PART ONE

The Setting
of the
Revolution

1

Background

The Seven Years' War—known in British North America as the French and Indian War—settled forever a century-long struggle between England and France for colonial supremacy in North America. The British victory in 1763 resulted in complete French expulsion from the North American continent; France retained only two insignificant islets off the coast of Nova Scotia and more valuable island possessions in the Caribbean.

It had been a long and costly war. Although the thirteen English colonies stretching along the Atlantic Ocean littoral had provided most of the army manpower for that part of the conflict fought in North America, numerous units of the British Regular Army had been sent from England, there had been a major commitment of forces by the Royal Navy, and the Royal Exchequer had footed all of the bills. In a postwar assessment, the British government found that the largely self-governing colonies had emerged from the war in better economic condition than the mother country. It seemed only right to the British Cabinet, to Parliament, and to young King George III that the colonists should pay for their own administration and security; their defense should no longer be a burden upon the British taxpayer.

The colonists, on the other hand, were people who had left England, or whose fathers had left England, because they sought greater freedom in the New World. They were as jealous of that freedom as they were proud of their British heritage. As free Britons, they were determined that they would not pay for, or accept, any obligations imposed upon them willy-nilly by a legislature three thousand miles away in which they had no vote. "Taxation without representation is tyranny," they said.

Colonial indignation mounted in the years after 1763, as the British Parliament's Sugar Act followed the Molasses Act, and the Townshend Acts of 1767 followed the Stamp Act of 1765. To avoid payment of taxes on many goods covered by the Townshend Acts, a great number of colonists refused to buy products made in England, and began to smuggle goods in from other countries. Local colonial governments sent appeals and petitions to the king and to Parliament; local groups of citizens, as well as congresses and assemblies representing several colonies, met to assert their rights as British subjects.

The British government, however, was equally determined that the laws should be enforced; Parliament was convinced that the colonists were trying to avoid financial responsibility by placing the burdens of colonial administration and security upon the people of England.

The people of Massachusetts took the lead in colonial opposition to the increasingly harsh enforcement measures. British troops were sent to Boston in 1768, leading to disorders that culminated in the so-called Boston Massacre in 1770. Violence and repression stimulated opposition throughout the colonies. In 1772, under the leadership of Samuel Adams of Massachusetts, local "Committees of Correspondence" were secretly formed, to begin planning for the use of force if necessary to protect their rights as Englishmen. Similar committees were soon formed in other colonies.

There was an outcry in all the colonies in 1773 when it was learned that Parliament had legislated a special heavy colonial duty on tea, although no such tax was being levied in England. The outcry became outrage when, soon afterward, large cargoes of heavily taxed tea arrived in colonial ports. Massachusetts again took the lead in active response; on December 16, 1773, citizens of Boston, dressed as Indians, boarded the three tea ships at the docks, and dumped their cargoes in the harbor—an event that came to be known as the "Boston Tea Party."

It was the turn of the British government to be outraged. Parliament responded with the "Coercive" or "Intolerable" Acts, closing the port of Boston, sending more troops to be garrisoned in the city to control its inhabitants, and repealing many of the people's traditional and treasured rights as British subjects. These acts went into effect on June 1, 1774.

Although the people of Boston were helpless under the iron control of the British Crown, things began to hum elsewhere in Massachusetts, and in other colonies as well. During August and September 1774, a convention of Massachusetts citizens met at Suffolk, and adopted a series of "Resolves" prepared by Dr. Joseph Warren, denouncing the Coercive Acts and calling for economic action and military preparation to resist them. Massachusetts leaders urged the other colonies to support the Suffolk Resolves, and to defend their liberty by force if necessary. Committees of Safety were soon established, prepared to take over the functions of government in the event of rebellion.

Colonists who plunged ever more actively into preparations to preserve their liberty by force if necessary called themselves "Patriots"; they were opposed by the "Loyalists," those who were horrified by the thought of violence or rebellion against the Crown. There was a more or less even division between Patriots and Loyalists throughout the thirteen colonies, save in Massachusetts, where the Patriots predominated and controlled most of the local governments.

Representatives of the colonies met at Philadelphia in September and October of 1774 to coordinate action in response to British repression. This First Continental Congress prepared a petition asking King George to recognize colonial rights. The radical Patriots of Massachusetts, meanwhile, were organizing themselves for more direct action. They took control of the colony's thirty militia regiments; one-fourth of the men of each regiment were appointed "minutemen," to be prepared to take up their arms to fight at a minute's notice. In open defiance of British authority, these militiamen trained and drilled on their village greens.

Commanding the British garrison in Boston was General

Thomas Gage, who was both the Royal Governor of Massachusetts and the overall commander of all British forces in the American colonies. Grimly he kept track of the activities going on throughout Massachusetts. He had reliable informants among the leaders of the colonial resistance movement—secret Loyalists pretending to be Patriots. He knew how much ammunition the colonists had collected; and he could draw maps of the places in the town of Concord where most of their arms and supplies were hidden. Similarly, the rebellious colonists had many willing agents of their own among the citizens of Boston, who constantly reported the movements of General Gage's highly visible red-coated soldiers.

Thus, in April 1775, Boston was a city dead to trade and commerce, cut off from the outside world by the closing of its port. Otherwise, however, it was very much alive; alive with rumor, watchful eyes, and concealed activity.

2

The Colonists

By 1770 the predominantly Anglo-Saxon population of the thirteen colonies by dint of necessity, ingenuity, and application had hewed out of the North American wilderness a viable—if amorphous—entity. It was an argumentative and competitive society—really thirteen separate societies—comprising some 2.4 million people, of whom 750,000 were black (most of them slaves). There were but two binders providing a sense of community to this fragmented society: the British Constitution, with its jealously cherished rights guaranteed to free Englishmen, and a common language. Considering themselves free Englishmen—regardless of origin—the colonists felt no urge for American independence. There was, however, one serious issue on which the colonists were almost unanimously aligned in opposition to the mother country. Since they had no representation in the British Parliament they strongly felt that only their own elected colonial assemblies had the right to tax them. And that, of course, was what in the end would cause all the trouble.

Internally, the colonists constituted a population in ferment; thirteen wrangling neighbors who had brought over with them all their differing Old World customs and prejudices to interact with new problems. Pennsylvania and Connecticut were coming to blows in the Yankee-Pennamite War for the possession of the Wyoming Valley. Up north in the New Hampshire Grants guerrilla warfare was being waged between New Yorkers and independent Vermonters who refused to be part of New York. Along the Hudson Valley the wealthy patroons were grinding their tenant farmers in a veritable serfdom. The roistering frontiersmen of the western fringe, mostly Scotch-Irish, cared little for any of their eastern neighbors.

New Englanders, steeped in rigid Protestant puritanism, viewed Marylanders and Virginians with some suspicion; there was too much frivolity and Papist taint down there. Southerners, in turn, already jelling in a different economic and social mold, scorned northern Yankees with their democratic egalitarianism and penny-pinching commercialism.

Minorities who also had sought freedom in North America— Germans (including many Rhinelanders from the Palatinate), Hollanders, French Huguenots, Swedes, and a scattering from most other European states—were further dilutants of homogeneity. Of these, the Pennsylvania Dutch and the Hollanders in the Hudson Valley would both stamp characteristic motifs upon the mixed pattern.

Each in its own way, the colonies were prospering; agriculture and industry throve. Innumerable mills provided water power to grind the corn and wheat, to saw the timber and run the ironworks already producing one-seventh of the world's pig- and bar-iron. A lusty shipbuilding industry was turning out vessels large and small. American-built ships, owned and manned by Americans, were plying the trade routes of the world. In 1747–1749 a Boston yard built two frigates for the British Admiralty—the *Boston* (24) and the *America* (44)—while the lofty American forests had long been producing a major proportion of the masts and spars of the Royal Navy. New England fishing fleets combed the Grand Banks, and New England whalers roamed the farthest seas.

Coastwise trade was prospering, too, for the lack of inland roads necessitated the shuttling of mercantile and passenger traffic between the seaports that dotted the Atlantic coast. Five of these had become major cities: Philadelphia (the largest), Boston, New York, Charleston, South Carolina, and Hampton, Virginia. Out of Philadelphia alone, in 1770, 769 vessels cleared, carrying 47,292 tons of cargo. Approximately one-quarter of this trade was coastwise within the colonies. Inbound to Philadelphia, that year, came 750 ships importing a cargo tonnage of 47,489, mostly luxuries.*

Principal colonial exports were iron, coal, tobacco, indigo, corn and wheat, rice, timber, dried fish, and furs (beaver skin was essential for the universally worn beaver hat). The cotton trade was not yet a major item (Eli Whitney, who invented the cotton gin, was only five years old in 1770).

And then there was the slave trade, which followed an odd triangular pattern. Fish and lumber from the colonies went to the West Indies, there to be exchanged for sugar and molasses brought back to New England distilleries. Their product, rum, traveled then to the west coast of Africa, to be bartered for the unfortunate black captives who would be sold in American ports to slavery. In principle, puritanical New Englanders frowned on this abominable trade, but many a Down East Yankee shipping fortune was founded on the profits from "Black Ivory."

Whether in the stately mansions of city aristocrats, or the neat row houses of their merchant neighbors, the plantation houses of

* Figures abstracted from the Department of Commerce's *Historical Statistics of the United States*, GPO, Washington, D.C., 1961.

the rural south, the log cabins of the frontier, or the frightful hovels of urban and rural poor, life's basic needs followed similar patterns. Chimneys, with huge fireplaces, provided the heat for cooking as well as warmth in the immediate vicinity of the roaring flames in winter, although the Franklin stove, invented by Ben Franklin in 1735, was becoming popular. Most of the houses, rich and poor, boasted a spinning wheel. And alike in mansion, farmhouse, and hovel, sanitation was primitive. Of indoor plumbing there was none; the "necessity" (privy) was outdoors, most vexing in winter and foul weather. As for baths, the portable tin tub, filled with hot water carried from the fireplace, was awkward at best, something to be avoided as much as possible. A trip to one of the many mineral baths or spas that had sprung up would provide a comfortable soaking, but that was only for those who could afford it. So, to put it bluntly, the average American stank (as did the average Briton and European).

An interesting product of winter chill and abominable roads was the New England practice of bundling. In the sparsely settled rural districts, the swain who went acourting and was caught by bad weather spent the night tucked in, fully clothed, beside his sweetie in one bed (thoughtful parents usually separated them by a long board, to prevent accidents). The practice later caused some astonishment and much comment among the young officers of Burgoyne's "Convention Army" during its melancholy two-year trek following the surrender at Saratoga.

The level of education in the colonies was not high, although a well-read and highly intelligent elite flourished. Of the common man little more was expected than the ability to count, to read the Bible, and to make his mark when formal signature was needed. But the seed of higher education was already bearing fruit. Harvard (founded in 1636), Yale, and Dartmouth colleges were functioning in New England; King's College (later Columbia) in New York; and the College of New Jersey at Princeton, while Virginia's William and Mary had been in existence since 1693. And, despite the fact that higher education for women was in general frowned upon, the Moravian Seminary at Bethlehem,

Pennsylvania, had opened its doors in 1740, attracting young ladies of quality from far and wide. Be it noted that the urge for higher education was rooted deep in religion. All the colonial colleges were denominational.

Medical science was still in its infancy; old family nostrums and even witchcraft vied with the physician to cure the sick. The study of natural philosophy had taken root; its high priest, Benjamin Franklin, was recognized both in America and abroad as one of the great scientists of the age. And, of course, American navigators, like their foreign compeers, had long known the rudiments of astronomy.

For all of the sharp contrasts between the regions and among the different social classes, the distinctions were less extreme than those that existed in Britain or on the continent of Europe. And, except for the unfortunate blacks in slavery, even the least advantaged individuals in the colonies could hope to enjoy opportunities that had been denied them and their parents in the "Old Country." They were very much aware that Colonial America was a land of promise, and that, despite human frustrations, that promise was being fulfilled.

3

The Continental Congress

The government of the rebellious colonies was a creature of chance and expediency, conceived in protest. As the taxation demands of George III and his government became ever more onerous and annoying to colonists who considered that their rights as Englishmen were being abridged, progressive Massachusetts leaders urged their counterparts in the other twelve colonies to join them in collective dissent. The result was an informal intercolonial association of Committees of Correspondence, pooling information, exchanging ideas, and coordinating protest.

It was Samuel Adams of Massachusetts who, at a Boston town meeting on November 2, 1772, recommended the establishment of local Committees of Correspondence. According to Royal Governor Thomas Hutchinson, by early 1773 there were more than eighty such committees in Massachusetts alone. Virginia leaders, in March 1773, suggested the establishment of central Committees of Correspondence for each of the thirteen colonies, which soon linked the entire Atlantic Coast region. This was a development that would later* be dubbed by the Tory *Massachusetts Guardian* as "the foulest, subtilist and most venemous serpent ever issued from the egg of sedition."

No attempt was made to conceal this activity. Since 1735, when editor Peter Zenger was acquitted of sedition charges made because he had dared criticize official actions, the colonies had enjoyed freedom of press, assembly, and speech. So the bulletins of the Committees of Correspondence received wide circulation and aroused the tumult and shouting of public opinion.

It must also be remembered that the colonies, with a long record of self-government behind them, had no dearth of politicians, many of them farsighted men: Tories, Whigs, and a hard core of radical firebrands, particularly in Massachusetts. Sam Adams of Boston was a rabble-rouser *par excellence*. But radicals flourished in other areas: Alexander McDougall in New York, Charles Thomson in Philadelphia, Patrick Henry in Williamsburg, Virginia, Christopher Gadsden and the Rutledge brothers in Charleston, South Carolina. Their continued spurring would be instrumental in changing the tune of loyal complaint into a demand for freedom.

The storm of popular colonial protest against the English government's 1774 "Intolerable Acts," punishing Boston for its "Tea Party" in December 1773, led the Committees of Corre-

* January 2, 1775.

spondence to arrange for an intercolonial assembly or congress, to consider a coordinated protest. This first Continental Congress—fifty-six delegates from twelve colonies (Georgia was missing)—met in Carpenters' Hall, Philadelphia, on September 5, 1774, selected Peyton Randolph from Virginia as its president, and agreed that one vote would be alloted to the group of delegates from each colony. This Congress voiced the rights of the colonies, decried all the repressive measures enacted by the Crown since 1763, laid down retaliatory economic sanctions, and then prepared and dispatched addresses of grievance to King George and to the peoples of both America and Britain. On October 26 it adjourned after agreeing to reconvene the following May if the wrongs had not yet been righted.

The possibility of an armed uprising against royal tyranny was discussed privately among many delegates to the Continental Congress. In Massachusetts, with Boston under the heel of British repression, such talk was becoming common. Farsighted leaders, however, were concerned lest such an uprising might lead to anarchy by destroying existing governmental authority. The result was the quiet establishment of a Provincial Congress in Massachusetts, which virtually assumed authority for all of the colony outside garrisoned Boston. When not in session, the Provincial Congress turned over its authority to a Committee of Safety, with membership almost identical to that of the earlier Committee of Correspondence.

On May 10, 1775, three weeks after the fighting at Lexington and Concord, the colonial delegates reconvened in the Philadelphia State House (Independence Hall) as the Second Continental Congress—still minus Georgia representation. Recognizing the fact of armed rebellion in Massachusetts, it began to function as a representative government. It drew up resolutions to put the colonies in a state of military readiness, to raise a contingent of riflemen, and to support the New Englanders then penning British troops in Boston; it drafted a plan for a Continental Army and appealed to Canada to join the revolt. John Hancock had succeeded Randolph as president of the Congress on May 24. On

June 15 George Washington of Virginia was elected general and commander-in-chief of the Continental Army. Four major generals—Artemas Ward, Charles Lee, Philip Schuyler, and Israel Putnam—and eight brigadier generals—Seth Pomeroy, William Heath, John Thomas, David Wooster, Joseph Spencer, John Sullivan, Richard Montgomery, and Nathanael Greene—were appointed. Horatio Gates was elected adjutant general to administer the armed forces. And then this penniless assemblage, dependent entirely on the goodwill of the thirteen uncertain and tentative colonial governments, voted to issue bills of credit (backed by promises alone)—amounting to $2,000,000—to finance military operations.

On July 5 the delegates—signing only as individuals and not as members of the Congress—adopted the so-called Olive Branch Petition, drafted by conservative John Dickinson, of Pennsylvania, and hand-carried to London. This petition, affirming American attachment to King George, urged him to cease further military action until reconciliation could be effected. It reached London on August 14. It was indeed an olive branch, but headstrong George refused to see the carrier, Richard Penn, or receive his petition. Meanwhile, Lord North's British plan for reconciliation—actually a reiteration of former grudging offers—was directed to individual colonies, thereby ignoring the Continental Congress, which rejected it on July 31, 1775.

On July 18 the Congress urged those colonies that had not already done so to establish Committees of Safety, like that which was governing in Massachusetts. Following that example, in most colonies the existing Committees of Correspondence became Committees of Safety, assuring an orderly transition from royal to colonial government.

After establishing a post-office department, with Benjamin Franklin at its head, and delegating commissioners to treat for peace with the Indians, the Congress adjourned for a brief recess on August 2. When it reconvened on September 12, 1775, a delegation from Georgia was in attendance, completing the representation of all thirteen colonies. Despite King George's rejection of the

Olive Branch Petition, the Congress made one last effort at reconciliation, reiterating its allegiance to the Crown, but not to Parliament.

Congress authorized a navy, then established a foreign ministry or state department in embryo: the Committee of Secret Correspondence, whose duties included the inauguration of treaties with European nations and negotiating loans from abroad to finance the war. Silas Deane, Benjamin Franklin, and Arthur Lee were appointed commissioners and soon left for Europe to take up these tasks. First, however, came the irrevocable step: the Declaration of Independence, voted July 2, 1776, and proclaimed two days later.

From that time until the conclusion of the War of the Revolution the fate of the American people lay in the hands of its representative Congress, while George Washington—subservient always to civil rule—carried out its wishes. His task was not easy. Political jealousies caused friction, and the Congress—collectively and as individual delegates—meddled in the details of military matters it had ostensibly entrusted to the commander-in-chief.

On December 12, 1776, when British arms threatened Philadelphia and the delegates scurried for shelter in Baltimore, the Congress almost gave up its task, granting dictatorial powers to Washington. The Congress returned to Philadelphia in March 1777, only to take flight again in September as Howe approached the city. Again, extensive powers, authority, and responsibility were dumped in Washington's lap by the fleeing delegates. For the next several months Congress met in York, Pennsylvania, after a brief stay in Lancaster. It was at York, in November 1777, that Congress approved the Articles of Confederation, the first real welding of a United States' structure. This document was finally ratified by all the states on March 1, 1781.

Meanwhile, during that winter of discontent—1777–1778—the Conway Cabal and Gates's jealous attempt to supplant Washington caused more friction, while the commander-in-chief at Valley Forge struggled successfully to preserve an army. Although Washington's firmness and forthrightness embarrassed and frustrated those delegates who connived secretly with Conway and Gates, congressional meddling would continue until Gates failed dismally in the South in 1780.

The Congress again returned to Philadelphia after the British withdrawal in the spring of 1778, in time to ratify the treaty of alliance with France on May 4. Thereafter it remained there in almost continuous session, confronting a wide range of domestic and foreign problems. It was replaced in May 1781 by the Congress of Confederation—which was virtually a continuation of the Continental Congress. (This, in turn, was succeeded by the present Congress of the United States on the adoption of the Constitution in 1789.) At one time or another 342 men served in the Continental Congress. Fifty-six others, although elected, never served. Its successive presidents numbered fourteen; of these two, Peyton Randolph (Virginia) and John Hancock (Massachusetts), held the office twice.

The defects of the Continental Congress were many and have sometimes tended to obscure its real accomplishments and fundamental importance. Although George Washington led American arms to victory, and his personality and genius were essential ingredients in achieving that victory, the Congress had picked him for the job, and without its support, wavering though it might have been at times, his contribution would have been a futile gesture. The Congress provided an essential linkage among the individualistic colonies, and from its flawed, experimental pattern was developed the representative government of free men by free men which has itself served as an ideal and a pattern for many others.

PART TWO

Narrative Summary
of the War
on Land and Sea

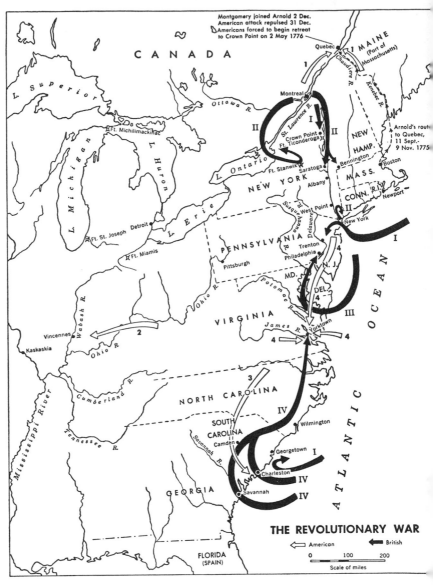

Map 1

American Offensives

(1) 1775—Invasion of Canada by Montgomery and Arnold

(2) 1779—Clark in the West

(3) 1781—Greene in the South

(4) 1781—Yorktown Campaign

British Offensives

(I) 1776—Three-pronged offensive: Lake Champlain, New York, Charleston

(II) 1777—Converging drives on Albany by Burgoyne, St. Leger, Clinton

(III) 1777—Howe's offensive to Philadelphia

(IV) 1780–1781—Invasion of South [by?] Clinton and Cornwallis

4

Lexington and Concord
April 19, 1775

General Gage, learning on April 14, 1775, that the turbulent Massachusetts radicals had collected a large quantity of military supplies at Concord, on April 18 ordered Lieutenant Colonel Francis Smith, 10th Foot, with his own regiment plus the grenadier and light infantry companies of the five regiments then in Boston, to "seize and destroy" the cache and then return "as soon as possible."

During the night of April 18–19 this elite expeditionary force, numbering in all some 750 men, assembled in secrecy and was lifted across the bay to Lechmere's Point by the assembled small boats of the British warships in the harbor.

With commendable foresight—Gage was under no illusions as to the temper and the number of his potential opponents—he also assembled a supporting force under Brigadier General Earl Hugh Percy: the 4th, 23rd and 47th Foot, and a battalion of marines from the warships; nearly two thousand men with two 6-pounder cannon. Percy was to move out six hours behind Smith, at four o'clock in the morning.

But the British garrison in Boston was in effect living in a goldfish bowl. Sharp eyes and ears had noted the abnormal bustle. By the time Smith's force began its march from Lechmere's Point, Paul Revere, William Dawes, and Dr. Samuel Prescott had spread the alarm, and the red-coated column moved in the brouhaha of an aroused countryside, clanging of church bells and the occasional boom of signal guns.

Dawn was breaking when Smith's advance guard, the light infantry, under Royal Marine Major John Pitcairn reached Lexington. Samuel Adams had fled two hours previous. On the common Captain John Parker's company of the Middlesex Militia Regiment, some seventy-odd men, stood in ragged line. Somebody—nobody will ever know who—loosed off his firelock and a British volley blazed. Disregarding Pitcairn's efforts to restrain them, the British came on with the bayonet, and the militia scattered, leaving eight of their men dead and three more wounded. Pitcairn's horse, grazed by a bullet, and one soldier wounded were the only British casualties.

The fat was in the fire now. Re-forming, the British column pushed on for Concord, four miles away, where most of the store of arms had been removed or hidden in feverish haste. Colonel Smith, fanning out part of his command protectively, set the remainder to searching for contraband, while on the heights behind the village a crowd of American militiamen gathered.

The British found little, but put what they gathered to the flames. The outraged mob looking on could stand it no longer. Captain Isaac Davis led his Acton company of the Middlesex Regiment down to the North Bridge, two fifers shrilling the "White Cockade." The outnumbered bridge guard opened fire, then recoiled. American muskets spoke, and the militia rushed the bridge. Two British soldiers had been killed; nine others, including four officers, wounded. Four Americans, including Captain Davis, were dead. The militia hesitated as Smith rushed up two companies of grenadiers to cover the fleeing bridge guard, but he made no counterattack. Instead, at noon he formed his troops in two columns and withdrew on the Lexington road.

Meanwhile the crowd of angry Americans was growing fast; men thronged all highways leading to the scene. At Meriam's Corner Smith's flank guards opened fire on a new influx of colonials, and answering fire began from behind woods, fences, and stone walls.

For sixteen long miles the British, exhausted by their long march, groped their way in a haze of powder smoke, leaving behind them a red fringe of their dead. Americans were crowding their rear and flanks. As one Englishman later put it, it seemed "as if men came down from the clouds." Ammunition was running low; British soldiers were half crazed by heat and thirst; discipline had reached its limit. They raced through Lexington to tumble into the serried ranks of Percy's relief force, deployed across the road.

Percy's cannon momentarily cleared the road behind the retreating column, and he realized that it was time to go. Herding Smith's men in front of him, he began a sullen withdrawal toward Cambridge, while fresh increments of militia—hornets in homespun—harried his way. Fearing that the Charles River bridge at Cambridge might prove to be a fatal bottleneck, Percy turned sharply to the northeast, reached Charlestown Neck by half past six and halted on the crest of Bunker's Hill. The pursuers, realizing that to brave the narrow causeway would be suicidal, halted, their fire dying away.

Gage, in Boston, the next day ordered Percy back from Charlestown. His heart was heavy. Four thousand disorganized American colonials had met some 1,800 British regulars and sent them packing. Sixty-five redcoats were dead, 173 more wounded, and 26 others were missing. Fifteen British officers, fine targets in their gold lace, white cross-belts, and shining gorgets, were casualties; one of them dead, the others wounded.

Ringing the city from Dorchester around to Chelsea, minutemen and regular militia units were thronging now in thousands; men from Massachusetts, New Hampshire, Rhode Island, and Connecticut. Fleet couriers were galloping southward to spread the good tidings of a glorious victory attained at a cost of 49 dead and 46 others wounded or missing.

George III, it seemed, had a real war on his hands.

5

Bunker's Hill
June 17, 1775

Two months later, on the sunny morning of June 17, 1775, beleaguered Boston woke to the sound of gunfire. Across the harbor a brown gash of new-turned earth slashed the crest of Breed's Hill, middle one of the three stepping-stone heights rising from the base of the pear-shaped Charlestown peninsula between the Mystic and Charles rivers. Admiral Sir Charles Graves's British warships in the harbor were taking potshots at the earthworks and the colonial militiamen who were digging on the hillside.

This threat was serious. Could the rebels mount heavy cannon on that hill, less than a mile from several anchored warships, Boston Harbor would be untenable. Gage reacted immediately. By noon twenty-eight large rowing barges carrying some 2,200 men and two light fieldpieces under Major General William Howe moved across the Charles River to the peninsula, to snuff out the impudent threat. It was a third of the entire British garrison, recently reinforced by sea.

It had been the arrival of these British reinforcements, in fact, that had led to the construction of the earthworks on Breed's Hill. The Massachusetts Committee of Safety, fearing that Gage might try to break the siege lines around Boston, assumed that the first British offensive move would be by way of Charlestown. Major General Artemas Ward, commanding Massachusetts troops and—by courtesy only—the other militia ringing Boston, was ordered to

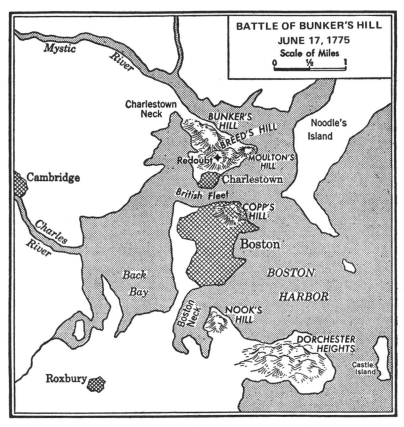

Map 2

fortify Bunker's Hill, highest point on the Charlestown peninsula, by a "strong redoubt."

At nightfall on the 16th, Colonel William Prescott with three little regiments, his own and two other Massachusetts units, moved out of Cambridge. Including a fatigue party and a two-gun artillery company, the task force numbered approximately 1,200 men.

In error, instead of occupying Bunker's Hill, the highest point, Prescott picked Breed's Hill, below it. (It was a serious mistake; Breed's Hill lacked the elevation of Bunker's Hill, and was several hundred yards closer to the guns of the British warships.) By dawn a substantial redoubt, 130 feet square and 12 feet high, had been gouged out. This was the object which had attracted the fire of the nearby naval vessels.

To protect his left flank, Prescott now had men digging a rude trench line to the Mystic, and had sent a company to occupy the village of Charlestown, on the waterfront to his right. Meanwhile Brigadier General Israel Putnam, who had volunteered to accompany Prescott, had galloped back to Ward in Cambridge, pleading for reinforcements. Grudgingly, two New Hampshire regiments, Stark's and Reed's, were ordered up, and Putnam brought back some of his own Connecticut troops to Bunker's Hill.

By this time British warships were bombarding the thirty-foot-wide neck of the Charlestown peninsula to prevent more reinforcement of the Breed's Hill fort, and attempting, not too successfully, to reach the rebels digging about the fort itself. This fire did little actual damage, but damped the enthusiasm of many defenders; some of them began dribbling away to safety.

As soon as he landed, Howe made a hasty reconnaissance. He decided to assault the fort from the Mystic River side to the north, while a secondary attack, under Brigadier General Sir George Pigot, moved toward Charlestown. Pigot's troops drew rebel fire from Prescott's troops in the village; so Admiral Graves drenched the village with red-hot shot, setting it aflame.

At the same time, on Howe's right, the light infantry skirted the Mystic shore, but turned inland before they reached Stark's and Reed's men, waiting behind an unsubstantial rail fence. In the center the grenadiers also moved ahead, as did Pigot, on the left. Forming two lines, the red-coated soldiers moved up the hill toward the fort. Someone in the redoubt—Putnam gets the credit —ordered, "Don't fire until you see the whites of their eyes!" There was a brief hush, punctuated by shouts of British sergeants dressing the marching lines. Then, at thirty-yards range, the earthwork erupted in a ragged volley.

Practically every musket ball found a mark. The British light infantry melted away. The grenadiers in the center, and Pigot's attack on the left, both recoiled. Howe, who had been following his skirmishers, was miraculously unharmed, but all of his staff officers were either killed or wounded. The British general personally rallied his shaken troops and they tried again, only to recoil once more when met by that terrible musket fire from the entrenched colonials.

Reinforced by four hundred additional troops, Howe tried a third time; the light infantry would merely demonstrate on the right; the main body, with bayonets fixed, toiled up the hill to the fort once more. Prescott's troops again opened deadly fire, but then their powder gave out. The redcoats came tumbling over the wall, and the defenders fled. There was no pursuit. Stark's and Reed's men over on the Mystic shore sullenly retreated without hindrance.

Howe had accomplished his mission, but at shocking cost. Of 2,400 men engaged, the British had lost 226 killed and 828 wounded. Eighty-nine of his casualties were officers: 19 killed and 70 wounded. Patriot losses were some 140 killed, 270 wounded, and 30 taken prisoner.

Boston's situation was unchanged; the British could not get out, the Patriots could not get in.

6

The Siege of Boston
1775–1776

Two days before the misnamed Battle of Bunker's Hill, the Second Continental Congress, meeting in Philadelphia, had passed two momentous resolutions. The first of these was to raise troops for a unified colonial, or Continental, army. The second was to select a man to command that army.

Reluctantly, on June 16, Virginia militia Colonel George Washington accepted the honor and heavy responsibility of military leadership of the combined forces of the thirteen rebellious colonies as general and commander-in-chief of the Continental Army. Promptly he assembled a small staff, then set out for Cambridge, to take command of the polyglot force of colonial militiamen ringing the port of Boston.

Discovering an uneasy stalemate, Washington promptly took steps to instill the rudiments of organization and discipline in the army besieging Boston. Seriously short of supplies, Washington established a small naval force to prey on British transports carrying supplies by sea to General Gage's beleaguered army. But his most serious deficiency was in artillery. Without large guns he could not hope to drive the British out of Boston, or to interfere seriously with the sea line of communications of the garrison of the seaport. Impatient to take the offensive, he sent his artillery chief, Colonel Henry Knox, to try to find some way to transport to Boston the heavy guns captured in May at Fort Ticonderoga, on Lake Champlain.

By the end of the year Washington could hope that, once he had some heavy artillery, he could take the offensive against Boston. He could take the offensive, that is, if he still had an army. On December 31 the enlistments of most of his soldiers expired, and all of the men were planning to go home. It was not that they were not patriotic. They simply felt that they had done their share, and that it was now the turn of other Patriots to take up the burden. Washington was able to persuade a few to re-enlist, and with great exertion he used this handful of half-disciplined "veterans" as the nucleus of a new army.

Inside Boston, General William Howe (Gage had gone home early in October) had prepared elaborate works on Bunker's Hill on the Charlestown side of his defenses, and at Boston Neck on the Dorchester side, impregnable to any American assault. By this time the British garrison had been reinforced to some eleven thousand men, but Howe's troops were rotting with scurvy and smallpox, rations were short, and there was little fuel. At year's end

Howe was desperately seeking an excuse to evacuate Boston, and to move his army someplace where it could maneuver and fight.

And then, in late January, Knox arrived at Cambridge with the cannon from Ticonderoga. It had been an amazing feat. Fifty-nine guns, the largest of them weighing 5,500 pounds, had been hauled a hundred miles through snow and ice, across frozen rivers, over mountains. With the guns Knox brought more than one ton of lead for musket balls.

Impatient Washington, whose new army was still less than eight thousand strong, was ready to move. Dorchester Heights was the target, the only eminence still unfortified by the British. Heavy cannon mounted there would dominate both the city and the harbor, compelling the British to "be so kind as to come out to us," as Washington put it.

To effect surprise Dorchester Heights must be seized and fortified in a single night. But what had been easy at Breed's Hill in June was seemingly impossible in wintertime, with the ground frozen to an eighteen-inch depth. At the suggestion of Colonel Rufus Putnam, a prefabricated fortification was prepared; heavy timber frames would be moved into position, then filled by logs, baskets of earth, and straw. Adjoining orchards would furnish sharpened stakes for the face of the ramparts, and barrels filled with earth and stones would crown the crest; these could be rolled downhill, if necessary, into the face of assaulting troops.

On the night of March 4, a working party 1,200 strong, with a covering force of 800 men, moved out of Roxbury to the Heights. With them creaked 360 oxcarts, carrying the prefab fortifications and the cannon. American batteries on the Cambridge side opened sporadic fire on the British lines to drown the noise of the caravan. At dawn Howe faced a *fait accompli*. To cap the climax, the British naval commander, now Rear Admiral Molyneux Shuldham, announced to Howe that under this new threat the fleet could no longer risk anchorage in Boston harbor. Howe must either storm the Heights or evacuate the city.

Howe had already determined to evacuate, but only at his own convenience. He ordered an immediate amphibious assault in force (any attempt to move by land over narrow Boston Neck would be too time-consuming). Five regiments, some 2,200 men, would go by water to Castle William and thence to the tip of Dorchester Heights. Two more regiments, with the grenadier and light infantry battalions of the garrison, would move by flatboat to the north side of the peninsula. The two landings were to be simultaneous, and—doubtless remembering Bunker's Hill—with the bayonet only.

A wild storm that night churned the shoreline, making attack impossible. For another day the heavy weather persisted, and then it was too late; Dorchester Heights now bristled with all of Ticonderoga's cannon, and Howe ordered immediate evacuation.

The exodus was pandemonium. The troops—able-bodied, sick, and wounded—plus more than a thousand Tory refugees, women and children, were crammed into small boats and lighters. They crawled toward the warships and transports lying out of the range of American guns. Howe had promised Bostonians that unless his troops were attacked he would not burn the city. Although Washington took no formal note of the promise, he held his fire.

By nightfall of March 17, St. Patrick's Day, the evacuation was completed. For five more days the British ships lay anchored five miles below the city in Nantasket Road, taking on water and distributing their human freight as best could be. Then they put out for Halifax.

7

The Invasion of Canada
1775–1776

From the outset of hostilities there was great interest in the Second Continental Congress—particularly among New England and New York delegates—in the possibility that anti-British sentiment among the predominantly French inhabitants of recently conquered Quebec would influence them to join the rebellion against the British Crown. Furthermore, the spreading of the revolt to Canada would have important military as well as political benefits for the rebels. In the first place, loss of Canada would severely handicap the British in any efforts to re-establish royal authority in the thirteen colonies. It would close a potential invasion route by way of the Lake Champlain-Richelieu River Valley, which had figured prominently in both French and British strategy in the French and Indian War. Thus, in May 1775, Congress made its first overtures to the "oppressed inhabitants of Canada."

This and subsequent efforts to attract the French Canadians to join in the revolt were, however, unsuccessful. The ardently Catholic people of Quebec were suspicious of the essentially Protestant inhabitants of New England and New York and saw little advantage in throwing off allegiance to the British Crown—which had treated them with consideration and tolerance—to join in a risky alliance with the anti-Catholic colonists to the south.

Despite this failure of diplomacy, many colonists thought that it would be an easy matter to gain control of the thinly inhabited St.

Lawrence Valley by force. The first attempt also came in May 1775. On the 10th a group of militiamen from Vermont (then called the New Hampshire Grants) and Connecticut, under Vermonter Ethan Allen, leader of the Green Mountain Boys (Vermont militia), seized Fort Ticonderoga on Lake Champlain. Accompanying that expedition was Colonel Benedict Arnold, of the Connecticut militia.

Following the seizure of Ticonderoga, Arnold and Allen led separate expeditions northward into Quebec, by way of the Richelieu River. Arnold captured Saint-Jean, but then retreated hastily as Canadian militia approached from Montreal. Allen, who had hoped to seize all Canada, was also deterred by this Canadian force; he quickly followed Arnold back to Lake Champlain.

After Congress established the Continental Army, in June 1775, it assigned command of the strategic northern theater to Major General Philip Schuyler of New York. Schuyler was directed to invade Canada and seize Montreal. By August he had assembled over a thousand men on the New York shores of Lake Champlain. He moved north toward Saint-Jean, which the British had strongly garrisoned following the Allen and Arnold raids. Schuyler besieged the town on September 6. Soon afterward, however, he became ill and, on September 13, was succeeded by young, able Brigadier General Richard Montgomery, who pressed the siege as aggressively as his limited resources would permit.

Meanwhile, soon after General George Washington had taken command of the colonial army outside Boston, he received a recommendation from Colonel Benedict Arnold that another expedition be sent to Canada, by way of Maine. Such a force could seize Quebec and cooperate with the Schuyler-Montgomery expedition in conquering the entire province of Quebec. Washington approved, and on September 12 Arnold and a force of 1,100 men left Cambridge to carry out Arnold's plan. Included in that force was a battalion of Pennsylvania and Virginia riflemen, commanded by Major Daniel Morgan.

While Arnold and his men toiled through the Maine wilderness, Montgomery pressed his siege of Saint-Jean. Operating with characteristic independence, impetuosity, and stupidity, Ethan Allen again tried to conquer Quebec single-handed, leading his Green Mountain Boys in a harebrained raid against Montreal. They were repulsed, and Allen was captured by the British.

On November 2, however, the six hundred defenders of Saint-Jean surrendered to Montgomery, who immediately pressed northward to Montreal. He defeated the small British defending force, commanded by Governor General Sir Guy Carleton, capturing the city and a tiny British river flotilla. Carleton, with only a handful of men remaining, withdrew northeastward, down the left bank of the St. Lawrence, to Quebec.

The British Governor General was almost intercepted. Arnold —whose command had been reduced to about six hundred men by desertion, illness, and death from privation—had reached the St. Lawrence River on November 8. By this time reliable Daniel Morgan had become Arnold's right-hand man. The Americans crossed the river to blockade the city on the 12th. Carleton evaded them and hastily prepared Quebec for defense. He had available a small force of British regulars, and the local city militia, almost all French Canadians. All together the defending force numbered about 1,800 men.

Montgomery left a small garrison in Montreal, and pursued Carleton to Quebec. He joined Arnold outside the city on December 3, and assumed command of the combined siege force of barely 1,100 men.

Aware that he was outnumbered by the defenders of Quebec's formidable walls, Montgomery was nonetheless determined to bring his so-far successful campaign to a glorious conclusion. Assisted by Arnold and Morgan, he prepared to take Quebec by surprise assault in bad weather. The Canadian winter soon provided the weather. Shortly after midnight on December 31, under the cover of a blizzard, the Americans made their attempt.

Montgomery had planned well. But he was opposed by one of the ablest British soldiers in America. Carleton recognized the danger of a bad-weather attack, and had made careful counterplans. The attackers were met by alert regular soldiers, sailors, and militiamen. Within a few minutes Montgomery was killed, and Arnold badly wounded. Intrepid Morgan, accompanied by a few of his men, fought his way through one of the city gates, but early the next morning the little band was surrounded and all were killed or captured. The disastrous assault had been completely repulsed; American losses were nearly one hundred men killed and wounded, and more than 450 prisoners—among them Morgan.

Despite his wound, Arnold retained command of the six hundred survivors, and ordered a withdrawal to a position overlooking the river, about a mile west of the city. There they erected ramparts of frozen snow, and awaited a British attack which never came. For four months they huddled there in frozen misery, isolated in the heart of Canada, short of rations, keeping only a tenuous line of communications with the garrison Montgomery had left in Montreal under Brigadier General David Wooster. In April Wooster arrived from Montreal with reinforcements; Arnold, whose leg wound had been aggravated by a fall from his horse, returned to Montreal.

In May ineffectual Wooster was replaced by Brigadier General John Thomas, who tried to organize the forlorn command for another attempt at Quebec before the expected arrival of British reinforcements from England. Actually the reinforcements, some eight thousand men, commanded by Major General John Burgoyne, were on a large fleet already moving up the St. Lawrence River. With support thus at hand, on May 6 Carleton made a surprise sortie from the walls of Quebec, and routed the more numerous Americans before Thomas could rally them. Thomas, already stricken by smallpox, bitterly followed the disorganized rabble to Sorel, near Montreal, where he died.

But now American reinforcements, also, were arriving. Brigadier General John Sullivan brought four thousand men from New York to Sorel, where he was joined by Brigadier General William Thompson, with two thousand Continentals from Boston. Sullivan sent Thompson down the river by boat to establish an advance post at Trois Rivières, midway between Montreal and Quebec.

Again the possibility of capturing Quebec seemed real to the Americans.

Sullivan was aware that British reinforcements were coming from England but apparently assumed they were only a few hundred men. Furthermore, he had no idea that Burgoyne had already landed his British and German regulars above Quebec and was also marching on Trois Rivières, accompanied on the river by much of the British fleet.

Before dawn on June 8, 1776, Thompson and his men landed near Trois Rivières. As they approached that town they were ambushed by a far larger force of British. At the same time they found themselves pounded by guns from the flotilla on the river. The Americans withdrew in confusion, closely followed by the British. After a three-day running fight Thompson and his surviving men were able to break contact, the British advance being slowed down by the marksmanship of a contingent of Pennsylvania riflemen. When the defeated troops reached Sorel, with the British close behind them, Sullivan realized that the whole American command was in danger of being cut off. He hastily withdrew southward toward Saint-Jean. Arnold, in command at Montreal, also retreated south, just in front of the British.

The Americans fell back to Ile aux Noix, at the upper end of Lake Champlain. Here Sullivan planned to stay, keeping a few acres of Canadian soil. It soon became evident, however, that it would be impossible either to live or to fight on the marshy, mosquito-infested island. Of the eight thousand troops there, two thousand were ravaged by smallpox, almost an equal number were suffering from either dysentery or malaria. In the final days of June the retreat was renewed by boat to Crown Point; a few days later it was continued back to Ticonderoga.

The invasion of Canada was over. Any further invading, it was clear, would be done by the British.

8

The Beginnings of the American Navy
1775

The first naval action of the Revolution took place on June 12, 1775, near the tiny coastal village of Machias, in northeastern Maine, then a part of Massachusetts. In early June HM schooner *Margaretta* (4) commanded by Midshipman Moore, RN, arrived in that port to arrange for a shipment of lumber to Boston. The people of Machias had learned about Lexington and Concord and the siege of Boston, and at first refused to enter into any dealings that might help the British. However, when the *Margaretta* came close to the town and pointed her 3-pounder guns at the houses, townspeople reluctantly began loading lumber on two coastal sloops being convoyed by the *Margaretta*.

On June 11, Sunday, a group of villagers planned to seize Midshipman Moore after he left the town's tiny church. But Moore, escaping, moved the *Margaretta* out of musket range, anchoring his vessel just inside the harbor entrance.

Early the next morning, June 12, Moore decided he could not get the lumber, and so weighed anchor to return to Boston. As the *Margaretta* was making sail, about forty lumbermen under their elected leader, Jeremiah O'Brien, seized the *Unity*, one of the lumber sloops, and sailed off in pursuit. Twenty more of O'Brien's men followed in another small schooner. Their arms were muskets, axes, handspikes and a small swivel gun on the *Unity*.

The *Margaretta* was a slow sailer, and the two American vessels soon came within range. The *Margaretta* opened fire but did only slight damage to the sails of the smaller sloop. A shot from the *Unity's* swivel gun killed the *Margaretta's* helmsman. Without rudder control, the British schooner turned suddenly into the wind. O'Brien quickly brought the *Unity* alongside, and the men of Machias then swarmed aboard the *Margaretta*. Moore was mortally wounded, and resistance quickly ended.

When word of this success reached Cambridge the Massachusetts General Court—the provincial parliamentary assembly—ordered that the guns of the unwieldy *Margaretta* should be put aboard the *Unity,* which was renamed *Machias Liberty*. A month later the newly christened vessel, still under Captain O'Brien, captured the British schooner *Diligent*.

Early next year the *Machias Liberty* and the *Diligent* were sent by the General Court to prey on British merchant ships in the Bay of Fundy. At first they were successful, but by October 1776, British warships arrived to patrol the bay area. The Machias ships were overwhelmed; O'Brien was captured and sent to prison. Evidently he soon escaped; the official *Naval Records of the American Revolution* lists the doughty Jeremiah as commanding no fewer than three successive privateersmen sailing out of Newburyport, Massachusetts, during 1780 and 1781.

Meanwhile, General Washington decided to take action against British supply ships carrying cargo into Boston Harbor. These vessels carried munitions, food, and equipment which he badly needed for his army.

Early in September, Washington ordered Captain Nicholas Broughton of the Marblehead Regiment to take some of his soldiers to man the schooner *Hannah* and try to capture some of the supply ships. Broughton soon captured a ship loaded with naval stores and lumber. Washington decided to commission five more schooners and brigantines, also manned by soldiers.

The men of Washington's little fleet were not happy about serving at sea when they had volunteered to fight on land. Nevertheless, they continued to operate during the winter, and by March 1776 had captured thirty-five British vessels. But after the British evacuated Boston, it became very difficult to find crews to man the fleet, and it was disbanded.

Meanwhile, in October 1775, the Continental Congress directed the preparation of two small armed vessels to intercept British transports. Soon afterward the Congress authorized two larger ships, one with twenty guns and the other with thirty-two. This was the real beginning of the United States Navy. A naval committee of Congress was appointed.

Work began at once at Philadelphia to convert four merchant vessels for naval use. While this was being done word reached Congress of a destructive British naval raid on Falmouth (now Portland), Maine. In indignant response, Congress ordered the acquisition of thirteen frigates; three carrying twenty-four guns each, five of twenty-eight, and five of thirty-two.

9

The Bahamas Expedition
February–April 1776

In October 1775 Congress appointed Captain Esek Hopkins of Rhode Island as the commodore of the new fleet it had authorized. In February 1776 he took to sea with the first converted ships of this new Continental Navy: the frigates *Alfred* (24) and *Columbus* (20); the brigs *Andrea Doria* (14) and *Cabot* (14); the sloops *Providence* (12) and *Hornet* (10); and the schooner *Wasp* (8).

Hopkins's first mission was to sail to the coast of Virginia and destroy or disable a flotilla of small craft which Loyalist Governor Dunmore of that Colony had commissioned. Then the squadron was to proceed to the coast of South Carolina, where another Loyalist coastal squadron was operating. Hopkins and his squadron set sail from Delaware Bay on February 17.

Despite his orders from Congress's naval committee, Hopkins had already decided upon another objective. Learning that the British had great stores of ordnance materials in the Bahamas, he headed for the islands. On March 3 he put 200 marines and 50 sailors ashore on New Providence Island, a few miles from the capital, Nassau, which was defended by two forts and 200 men. The Nassau garrison showed little fight. Hopkins's men occupied the town and seized 88 cannon, 15 mortars, quantities of cannonballs, shells, fuses, and 24 casks of powder.

Leaving the Bahamas, Hopkins headed for Newport, Rhode Island, still ignoring his original mission from Congress. On the way he met and captured two small British warships and two merchantmen. From his prisoners Hopkins learned that a strong British fleet was in Narragansett Bay. To avoid a disastrous encounter with a superior force, he changed course for New London.

During the night of April 5 lights of a strange vessel were sighted by the squadron. Suddenly, as she showed more lights and her British colors, she fired on the nearest American ship, the *Cabot*. The stranger proved to be a sloop of twenty guns, HMS *Glasgow*. Although outnumbered and outgunned she was more than a match for the inexperienced crews of the American ships. After damaging several of her opponents, the *Glasgow* suddenly sheered away and escaped. As a result of the action the master of the *Providence* was dismissed for cowardice, and Lieutenant John Paul Jones was given command of the ship.

Hopkins was soon summoned to Philadelphia by Congress to explain why he had failed to follow orders. Despite hearty support from John Adams, and from his brother, delegate Steven Hopkins of Rhode Island, Congress in June voted to censure Hopkins for disobedience. In January 1777 he was dismissed from the new navy. His squadron, which had been undermanned ever since its return from the Bahamas, never again operated as a unit.

10

Sullivan's Island
June 28, 1776

At first revolutionary activity in the southern colonies was less dramatic than the revolt in the North. Nevertheless, in the summer of 1775 as Patriot leaders seized control of three colonial governments three royal governors of southern colonies were forced to take refuge on British warships; Earl John Murray, Lord Dunmore, of Virginia; Josiah Martin of North Carolina; and Lord William Campbell of South Carolina.

The British government's plan for 1776 was to send three expeditionary forces to America to suppress the rebellion. The northern force, under General Burgoyne, was to regain control of Canada and the St. Lawrence Valley. The main expedition, under brothers Admiral Lord Robert Howe and General Sir William Howe, was to occupy New York and the Middle Atlantic colonies. The southern force, under General Sir Henry Clinton, was to restore royal authority in the South, then rejoin General Howe at New York.

On February 13, 1776, 2,500 troops for this southern expedition, commanded by Major General Earl Charles Cornwallis, set sail from Cork in thirty transports, escorted by eleven warships under Admiral Sir Peter Parker. At Cape Fear, North Carolina, Clinton, bringing a small force from Boston, would join the expedition and decide whether to start the southern campaign in Virginia or the Carolinas.

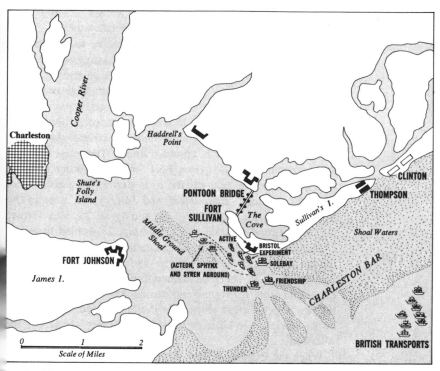

Battle of Sullivan's Island.

Map 3

Clinton and his small contingent of troops sailed from Boston in January. He picked up Governors Martin and Campbell, whose warship homes were anchored inside Sandy Hook at the entrance to New York harbor. He then proceeded to the mouth of the Cape Fear River to await the arrival of the convoy from Ireland.

Washington, meanwhile, had learned that the British were planning to send some troops south from Boston. Uncertain where they were going, he assumed it was to New York. He detached his second-in-command, Major General Charles Lee, and sent him to strengthen the defense of New York. At the end of February, however, the Continental Congress ordered Lee to command the

Southern Department, to check increasing Royalist activity in the South, and to prepare for the possibility of rumored British plans for military operations in that region.

The British convoy, scattered by storms, finally reached Cape Fear between April 18 and May 3. Parker and Clinton conferred, and decided that Charleston was the best place to attack first. On May 30 the British set sail from Cape Fear, arriving off the Charleston bar on June 4, 1776.

Lee, who had arrived in North Carolina, moved to the coast with about 1,900 Continental soldiers from Virginia and North Carolina as soon as he learned of the arrival of the British fleet off Cape Fear. When the British sailed south, Lee and his command marched to Charleston, arriving there on June 5.

Lee found that Charleston was defended by about 4,700 militiamen. Of these, 450 were with Colonel William Moultrie at Fort Sullivan on Sullivan's Island. Across the harbor mouth at Fort Johnson, on James Island, were another 400, under Colonel Christopher Gadsden. The two forts commanded the harbor entrance. Fort Sullivan was the more important of these posts, but its defenses were still unfinished. The northern and western sides of the fort were unprotected, and were vulnerable to an attack by troops landed at the northeastern end of the island.

Lee believed that the unfinished fort should be abandoned, but he yielded to the urgings of Colonel Moultrie and Governor John Rutledge. Both men had faith that the parallel palisades of palmetto logs—twelve feet high and with sixteen feet of sand between them—on the southern and eastern sides of Fort Sullivan would resist any naval guns. They also believed that a land attack was unlikely. Lee reinforced the fort's garrison, and sent troops to protect the northern part of Sullivan's Island against a possible attack by land. He also had a ponton bridge built from the island to the mainland, so that Moultrie's men would have a way of retreat if this should be necessary.

Like Lee, General Clinton quickly recognized the vulnerability of Fort Sullivan's land defenses. The British general put most of his men ashore on Long Island, north of Sullivan's Island and separated from it only by a narrow channel. Lee responded by sending about eight hundred men to entrench on the north end of Sullivan's Island. To Clinton's surprise, however, the tide-whipped channel proved almost impassable, for it varied in depth from a few inches to more than seven feet and could be neither forded nor crossed in boats. After the few Britishers who managed to get across were driven off by the American defenders, Clinton abandoned the effort.

Meanwhile Sir Peter Parker was preparing for a naval attack against Charleston. However, it took about two weeks for him to get his two heaviest ships—the exceptionally large frigates *Bristol* and *Experiment,* each of fifty guns—over the bar. He had to unship their guns to lighten the vessels and raise them high enough in the water to cross. Then the guns had to be reshipped.

Finally, in the early morning of June 28, 1776, the British squadron approached Sullivan's Island, supported by fire of 10-inch shells from the mortars of the ketch *Thunder Bomb.* The ships dropped anchor about two hundred yards from Fort Sullivan in order to bring their broadsides to bear on the fort. *Active* (28), *Bristol* (Parker's flagship), *Experiment,* and *Solebay* (28) were in the front line; *Acteon* (28), *Sphynx* (20), and *Syren* (28), were farther out, with *Thunder Bomb* and *Friendship* (28) behind them.

Moultrie's confidence in the palmetto walls proved justified. The soft wood did not splinter and few of the balls penetrated. His men, short on ammunition, took careful aim for every shot from their guns and caused considerable damage to the two largest British ships. On the *Bristol* all of the officers were killed or wounded, Admiral Parker among the wounded.

The frigates *Acteon, Sphynx,* and *Syren* tried to move around to the unprotected west end of the island, to drive the defenders out of the fort. However, they all ran aground on shoals. Then, as they tried to pull themselves off, *Acteon* and *Sphynx* collided. *Acteon* remained aground and the following morning was burned and abandoned by her crew. The other two vessels, although badly damaged by fire from the fort, managed to get off the shoals and retire out of the harbor entrance.

The British now realized that they could not take the fort. At 9:30 P.M. the remaining warships ceased firing. An hour and a half later they slipped their cables and withdrew out of range. Charleston remained in Patriot hands.

Clinton's troops stayed on Long Island until early July, when he embarked them and took them up to join General Howe at New York. Parker's ships remained just out of range, undergoing repairs, until August. Then, after the laborious task of floating the two largest vessels back over the bar, they too sailed for New York.

11

The *Turtle* vs. Lord Howe
September 6–7, 1776

In 1775, shortly after the outbreak of hostilities, inventor David Bushnell of Connecticut persuaded that colony's Council of Safety to provide him with funds to produce a submarine vessel he had designed. By midsummer of 1776 this vessel, christened the *Turtle,* was ready for operational testing.

Shaped like a large clam, the submarine was constructed of large oaken timbers, fitted closely together and scooped out to form a chamber large enough for one man to stand or sit and work its mechanisms. To make it watertight it was bound by iron bands, the seams were caulked, and the entire surface was covered with tar. Entrance was from the top through a watertight hatch with a hinged iron cover. Six small pieces of thick glass were inserted in the top around the hatch; these gave enough light on a clear day to permit reading when the *Turtle* was eighteen feet below the surface.

Except when deliberately submerged, the *Turtle* floated with the hatch housing out of the water; there were three small holes in the housing that permitted air to enter. These could be closed when the submarine submerged, leaving enough oxygen inside for the operator to breathe comfortably for more than an hour. The craft could be submerged by letting water into a tank in the bottom of the hull; the operator could open the water inlet by pushing a spring with his foot.

Attached to the bottom of the *Turtle* were seven hundred pounds of lead to keep her upright; two hundred pounds of this weight could be readily released in order to permit her to rise if the foot-operated pumps that normally controlled the depth failed to function properly. Propulsion was provided by two paddles, twelve inches long and four inches wide, set like a windmill in front of the submarine. The man inside turned these paddles by means of a crank operated with one hand, and steered with a tiller held in the other. In still water the tiny submarine could attain a speed of three knots. Two smaller paddles on top, also turned by a crank, helped the craft to rise or descend.

Attached to the back of the *Turtle* was a magazine, also built of closely fitted, tar-covered oak. The magazine contained 130 pounds of gunpowder, a clock, and a gunlock. A screw held this device to the submarine and also held the clock's spring to keep it from running. When the screw was withdrawn from the inside, the clock would start. After twenty to thirty minutes the clock would run down enough so that the gunlock would operate, creating a spark and igniting the powder. The time delay was necessary to permit the operator and the submarine to escape the explosion. From the top of the *Turtle* protruded a sharp iron screw, which the man inside could manipulate. By turning a crank he could make the screw bore into the wooden bottom of a ship. The screw was attached by a line to the magazine, so that when the operator detached them both from the *Turtle,* the clock would automatically start, and the magazine would be in position to blow up the vessel.

With the arrival of the British expedition off New York, on June 25, 1776, Bushnell suggested to General Washington that the *Turtle* should be used to destroy one of Lord Howe's vessels. Washington approved the idea, and Sergeant Ezra Lee, who had been trained by Bushnell to operate the submarine, was selected for the job. Late on the night of September 6, 1776, the *Turtle* was towed down the harbor as close to the fleet as possible. Then Lee entered his craft and was set adrift.

The tide was running out, and Lee was carried down below the fleet, but he managed to get his craft turned around and headed back up through the Narrows. Cranking vigorously for two hours and a half, he brought the submarine under the stern of one of the British ships, just at dawn. Then he dived and went under the ship's bottom. Try as he would, however, he could not drive the screw into the timbers. Perhaps he hit a part that was bound in copper; perhaps the pressure from below was not sufficient. Each time he tried, the submarine merely bounced off the vessel above her. On the last attempt the little craft rose to the surface beside the British ship. Fearing he would be detected in the growing daylight, Lee decided to give up the effort.

It was four miles to friendly shores, but now the tide was running in. As the *Turtle* passed Governors Island she was spotted from shore. A group of men launched a boat and rowed toward this strange object. Lee then released the magazine, which alarmed the pursuers and caused them to turn back. Lee continued to the Manhattan shore, where he was sighted by his party. They rowed out and towed the craft ashore. The magazine floated into the East River, and there exploded, causing much excitement but no damage.

Lee later tried to attach a magazine to a British frigate moored in the North (Hudson) River. But he was discovered and had to give it up. By this time the British had seized New York, and there were no further submarine operations.

12

Long Island
August 27, 1776

When the British evacuated Boston, Washington expected that they would attempt to re-establish control of the Middle Atlantic colonies by seizing either New York or Philadelphia. New York seemed the more likely target. So he marched south to that city from Boston.

In fact the British government had already decided to seize centrally located New York, with its magnificent harbor. Admiral Lord Richard Howe (elder brother of General Sir William Howe) was placed in command of a great amphibious expeditionary force being formed in England for the invasion. This force included a fleet of ten ships of the line, twenty frigates, and several hundred transports, manned by ten thousand British sailors. The land force contingent was thirty-two thousand professional soldiers—part British regulars and part German mercenaries—the largest expeditionary force that had ever been sent out from Great Britain. General Howe, who had gone to Halifax from Boston, would join the expedition at Halifax to become leader of the army contingent.

On June 25 the first ships of this vast British armada appeared off Sandy Hook, at the entrance to New York Bay. In early July General Howe's troops began to land on Staten Island. Washington's resources were woefully inadequate to oppose this superb British army. Even after repeated pleas to the Continental Congress, by the end of July he had fewer than twenty thousand troops. Of these about half were relatively reliable Continental

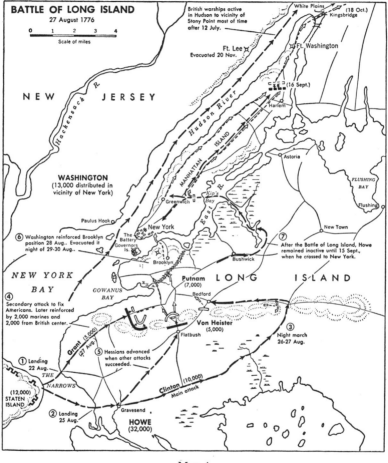

BATTLE OF LONG ISLAND
27 August 1776

Scale of miles
0   1   2   3   4

British warships active in Hudson to vicinity of Stony Point most of time after 12 July.

White Plains   (18 Oct.)
Kingsbridge

Ft. Lee
Evacuated 20 Nov.

Ft. Washington

NEW   JERSEY

Hackensack R.

Hudson River

(16 Sept.)

Harlem

MANHATTAN ISLAND

Astoria

FLUSHING BAY

Flushing

WASHINGTON
(13,000 distributed in vicinity of New York)

Kip's Bay

East R.

Greenwich

Paulus Hook

New York

New Town

⑥ Washington reinforced Brooklyn position 28 Aug.. Evacuated it night of 29-30 Aug..

The Battery
Governors Is.

Brooklyn

Bushwick

⑦ After the Battle of Long Island, Howe remained inactive until 15 Sept., when he crossed to New York.

NEW YORK BAY

GOWANUS BAY

Putnam (7,000)

Bedford

LONG   ISLAND

④ Secondary attack to fix Americans. Later reinforced by 2,000 marines and 2,000 from British center.

Grant (5,000)
27 Aug.

⑤ Hessians advanced when other attacks succeeded.

Flatbush

Von Heister (5,000)

③ Night march 26-27 Aug.

① Landing 22 Aug.

THE NARROWS

(12,000) STATEN ISLAND

② Landing 25 Aug.

Gravesend

Clinton (10,000)
Main attack

HOWE (32,000)

Map 4

soldiers; the rest were short-term militiamen. Washington orga-nized his troops into five divisions, headed by Major General Israel Putnam (who had been at Bunker's Hill), Brigadier General Joseph Spencer, recently promoted Major General John Sullivan,

Brigadier General William Heath, and Major General Nathanael Greene.

Washington realized that he could not possibly stop a major and determined British effort to capture New York. The combination of land and sea power available to the Howe brothers was overwhelming in its superiority to his own weak resources. But Congress ordered him to defend the city. So he was determined to do all he could to delay the British and deter them by harassment.

Washington ordered hulks sunk in Buttermilk Channel and the lower East River. Earthworks, batteries, and barricades were built all around lower Manhattan Island, at key points on the New Jersey shore across the Hudson River, and at several other places farther up Manhattan. To protect the approach to the city from Long Island, fortifications were built along Brooklyn Heights.

On July 12 Lord Howe made his first move to test the city's defenses. He sent two frigates up the Hudson River past Manhattan Island. The few shots that were fired at them did no damage. The British ships stayed for about a month in the Tappan Zee, north of the city, and then returned safely.

This small naval operation demonstrated to Washington that, no matter what he did in Brooklyn and lower Manhattan, the British could make their way up the Hudson and land behind him, cutting off and destroying his army. But he had received orders from Congress to try to hold New York, and he realized the city's great strategic importance. He decided to do his best. He sent Greene's, Sullivan's, and Putnam's divisions to hold the Brooklyn Heights fortifications, under the overall command of Greene. He kept Heath's and Spencer's divisions under his own direct command on Manhattan.

A force of fifteen thousand British troops crossed the Narrows from Staten Island to Gravesend Bay, Long Island, on August 22. The few Americans guarding southwestern Long Island quickly withdrew. The British troops, under General Earl Charles Cornwallis, advanced north and took Flatbush. Two days later five thousand Hessian troops, under Major General Leopold von Heister, also crossed over from Staten Island.

Meanwhile General Greene, commanding American forces on Long Island, became ill. He was replaced by General Putnam. Putnam's command, about ten thousand troops, was based on the fortified area of Brooklyn Heights, in the northwestern corner of Long Island. About half of the force, under Sullivan's command, was deployed on Long Island Heights, to cover the approaches to the fortifications. Long Island Heights was a long east-west ridge separating the southern flatlands, now held by the British, from the northern part of the island. The two main passes across Long Island Heights—Flatbush Pass and Bedford Pass—were strongly held, and a line of outposts protected the ridge line. Far to the east was Jamaica Pass, which was kept under observation by a mounted patrol.

After reconnoitering the American defenses, Howe made plans for an attack on August 27. He decided to take his main body, ten thousand strong, around the left flank of Sullivan's line, crossing Long Island Heights through the undefended Jamaica Pass. This force, under the command of General Clinton, started its enveloping march from Flatbush at 9:00 P.M. on the evening of the 26th, just after dark.

To divert American attention from this main effort, Howe ordered Major General James Grant, with five thousand men, to make a predawn attack on the right flank of the American line, anchored on Gowanus Bay. At the same time General von Heister, also with about five thousand men, was to bombard the defenses of the Flatbush and Bedford passes with the Hessian artillery.

These diversions were completely successful. Soon after dawn the British main force swept easily through Jamaica Pass, capturing a five-man cavalry patrol before anyone could even fire a shot to give warning. Northwest of the pass the British surprised and overran the Pennsylvania regiment of Colonel Samuel Miles, some five hundred men. A few horsemen of Miles's command escaped and galloped to Brooklyn Heights, where they informed Putnam. Inexplicably he took no action; nor did he inform any of his subordinates.

Sullivan's first warning of the envelopment came at 9:00 A.M., when he heard two guns fired behind him. This was General Clinton's signal to von Heister and to Grant, informing them that the main body was behind the Americans. Sullivan immediately rushed a regiment toward Bedford, but it was thrown back by Clinton's advancing troops; at the same time, von Heister responded to Clinton's signal by smashing through Flatbush Pass with a bayonet attack. Sullivan, hopelessly trapped between two fires, was captured along with several hundred of his surviving men.

Grant could not make his attack simultaneously with von Heister's, because he was waiting for ammunition to replenish what he had used up in his early-morning diversion near Gowanus Bay. By 10:00 A.M., however, he was ready; reinforced by two thousand Royal Marines, he attacked northward.

Opposing Grant's attack was a brigade of 1,500 men under Brigadier General William Alexander (known as Lord Stirling). At first Stirling's men checked the British attack. Then Stirling heard firing to his left rear, and realized that the British were behind him and that his retreat was cut off. To his right rear lay the supposedly impassable Gowanus Marsh. Stirling, however, had seen some of his men carrying wounded back along a trail through the marsh, and he decided that it had to be tried. But first he had to hold off Clinton's threat to his left rear. Ordering two of his regiments to retire slowly before Grant and to work their way back through the marsh, Stirling took five hundred Maryland Continental troops under Colonel William Smallwood and launched a counterattack against a British force under British General Lord Cornwallis, approaching from Bedford.

General Washington, who had arrived at Putnam's headquarters at 9:00 A.M., was observing the action from the high ground inside the fortifications of Brooklyn Heights. Seeing what Stirling was doing, he quickly sent a detachment to help cover the withdrawal across Gowanus Marsh. Stirling himself and Smallwood's men, after charging five times, were finally surrounded and captured by

Cornwallis. "Good God, what brave men must I lose this day!" Washington is reported to have exclaimed as he watched Stirling's attacks.

By noon the battle was over, and the surviving Americans had retreated into the Brooklyn Heights fortifications. Washington expected the British to assault Brooklyn Heights that afternoon; if they succeeded ten thousand men would be lost—half of his entire New York army. Yet he did not have time to organize an evacuation across the East River. He therefore decided to hold at all costs, and sent for reinforcements. He was determined to hold Brooklyn Heights long enough to permit a deliberate decision.

Howe, meanwhile, had decided not to make an immediate assault on the Brooklyn Heights position. He remembered the terrible losses his troops had suffered at Bunker's Hill in attacking an American fortification. So he began making preparations for a siege.

When Washington saw the British trenches next morning, he realized what Howe had in mind. There would be a systematic hammering of the American defenses by British siege artillery and finally a well-prepared attack by greatly superior forces. Admiral Howe could send men up the Hudson to land behind him, as Washington had known all along. And the admiral's naval guns could be used along with General Howe's siege guns to batter the Brooklyn fortifications. It was obvious, therefore, that Brooklyn Heights could not be held for long. Washington decided to withdraw from Brooklyn.

Because of the British numerical superiority, however, the withdrawal had to be carried out in secrecy. Otherwise the American force—now about three-fifths of Washington's army—would surely be destroyed when defending troops were pulled back to the river. Since he knew that there were Loyalist spies all around him, Washington did not tell anyone of his decision until late in the afternoon of August 29. Then he told his senior officers that the evacuation would take place that same night.

A covering force of about two thousand men held the fortifications, while the remaining troops embarked for Manhattan in rowing boats manned by Glover's Marblehead Regiment—fishermen accustomed to small-boat handling. The troops were told that reinforcements from Manhattan were relieving them, and that they should withdraw and embark. The operation began at dark. At 4:00 A.M., the covering troops left their positions and began embarking just as the early dawn was breaking.

It was about 6:00 A.M. when the British discovered that the American trenches were empty. Pushing forward cautiously, they reached the river a little before 7:00 A.M., just as the last American boat, carrying General Washington, was pulling away from the Brooklyn shore.

The Americans had lost about 1,500 men in the battle of Long Island, 1,100 of them captured. The British had lost about 300 killed and wounded, plus 23 captured.

Washington had made many mistakes during this brief campaign. He had attempted to hold an untenable position, and had placed undue confidence in unreliable General Putnam. Washington had also failed to protect his plans and dispositions from the many spies in Loyalist-inclined New York. He had waited too long before taking personal command of the forces on Long Island.

However, Washington had the priceless ability to learn from his mistakes. The sound decision on the 27th to reinforce his panic-stricken men, the sound decision on the 28th to evacuate, and the flawless way in which the evacuation was planned and carried out on the 29th—all showed how quickly he could learn.

13

Kips Bay and Harlem Heights
September 15–16, 1776

On Sunday morning, September 15, British troops in small boats made an amphibious assault across the East River, landing at Kips Bay, on Manhattan (near the foot of modern 34th Street). The American defenders, mostly New Englanders, made little effort to halt the attack, and fled shamelessly from the threat of gleaming British bayonets. Washington, alarmed by the sound of firing, rushed to the scene and vainly tried to rally the fleeing American defenders. One of his aides heard the general groan: "Are these the men with whom I am to defend America?" He took off his hat and threw it on the ground in a fit of helpless rage. As the British infantrymen rushed forward, one of his aides seized the reins of the general's horse and led him at a gallop behind the scampering New Englanders, as British musket balls whistled past them.

Washington quickly recovered his composure, and issued orders to save what he could from the disaster. His troops had already begun their evacuation of lower Manhattan, and Washington sent General Putnam galloping off to the south to lead the troops out of New York City and up the west side of Manhattan to Harlem Heights. A messenger was sent north to Heath, ordering him to man prepared entrenchments along the Harlem Heights. Then Washington slowly followed his broken, fleeing troops northward.

The initial British landing force had been about four thousand men, of whom three-fourths were British light infantry, grenadiers, and Guards; the remainder were Hessian jägers. Lord Cornwallis was in command of this leading division, and General Howe also accompanied the assault wave. Reaching Murray Hill (about 39th Street and Park Avenue) the cautious British commander ordered a halt, fearful that if his relatively small attacking force were overextended the much more numerous Americans might rally and drive him back into the river. Possibly he was right, but it is doubtful if anything could have rallied the Americans that afternoon.

British and Hessian reinforcements did not arrive until mid-afternoon. Howe immediately began a pursuit north toward Harlem Heights with the bulk of his army, while sending several battalions southward to seize abandoned New York.

As the leading elements of the British main body reached McGowan's Pass (near the northeast corner of modern Central Park) at dusk, they came under long-range fire from the Americans entrenched on Harlem Heights. Howe halted for the night.

It is doubtful that the British lost as many as ten men that day. Probably not more than 30 Americans were killed or wounded, but about 350 men, and about 55 abandoned cannon, were captured in New York, as well as much ammunition and considerable quantities of supplies that could not be evacuated in time.

During that late afternoon and early evening Washington labored to reorganize his army. He had about 16,000 men, 6,000 of these protecting King's Bridge against a possible British turning movement through the Bronx—Washington's greatest worry. The remaining 10,000 manned three lines of entrenchments extending in depth roughly between modern 130th and 150th streets. Washington doubted, however, if his men would stand up against another British attack, despite the advantage of high and rocky ground and the protection of earthworks.

Shortly after dawn, Lieutenant Colonel Thomas Knowlton's battalion of Connecticut rangers, about 150 men, began to reconnoiter across the "Hollow Way," a then-wooded valley where 130th Street now lies. As they were approaching the high ground where Grant's Tomb now stands they were met by British regulars.

Knowlton drew his men back in good order to the high ground on the north side of the Hollow Way just as Washington arrived.

When Washington heard Knowlton's report, he saw an opportunity to teach the pursuing Englishmen a lesson. He ordered Knowlton, accompanied by three companies of Colonel George Weedon's Virginia Regiment under Major Andrew Leitch, to go back across the Hollow Way, farther to the east, to get around behind the Britishers. At the same time, the remainder of Weedon's regiment, and other troops in the line, were to attract the attention of the British from the front by heavy musket fire and a feigned advance. Washington sent his adjutant general, Colonel Reed, with the enveloping force, which was probably about three hundred men. One other senior American officer—never directly identified by either Washington or Reed—accompanied the column as a self-appointed volunteer. Apparently it was either General Putnam or Brigadier General George Clinton. It was by this time nearly noon.

The holding attack quickly accomplished its purpose. As Weedon and his men moved forward into the Hollow Way, the challenge was answered by the British, who began to advance to make contact in the valley. Suddenly, to Washington's annoyance, firing broke out on the British right flank on Vanderwater (now Morningside) Heights. The general had hoped that Knowlton and Leitch would work their way completely around behind the British before opening fire. Reed later reported to Washington that, despite his protests, the accompanying general officer had ordered Knowlton to open fire prematurely.

The results of the envelopment were therefore less decisive than Washington had hoped. However, the British immediately fell back to the high ground south of the Hollow Way, pressed vigorously by Knowlton, Leitch, and Weedon. At this time, however, both Knowlton and Leitch fell, mortally wounded. Fearful that the impetus of the drive would slacken with the loss of these two energetic leaders, Washington sent a Maryland regiment and some New England units to bolster the enveloping force. Despite reinforcements rushed to the front by British Brigadier General Alexander Leslie, the American advance continued, and the British regulars fell back in some confusion.

By now there were close to five thousand troops engaged on each side, and through his glasses Washington could see additional British units moving up. He was pleased with the manner in which his troops had performed, and decided to call off the battle while he was still ahead. Despite the enthusiasm of the chase, his troops responded well, and withdrew in good order. By the time the advance ceased, the Americans had reached about to modern 108th Street, approximately a mile from the initial point of contact in the Hollow Way.

Casualty reports were conflicting and vague. The British lost about 70 killed and 200 wounded in the six-hour fight, while the Americans had 30 killed and 90 wounded. A relatively minor action, this battle of Harlem Heights did much to help American morale. Howe and his subordinates, amazed by the American resiliency and determination, became more cautious in their subsequent actions.

A lull of several weeks followed, while Howe cautiously prepared for his next move. He was still determined to avoid a frontal assault against American marksmen in prepared entrenchments. His timetable was set back still further by a great fire which broke out in New York on September 20, and which raged for nearly two days. Howe was furious, since he assumed (perhaps correctly) that the fire was deliberate sabotage.

One demonstration of Howe's fury was action against a young American spy, Connecticut Captain Nathan Hale, who was captured on Long Island on September 21. Without benefit of a trial, Hale was summarily sentenced to death and hanged in New York City the following morning. His last words became a slogan for his surviving fellow Patriots: "My only regret is that I have but one life to give for my country."

14

Valcour Island
October 11–12, 1776

After the failure of the invasion of Canada in June 1776, General Sullivan led the retreating troops back to Fort Ticonderoga on Lake Champlain. Sullivan was then ordered south to join Washington's army in the defense of New York, and the command at Ticonderoga fell to energetic Brigadier General Benedict Arnold. General Schuyler, still in overall command in the North, endorsed Arnold's plan to build a fleet on Lake Champlain, to prevent or hinder the expected British invasion of northern New York.

Arnold already had two schooners—the *Royal Savage* (12) and the *Liberty* (8)—and a sloop, the *Enterprise* (12), all of which had been captured the year before when the Americans seized control of the lake. He immediately sent out calls for materials and for men skilled at shipbuilding. The builders went to work at Ticonderoga on another schooner, the *Revenge,* to carry eight guns. At nearby Skenesboro (now Whitehall), they set up another shipyard, and turned out four large row galleys (each to carry ten or twelve guns) and eight or nine smaller, flat-bottomed gundalows, or gondolas, as they were commonly called, to carry three guns each.

The British meanwhile were also building up a fleet at the northern end of the lake. Some of the vessels were transported overland, in pieces, from the St. Lawrence River to the northern shore of the lake, and reassembled. These included a three-masted

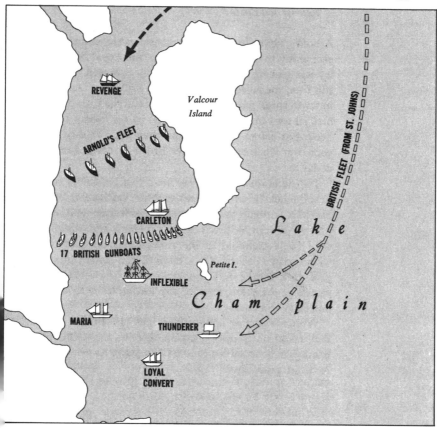

Battle of Valcour Island.

Map 5

oceangoing ship, the *Inflexible* (18), two 12-gun schooners, the *Maria* and the *Carleton,* and a large flat-bottomed radeau, or barge, the *Thunderer,* which carried two howitzers, six 24-pounders, and six 12-pounders. They had seized a small schooner (the *Loyal Convert,* with eight or ten guns). At Saint-Jean, on the Richelieu River, they built twenty gunboats (each with one gun), four longboats (each with a field gun), and twenty-four provision boats or bateaux. Commanding this formidable squadron was Captain Thomas Pringle, RN.

On October 4, 1776, Pringle sailed south. His craft were manned by more than a thousand sailors of the Royal Navy, while the 29th Foot, some five hundred strong, was parceled out as marines.

Arnold's little fleet was also ready by this time. Anticipating the British move, he had gone partway down the lake to meet Pringle. Thinking to ambush the enemy, Arnold anchored his ships behind Valcour Island, south of Plattsburg. He moored his vessels fore and aft in a crescent line, permitting them to fire broadside at enemy vessels, which, once they discovered the Americans, would have to approach, bow-on, from the south.

Running before the wind on a clear, sunny morning, October 11, 1776, Pringle's squadron, led by the *Inflexible,* headed south. Not until they cleared the southern tip of Valcour Island did the British discover the Americans hiding behind it. Arnold sent the galleys and the *Royal Savage* out to attack the enemy, and to entice them to pursue under the guns of the remainder of his fleet. As the British followed her, the *Royal Savage* ran aground, and was later set afire and abandoned by her crew.

The larger British ships were unable to beat up against the wind to where the American vessels were anchored behind the island. So they dropped anchor and opened fire from a distance. The *Carleton* and the gunboats, however, worked their way to about 350 yards from the American line before they dropped anchor and opened fire. In the ensuing fierce gun battle, American fire was concentrated on the British schooner, which was finally towed out of the fight by two longboats, leaking badly and with half of her crew dead or wounded.

Late in the day the *Inflexible* managed to claw her way against the breeze into close range. This was the turning point of the battle. Five times she raked the American vessels with a full broadside, causing severe damage and many casualties. By now, however, it was dusk. The British broke off the fight and anchored for the night across the channel. They would wait for morning to finish off the Americans.

Arnold's ships had already suffered considerable damage, before the final cannonade from the *Inflexible* sank one galley and severely crippled two others. Defeat was inevitable. With the wind still from the north, and a night fog settling in, Arnold decided to try to sneak past the British and head for Crown Point. With muffled oars the Americans slipped by the enemy vessels unnoticed. But before long the wind changed, and they were only a few miles away when the British discovered their absence at dawn.

Pringle hoisted anchor and set off in pursuit. His vessels, able to sail closer to the wind, quickly overhauled the Americans. When the leading British ships came within range, three of the American craft struck their colors. Three others made good their escape to Ticonderoga. Six, including Arnold's *Congress,* were further damaged in the ensuing running gun battle, and were finally beached. There Arnold burned them, then led the two hundred survivors to Crown Point, and on to Ticonderoga.

Winter was now approaching, and the British decided that they could not properly exploit their victory until spring. An uneasy calm settled over the waters of Lake Champlain, now firmly in British possession.

15

Cruise of the *Reprisal*
1776–1777

During 1776 Congress approved the commissioning of several additional warships in the Continental Navy. One of these was the brig-rigged sloop of war *Reprisal* (16). Under Captain Lambert Wickes she sailed for Martinique in the French West Indies in July, carrying to his post William Bingham, recently appointed commercial and naval agent by the Continental Congress for the purchase and shipment of munitions.

On the way, Wickes captured three British merchant ships. Then, off the entrance to St. Pierre, Martinique, he encountered the British sloop of war *Shark* (16). There was a sharp action, but the British vessel broke it off before much damage had been done to either vessel. Wickes continued into the harbor and landed his passenger. The *Reprisal* then returned to Philadelphia.

In October the Continental Congress gave Wickes another important nonmilitary assignment. This time he was to carry Benjamin Franklin to France, to become a very successful ambassador and peace negotiator. Wickes landed Franklin safely at St. Nazaire and then sailed with the *Reprisal* on a raid into British waters.

In January 1777 Wickes cruised in the English Channel, capturing five merchant vessels. Returning to St. Nazaire, he sold his prizes and distributed prize money among his crew. He used part of the prize money to fit out a schooner, *Dolphin,* as a companion to the *Reprisal.* Then in May, as commodore of this two-vessel squadron, Wickes again went raiding in British waters. Joined by the brig *Lexington* (16), under Captain Henry Johnson, Wickes's squadron captured eighteen vessels off the Irish coast. Then, on June 26, off Ushant on the coast of England, the three American vessels met up with HM ship of the line *Burford* (74). This was too formidable an opponent. The three small vessels scattered, and the *Burford,* with the wind behind her, pursued the *Reprisal* toward France for eight hours. Wickes threw all his guns overboard to lighten his vessel, but the *Burford* held her distance, and hit the *Reprisal* several times with her bow guns. Only when daylight faded and the ships approached a rocky lee shore, did the English captain give up the chase. Wickes again returned to St. Nazaire.

The British government protested to France over Wickes's use of neutral French ports. The French government was not yet ready to enter the war on the American side, and ordered Wickes out to sea. He was given time, however, to refit his ship with guns and to repair the slight damage suffered from the *Burford*. The *Reprisal* finally sailed on September 14, 1777. British warships were off the French coast looking for her, but she eluded them and made for home. Off the coast of Newfoundland, however, the *Reprisal* ran into a gale and was lost with all hands. So ended the promising career of Lambert Wickes, America's first naval hero.

16

White Plains
October 28, 1776

For nearly a month after the engagement at Harlem Heights the American and British armies held their ground, as Howe pondered his next move. The Americans held the northern, narrow, "handle" of Manhattan; the British the rest of the island. American guns and troops on the rugged heights overlooking the narrow Harlem River discouraged the British from making a close-in envelopment. What Washington feared, however, was that the British fleet would carry troops up the Hudson River, or up the East River into Long Island Sound, to land troops in the Bronx, or Westchester, to cut off the American retreat. On the other hand, because of the orders he had received from Congress, he felt he could not abandon Manhattan Island until the British made an overt move.

Howe, for his part, was well aware of the advantage given him by his brother's naval control of the waterways around New York. Yet he had had enough evidence of Washington's military competence, and had seen enough instances of good fighting by the American soldiers, to be wary. Any landings behind the American lines would have to be close to Howe's main army, to avoid giving Washington a chance to defeat the detachments in detail.

On October 12 Howe finally made his move. Leaving half of his army to hold lower Manhattan Island, he took the remaining ten thousand by water up the East River, to a peninsula on the Bronx shore known as Throg's Neck. However, in his desire to avoid having the two parts of his army too far separated from each other, Howe had failed to take full advantage of his command of the water, and had landed too close to Washington's troops in the Bronx-King's Bridge area. The leading British division, under energetic Lord Cornwallis, was held up on the peninsula by the determined defense of Colonel Edward Hand's 1st Pennsylvania Rifle Regiment. Before the British could push these defenders aside, reinforcements arrived to strengthen the defense of Throg's Neck. Although the British still had a numerical preponderance of force, they were able to bring only a few of their troops into action on the narrow neck. Held up by 1,800 Americans, some 4,000 British were bottled up on a point of land less than a square mile in area.

It was obvious to Washington, however, that this British setback could only be temporary. They could land anyplace they wanted above Throg's Neck, or on the Hudson shore above King's Bridge. He did not have enough men to hold the entire shoreline. On October 16, therefore, he decided to withdraw from Manhattan, and move up to White Plains, where the army would no longer be in danger of being cut off. Because of specific instructions from Congress, however, he decided to leave about two thousand troops in the fortification of Fort Washington, near the highest point in Manhattan, overlooking the Hudson River. Another three thousand troops were sent across the river to Fort Lee, on the Jersey Palisades, opposite Fort Washington.

With the remainder of his army, about 14,500 men, Washington began a deliberate withdrawal from Manhattan, carrying all of his supplies with him.

On December 18 General Howe made the move up the East River that Washington expected. Cornwallis's light division was again the spearhead, this time landing at Pell's Point, near modern Pelham. Once more the British advance was blunted by the alertness of the American defenders, this time a Massachusetts brigade under Colonel John Glover. However, the terrain was not as easily defended as Throg's Neck, and the British slowly forced the Massachusetts men back to the Post Road, and then seized New Rochelle, where Howe concentrated his army.

Washington, at White Plains, again reorganized his army. There were now seven divisions, commanded respectively by Generals Lee, Greene, Putnam, Sullivan, Spencer, Heath, and Benjamin Lincoln. Greene's division was holding forts Washington and Lee; the others were with Washington at White Plains.

On October 23 Howe began a slow advance northward, culminating in a skirmish against American outposts four miles south of White Plains on the morning of the 27th. Washington expected an immediate British attack. However, Howe contented himself with thorough patrolling and reconnaissance.

The American position was on a line of low rolling hills just south of the village of White Plains; the right flank protected by the shallow Bronx River, the left on a millpond. The right of the American line was dominated by high Chatterton's Hill west of the Bronx River, where two small militia regiments under Colonel Rufus Putnam were entrenched. Late on the 27th, when Washington noted British reconnaissance interest in Chatterton's Hill, he decided to reinforce Putnam. Shortly after dawn on the 28th he sent over Colonel John Haslet's Delaware regiment, and then, possibly as an afterthought, followed this with General Alexander McDougall's brigade—bringing the force on the hill to about 1,600 men in all.

Part of Spencer's division, probably about 1,000 men, held a delaying position approximately half a mile south of the main line. Deployed behind farm stone walls, Spencer's troops met the British advance, early on the 28th, with strong and concentrated fire. As more British troops arrived, and prepared to attack, however, Spencer, in accordance with his instructions from Washington, pulled back to the main position.

Again Howe avoided a frontal assault. His reconnaissance of the 27th had convinced him that Chatterton's Hill was the key to the American position. He sent a combined British and Hessian force of more than four thousand men west of the Bronx River to take it.

With intense artillery support, the British and Hessians crossed the stream and slowly started up Chatterton's Hill. The militia regiments immediately ran. The Continentals attempted to hold the crest for a while, but the British and Hessians pressed forward, extending their flanks around the base of the hill. To avoid being cut off, the Continentals then fell back, covered by the slow and deliberate withdrawal of Haslet's regiment. The Hessians and British quickly seized the crest and began to organize for further advance while artillery was being dragged up the hill behind them. In the face of this threat, Washington ended the battle by withdrawing his right flank north of White Plains, to a new position between the Bronx River and St. Mary's Lake.

American losses were probably slightly more than 250 men, of whom some 50 were killed. British losses were approximately 240, also with about 50 dead. About one-third of these casualties were suffered by the Hessians.

For three days the two armies faced each other, while Howe received reinforcements from Manhattan and Staten islands, bringing his strength up to nearly twenty thousand. During the night of October 31–November 1, therefore, Washington made a night withdrawal to higher and more commanding ground on North Castle Heights. A pause of several days followed, while the British, moving into White Plains, probed cautiously against the American defenses.

With his usual distaste for frontal assault of American entrenchments, Howe saw no further reason for operations northward into Westchester. He decided instead to clear the Americans from Fort Washington and the north tip of Manhattan Island, thus opening up a land line of communications to New York. Then, after consolidating the areas on both sides of the lower Hudson, he intended to put his troops into winter quarters around New York, in preparation for what he confidently felt would be the culminating campaign against the rebels in 1777.

During the night of November 4–5, therefore, the British made a night withdrawal to the southwest. Though many Americans were prematurely jubilant at this apparent British retreat, Washington realized the likelihood that Howe was planning an attack on Fort Washington. He feared this would be followed by an advance into the Jerseys.

17

Fort Washington
November 16, 1776

Howe's next objective was to capture Fort Washington, the last remaining American foothold on Manhattan Island. This would make more secure the proposed British winter quarters in New York. It would also open the way for a thrust across the Hudson River through New Jersey to Philadelphia—the rebel capital— either in the late fall or in the spring.

Fort Washington, located on a bluff 230 feet above the Hudson, was formidable principally because of its location and the extremely rugged, rocky slopes which it overlooked. It was a simple, open earthwork, pentagonal in shape, with a bastion at each corner. Washington doubted that the fort could hold out against an intensive British attack, but Greene, Israel Putnam, and Colonel Robert Magaw, the garrison commander, were all confident of its strength. Washington's doubts were intensified on November 7 when three British warships moved upstream, successfully avoiding the obstacles in the river which forts Washington and Lee were intended to protect. Despairing now of any possibility of preventing the British from using the river, Washington could see little reason for maintaining a garrison of two thousand men precariously isolated on Manhattan. However, since Congress wanted the fort held if possible, and since Greene was on the spot and better able to assess the situation, Washington left the decision to him.

When Howe marched back south toward Manhattan, Washington began to shift his main army to meet the two major likely British threats. The first of these was the dangerous possibility of a British advance up the Hudson to Albany. To block this, Washington left General Lee with approximately seven thousand men at North Castle. The other possibility, of course, was the feared thrust across the Hudson toward Philadelphia. To hinder this, on November 9 Washington personally led some two thousand men to join the three thousand under Greene in and around Fort Lee on the west bank. With his army thus divided, Washington felt it important to hold the Highlands region of the Hudson and maintain communications between these two major portions of his army. To perform this task, Heath with approximately four thousand men was ordered toward Peekskill.

These decisions divided Washington's already weak army into four major groups (his own and Greene's force west of the Hudson, Lee to the northeast, Heath to the north, and Magaw at Fort Washington). This left Howe on interior lines, able to concentrate his larger army against any one of these contingents. However, experience had shown Washington that the British would not move rapidly. His dispositions allowed for forces sufficiently substantial to delay any British move to the north or west, and by securing the Hudson Highlands crossings he believed he would be able to concentrate his army rapidly once Howe's intentions were clearly indicated. Having properly decided upon a defensive strategy, there was not much else that Washington could have done under the difficult circumstances—other than to withdraw the exposed force from Fort Washington.

Worried about that position, on November 12 Washington visited Greene at Fort Lee to discuss the situation. Greene again expressed confidence in the impregnability of the fortress, but Washington remained undecided. The two generals were rowed over to Fort Washington to inspect Magaw's defenses on the 14th, and Washington still found his better judgment completely contradicted by the enthusiasm and confidence of his subordinates. So he again postponed a decision to abandon the fort.

The extensive outworks of the fortress extended across Manhattan Island from the Hudson to the Harlem River, and from the old entrenchments overlooking the Hollow Way almost to King's Bridge in the north. This line required more troops than Magaw had; so Greene reinforced the garrison to a strength of nearly three thousand men—evidently without consulting Washington, who still believed its strength to be fewer than two thousand.

By November 15 British troops were concentrated north and south of Magaw's lines. General Howe sent a message to the fort demanding surrender. Magaw declined, and sent a report to Greene and to Washington.

At dawn the next morning—November 16—Washington had himself rowed across the river to inspect the fortress personally and to make a final decision whether to hold it or abandon it. Just as he was leaving the Jersey shore, heavy firing broke out south and north of the fort, but Washington continued across the river. Arriving at the fort, he found that British and Hessian troops were attacking the outworks from north and south. He decided that his presence was merely an embarrassment and an encumbrance to Magaw, who had a battle to fight. Restraining his impulse to take personal command, Washington returned across the river to Fort Lee to await developments.

Howe had assembled eight thousand troops to assault the fort. The main effort was to be made from the north, by some three thousand Germans under Knyphausen. To the east, two small columns totaling another three thousand men, under Generals Edward Mathew and Cornwallis, were to make assault crossings over the Harlem River, and then drive westward against the face of the fort. Lord Percy was advancing northward from central Manhattan with a mixed British-Hessian force of two thousand men.

Percy had opened the action shortly after dawn with an intensive bombardment across the Hollow Way, followed by a general advance all along the line. The thinly spread out Americans were quickly pushed back, but Percy halted when he discovered that Cornwallis and Mathew were having troubles getting across the Harlem River. Meanwhile, shortly before 10:00 A.M., Knyphausen's Germans had begun their assault through the wild and rocky area to the north. Despite stubborn resistance, the Germans pushed forward aggressively. For more than three hours, the hardest fighting of the day raged amidst the boulders and ravines north of Fort Washington.

Shortly before noon Mathew and Cornwallis successfully assaulted over the Harlem River, despite heavy American fire from the west bank heights. Then all four British columns began to forge ahead, and by early afternoon Rall's Hessian regiment was close to the fort itself, on the crest above the Hudson. As the other three columns continued to close in, Rall demanded Magaw's surrender.

Washington and his companions at Fort Lee heard the firing grow in volume and approach the fort from both directions. By early afternoon he was convinced that the fort could not be held. He sent a message to Magaw, ordering him to cling to his remaining positions until nightfall, and then to evacuate to the Jersey shore. Washington had Greene collect boats and make preparations for the evacuation.

Meanwhile Magaw, to gain time, had attempted to discuss surrender terms with Rall. By this time he realized that, though he had too few troops to hold his extensive outworks, he had far too many to be crowded safely into the relatively small, open area of Fort Washington itself. When Rall, and then General Knyphausen, ordered immediate surrender, without further negotiations, Magaw gave up. He was fearful of the casualties which artillery fire would cause among the crowd of troops huddled in the fort. It was at this moment, probably near 3:00 P.M., that he received Washington's message to hold on until nightfall. Magaw responded that he had so committed himself to surrender that he could not with honor obey the order. So fell Fort Washington.

American losses were 53 killed, 96 wounded, and 2,722 unwounded captured. The British lost 77 killed, 374 wounded, and 7 missing; nearly three-fourths of these casualties were Hessians. They captured 43 artillery pieces, and great quantities of artillery and small-arms ammunition.

The loss of nearly three thousand men was serious to Washington, while the relatively easy capture of the supposedly impregnable fortress by the British struck another sharp blow at American morale. Greene, realizing that his insistence had caused Washington to agree to the defense of the fort, was particularly depressed by the catastrophe.

The blame, however, was Washington's. His estimate had been that the fort was indefensible. He had skillfully disposed the remainder of his forces so that the retention of the garrison of Fort Washington on Manhattan was not only unnecessary, but dangerous. A firm decision had been necessary, and Washington had vacillated. He had to face the consequences.

18

Trenton
December 26, 1776

On Christmas Day, 1776, the Patriot cause appeared to be approaching a tragic end. In the weeks following the surrender of Fort Washington, Washington and his Continentals had been harried from the Hudson through New Jersey. Now the remnants of his army, some 2,400 strong, lay on the west bank of the

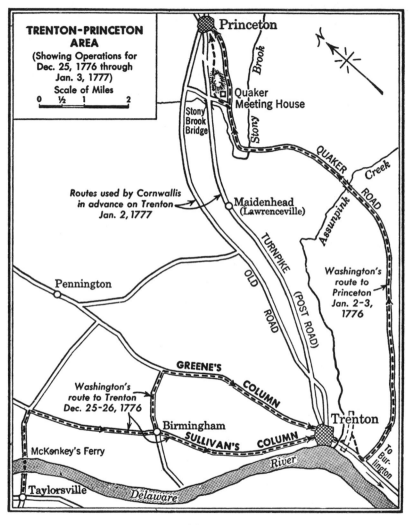

TRENTON-PRINCETON AREA
(Showing Operations for Dec. 25, 1776 through Jan. 3, 1777)
Scale of Miles
0   ½   1   2

Princeton

Stony Brook

Quaker Meeting House

Stony Brook Bridge

QUAKER ROAD

Assunpink Creek

Routes used by Cornwallis in advance on Trenton Jan. 2, 1777

Maidenhead (Lawrenceville)

TURNPIKE (POST ROAD)

OLD ROAD

Washington's route to Princeton Jan. 2-3, 1776

Pennington

GREENE'S COLUMN

Washington's route to Trenton Dec. 25-26, 1776

Birmingham

SULLIVAN'S COLUMN

Trenton

To Burlington

McKonkey's Ferry

Delaware River

Taylorsville

Map 6

Delaware not far from Trenton. Safe for the moment because they had garnered all river craft to their side, they had been joined by about two thousand additional short-term Pennsylvania militia. But a great proportion of the Continental enlistments would expire at year's end, leaving only about a thousand men still under arms.

Howe had gone into winter quarters. About half of his troops were in the New York area; the remainder, thirteen thousand men, was comfortably disposed throughout central New Jersey, with advanced posts at Princeton and on the east bank of the Delaware at Trenton and Bordentown, where the Hessian division, some three thousand men, was ensconced. Come spring, Sir William intended to overwhelm the ragged rabble huddled across the Delaware. Meanwhile, as Christmas approached, wine, women, and wassail would entertain His Majesty's troops.

But Christmas afternoon, Washington's Continentals were assembling in a valley close by McKonkey's Ferry, nine miles north of Trenton. Their uniforms were ragged, their footgear deplorable. But each man carried forty rounds of ammunition, three days' rations, and a blanket. Washington had decided to dare all in a dramatic effort to revive Patriot spirit. His main body would strike Trenton at dawn the next day and, if successful, thrust to the British depot at New Brunswick with its supplies of clothing, food, and ammunition. Secondary crossings by the militia completed the plan; Ewing just south of Trenton, to cut the enemy retreat path at Assunpink Creek; and Cadwalader near Bristol, to prevent Hessian reinforcement from Bordentown.

The winter weather was abominable—wind, rain, sleet, and snow flurries. Ice cakes bobbed on the fast-flowing river. But Glover's amphibious Marblehead regiment manned stout, 50-foot-long "Durham" boats and before dawn Washington's 2,400 men and 18 fieldpieces with their teams were shivering on the muddy east bank of the river.

Meanwhile, both Ewing and Cadwalader, discouraged by the weather, had failed to accomplish their parts of the plan. Ewing gave up entirely; Cadwalader, after making a timid attempt to cross, remained on the west shore. Washington would have to go it alone.

The nine-mile march to Trenton was made in two columns; Greene's division on the Pennington Road debouching in the northern entrance to Trenton; Sullivan along the River Road, to box in the garrison from the south. Rain' and snow had rendered useless most of the flintlock muskets. Washington, learning this in a message from Sullivan, retorted: "Tell General Sullivan to use the bayonet. I am resolved to take Trenton!" But the cannon were not affected; half-frozen gunners shielded the touchholes from the rain with wrappings, and even with bare hands as they trundled along; cartridges and powder were protected in limbers and caissons.

In Trenton, Hessian Colonel Johann Rall, contemptuous of American fighting spirit, had made no attempt to fortify his cantonment, although he had posted picket guards on the roads. Rall's brigade was composed of three regiments: his own, Kynphausen's, and von Lossberg's. There was also a company of jägers and a twenty-man platoon of the British 16th Light Dragoons; in all, something more than a thousand men, with six cannon. Rall and his command, relaxed by their Christmas celebration, slept sound that night, but the pickets were on the job.

It was broad daylight when the Hessian pickets, discovering the Patriot advance on both roads, opened fire, but were driven in. On the north Stirling's brigade began pushing down parallel King and Queen streets, while Hamilton's and Forrest's batteries dropped trail, hub to hub, to sweep the narrow streets. Mercer's brigade pushed into the village from the northwest, Stephen's from the northeast. On the south, Sullivan's division rushed the River Road to seize the Assunpink Creek bridge.

Between these converging thrusts lay the Hessian quarters, close-packed, in the center of the village.

Boiling out of their quarters at the alarm, the Hessians found themselves hemmed in by American infantrymen and by the close-range fire of artillery sweeping the streets. A short, sporadic resistance ended when the Rall and Lossberg regiments surrendered to Greene's men in a field east of the village. The Knyphausens, pinned against the creek, then threw down their arms to St. Clair's brigade of Sullivan's division.

It was all over within an hour. Hessian dead, von Rall among them, numbered 22; 948 were bagged, some 400-odd others, including the dragoons, escaped to the south. Two Americans had frozen to death during the river crossing, and four others were wounded in the fight.

Washington, his victory won, faced an immediate decision. His secondary attacks having aborted, his tired men would be no match for the now alerted enemies who would be racing down from Princeton and Bordentown. So, herding their prisoners, the captured enemy guns, and several wagonloads of booty, the Continental Army plodded back to its waiting boats and another bitter river crossing, during which three more men were frozen to death. By early evening the troops were safe in their west bank bivouacs.

Washington had accomplished his purpose. As writes Trevelyan, the British historian: "It may be doubted whether so small a number of men ever employed so short a space of time with greater or more lasting results upon the history of the world."

General Howe, shocked to find that "three old established regiments of a people who make war a profession, should lay down their arms to a ragged and undisciplined militia," sent Cornwallis south with eight thousand men, to retrieve the situation along the Delaware.

19

Princeton
January 3, 1777

Two militia units had been ordered to participate in the Trenton operation with Washington's command, but the miserable weather Christmas night had deterred both of them from crossing the river. Early the next morning Colonel John Cadwalader, commander of one of these units, wrote to Washington: "I imagine the badness of the night must have prevented your crossing, as you intended." When he learned, a few hours later, that Washington's men had been fighting their way into Trenton at the very hour he was writing his letter, Cadwalader was stung into belated action, apparently hoping to share at least part of Washington's glory. Early on the morning of the 27th he took his two thousand men across the river, without asking permission, and without even informing Washington of his intentions.

Not till he had rashly pushed through Brunswick—now abandoned by the Hessians—and advanced to Crosswick did Cadwalader send a message to Washington. Not realizing how precarious was his situation, Cadwalader urged the general to join him. Washington knew that Cornwallis, with a large British force, was already advancing from central New Jersey toward Trenton. If Cadwalader should be overwhelmed, this could seriously diminish the effect of the victory at Trenton. If he should order Cadwalader to recross to the west bank of the Delaware, this ignominious retreat would also certainly diminish those effects. Yet if he were to order his exhausted soldiers to cross back to the east bank, he might well discourage them from re-enlisting when their terms of enlistment expired on December 31; even worse, his command and Cadwalader's would be outnumbered by Cornwallis, and both might be defeated.

Faced with such difficult choices, Washington characteristically chose boldness. He ordered Cadwalader to fall back to Trenton, while he and his men made their third crossing of the Delaware River in three days.

A skillful delaying action slowed Cornwallis's advance sufficiently to permit Washington to establish an entrenched position near Trenton, south of Assunpink Creek. The British general, with about 5,500 men, arrived at nightfall, but delayed an assault until the next morning. About 2,500 more British troops, at Princeton and Maidenhead, were expected to arrive shortly after noon. The Continental Army, shrunken by expiring enlistments, now numbered only 1,600 men, but there were also about 3,000 militia with them. Boxed between the Atlantic Ocean on one side and the unfordable Delaware on the other, the Americans would be an easy victim to Cornwallis's superior force.

But next morning Washington was not there. Leaving a detachment to keep his campfires burning, he had moved in the night around the British left and was on the way to Princeton, far in Cornwallis's rear.

At Stony Brook bridge, two miles short of Princeton, Mercer's brigade, covering the Continental left, met British Colonel Charles Mawhood's brigade, eight hundred strong—two regiments of infantry, a cavalry detachment, and two guns, who had hurried out of town at Cornwallis's order, to join the proposed assault across Assunpink Creek. Both sides rapidly deployed between the Stony Brook and Post roads, and the efficient Mawhood at once attacked.

Washington, hearing the fusillades, galloped to the scene, ordering Cadwalader's Pennsylvania militia, the Associators, to reinforce Mercer. At this moment, however, Mawhood's British regulars broke Mercer's ranks with a bayonet charge; Mercer fell, mortally wounded. Meanwhile, however, an American two-gun battery on Mercer's right opened up against the British left flank. Mawhood, halting to take care of the artillery fire, now saw Cadwalader's militia advancing out of the woods to his front. He reorganized his line on the crest of a rise, with his left flank refused to get it out of range of the cannon.

Cadwalader's troops, shaken at the sight of Mercer's retreating men, received one volley from the British infantry and took to their heels. At that moment Washington's rear guard, Hitchcock's brigade of New England Continentals, appeared. (The main body, under Sullivan, was still marching toward Princeton.)

Washington, ordering Hitchcock's men to deploy on the right, spurred his horse into the midst of Mercer's and Cadwalader's fugitives, shouting for them to stop their disgraceful flight. The effect was miraculous; Mercer's shaken men halted, then turned to follow their commander, as he galloped to the front waving his hat.

For an instant his form disappeared in the smoke of crossfire as both sides opened up. Then he reappeared, untouched.

"Bring up the troops!" he called. "Bring up the troops, the day is ours!"

That did it. With Hitchcock enveloping one British flank and Mercer's men the other, Mawhood abandoned his own guns, and by a desperate bayonet charge got safely across the Stony Brook bridge. Washington, leading his own guard, a platoon of the Philadelphia Light Horse, pursued.

The fifteen-minute-long skirmish—it could hardly be called a battle—was over. Mawhood's troops, harried by the Pennsylvania cavalrymen, disappeared toward Trenton. Washington, drawing rein, gave up the chase and galloped back to join Sullivan's march to Princeton. British losses were 60-odd killed or wounded, and 35 more made prisoner. The Patriots lost 40 killed or wounded.

At Princeton, the small remaining British depot force was easily dispersed.

Collecting 115 prisoners, Washington, knowing full well that by this time Cornwallis must be hurrying back, contented himself with a pell-mell looting of British stores to let his men grab shoes, clothing, and food; then he put the remainder to the flame. By the time the frustrated Cornwallis reached Princeton, the Continental Army was safely on the way to Morristown, where it went into winter quarters. All the British commander could do was to make another forced march back to New Brunswick to protect his depot. In the nine-day campaign embracing Trenton and Princeton, Washington had driven the British from all their New Jersey posts except New Brunswick and Amboy, had blunted the previously irresistible British advance, and fanned the dying embers of American independence to roaring flame. Cornwallis, after his surrender at Yorktown two years later, put it well when he told Washington:

"Fame will gather your brightest laurels from the banks of the Delaware rather than from the Chesapeake."

20

The British Plans for 1777
January–May 1777

Early in 1777 Major General John Burgoyne, returning to England, laid before King George and Lord George Germain, Secretary of State for the Colonies, a most enticing plan to end the troubles in North America. He proposed splitting the recalcitrant colonies. A powerful force would drive from Canada down the Lake Champlain–Hudson Valley route, assisted by a simultaneous secondary effort eastward from Lake Erie up the Mohawk Valley. Meeting at Albany, the combined forces would link with a full-scale converging thrust by Howe up the Hudson from New York. New England would thus be split away from the other colonies, King George's troops would be securely united in the very heartland of the insurrection, and the revolution could be quickly snuffed out.

Burgoyne's pitch was alluring but shallow; no consideration had been given to the enormous logistical problem involved in its execution. Worse still, Germain, while approving "Gentleman Johnny's" grandiose scheme, at the same time approved an entirely different plan submitted from New York by Howe. This was for a major drive south against Washington's main army, and capture of Philadelphia, capital of the rebellious colonies. Germain at best was not a bright man; how these two plans, diametrically opposite in direction, would be coordinated does not appear to have penetrated his mind. In any event, he issued no direct order to Howe to cooperate with Burgoyne, although Howe does seem to have been informed of Burgoyne's plan to advance to Albany from Canada. Burgoyne assumed from his conversations with Germain that Howe would be ordered to cooperate with him by advancing up the Hudson from New York to Albany. He made no personal effort, however, to coordinate his plans with Howe's.

Howe, on the other hand, after receiving Germain's approval of his plan in April, was careful to inform General Sir Guy Carleton, British commander-in-chief in Canada, of his intentions. Howe warned Carleton not to expect his cooperation in the north, although he promised to "have a corps on the lower part of the Hudson's River sufficient to open the communications for shipping through the Highlands . . . which corps may afterwards act in favor of the northern army." He sent a copy of his letter to Germain. Burgoyne learned Howe's intentions when he returned to Canada from England, for Carleton at once showed him Howe's letter. The letter had no appreciable effect on Burgoyne, however, who completed preparations for his advance into New York state.

In this atmosphere of blissful uncertainty shot through with squalls of cross-purpose, both of the northern expeditions assembled; Burgoyne at Saint-Jean, south of Montreal, and Lieutenant Colonel Barry St. Leger (temporary brigadier general) leading the secondary effort on the St. Lawrence at Lachine.

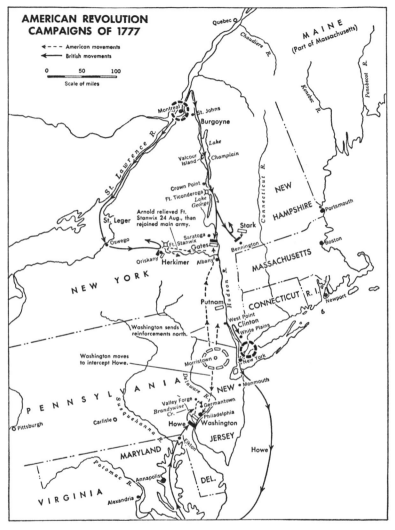

AMERICAN REVOLUTION CAMPAIGNS OF 1777

← - - - American movements
←———— British movements

0   50   100
Scale of miles

MAINE (Part of Massachusetts)

Quebec

Chaudiere R.

Kenebec R.

Penobscot R.

St. Lawrence R.

Montreal

St. Johns

Burgoyne

Lake Champlain

Valcour Island

Crown Point

Ft. Ticonderoga

Lake George

Arnold relieved Ft. Stanwix 24 Aug., then rejoined main army.

St. Leger

Oswego

Ft. Stanwix

Oriskany

Herkimer

Gates

Saratoga

Albany

Stark

Bennington

Connecticut R.

NEW HAMPSHIRE

Portsmouth

Boston

MASSACHUSETTS

CONNECTICUT

R. I.

Newport

NEW YORK

Putnam

Hudson R.

Washington sends reinforcements north.

West Point

Clinton

White Plains

New York

Washington moves to intercept Howe.

Morristown

NEW

Monmouth

JERSEY

Howe

Delaware R.

Valley Forge

Brandywine Cr.

Germantown

Philadelphia

Washington

Howe

PENNSYLVANIA

Susquehanna R.

Pittsburgh

Carlisle

Elkton

MARYLAND

Potomac R.

Annapolis

DEL.

VIRGINIA

Alexandria

Map 7

21

Ticonderoga
June–July 1777

The Patriot Northern Department was commanded by Major General Philip J. Schuyler, New York patroon whose aristocratic aloofness made him highly unpopular with the New England militiamen and Continentals who made up the majority of his force. The remnants of the Continentals who had been engaged in Montgomery's ill-fated invasion of Canada, plus some newly raised militia, approximating three thousand in all, garrisoned the guardian of the classic invasion route, Fort Ticonderoga, near the head of Lake Champlain.

At its southern end the lake was but a quarter-mile wide. Fort Ticonderoga itself, with a star-shaped masonry citadel—built originally by the French—lay on the west shore. Across the lake were Mount Montgomery's fortifications, constructed by Colonel Thaddeus Kosciusko, the Polish engineer. A boom and a footbridge spanned the lake, and behind them lay the remnants of Arnold's squadron of the year previous, together with some two hundred bateaux and other working craft.

Seemingly impregnable, this complex had one major defect: a precipitous conical hill called Sugar Loaf, one mile to the southwest on the New York side, commanding Ticonderoga, had been left unfortified. General Horatio Gates, charged with the renovation of the fortress in 1776, had contemptuously disregarded recommendations that Sugar Loaf be fortified; he considered it to be inaccessible.

To man the entire complex would have necessitated a garrison of 10,000 men. Major General Arthur St. Clair, its commander, had only about 3,500; of these 2,500 were Continentals in ten thin regiments, organized in three brigades: Poore's, Patterson's, and Fermoy's. Two additional militia regiments, totaling about a thousand men, poorly armed and untrained, had been added to this force in July. This garrison was poorly clothed, inadequately armed, and shot through by disease and malnutrition.

Burgoyne's army, 7,500 strong, with 42 light field guns, left Saint-Jean during the third week of June 1777, and paraded up Lake Champlain in "an enormous regatta" of sailboats, row galleys, and the radeau christened *Thunderer*. A naval contingent of two small frigates and a cluster of smaller craft preceded, while Indian auxiliaries, 400 of them, paddled alongside and ahead in a covey of canoes. Behind, came a large baggage train including, fantastically, more than 500 camp followers, women and children.

Major General William Phillips commanded the British increment of some 4,500 men; Brigadier General Simon Fraser, Master of Lovatt, led the advanced corps of light infantry and grenadiers; Brigadier General Powell the 1st Brigade, consisting of the 9th, 47th, and 53rd Foot; Brigadier General Hamilton the 2nd Brigade: the 20th, 21st, and 62nd Foot.

Major General Baron Friedrich Adolph von Riedesel, in theory Burgoyne's second-in-command, led the three-thousand-strong German contingent: Lieutenant Colonel von Breymann's advanced corps of one grenadier battalion, a jäger company, and a detachment of picked British marksmen; Brigadier General von Specht's 1st Brigade, his own regiment, and those of Riedesel and Rhetz; Brigadier General Gall's 2nd Brigade consisting of the Prinz Friederich and Hesse-Hanau regiments. In reserve was a battalion—fewer than five hundred men—of dismounted dragoons.

Except for the Hesse-Hanau contingents, all the Germans were Brunswickers (see p. 210). The artillery of the expedition was manned by detachments of Royal Artillery, Hesse-Hanau gunners, and men drafted from the British infantry.

At Crown Point Burgoyne's expedition disembarked. Fraser's

advance corps led the way down the New York side, followed more slowly by the remainder of the British division; the Germans took to the Vermont side. The naval flotilla dropped anchor just out of cannon range from the Ticonderoga complex.

After some preliminary skirmishing and reconnaissance, Burgoyne's engineers discovered Sugar Loaf, promptly christened it Mount Defiance, and set to work. By the morning of July 5 two 12-pounder brass guns glinted on its crest, dominating the Ticonderoga complex, all within easy range.

Should St. Clair stay, defeat was certain; if he retreated he knew he would be damned as a coward, a traitor, even. But he would still have a fighting force in being. He ordered immediate evacuation under cover of darkness that night. The baggage and as much light artillery and stores as could be moved would go by boat to Skenesboro (now Whitehall), with one regiment as escort. St. Clair hoped the boom would impede British pursuit by water. The bulk of the command, fleeing eastward across the footbridge, would move across country to Hubbardton, via an abominable stump-studded trail called the Military Road; thence south to Castleton, and rendezvous with the train at Skenesboro to the west. Two ready-loaded cannon at the eastern end of the footbridge would check any British attempt at immediate pursuit.

At nightfall the evacuation proceeded in a fever of confusion and—among the militia—stark fear. St. Clair ordered a heavy cannonade which would—he hoped—drown the noise. But all effort at secrecy failed when the futile Frenchman Fermoy, one of St. Clair's brigade commanders, set fire to his own quarters on Mount Independence.

At 4:00 A.M., July 6, the last American cleared the footbridge. Thirty minutes later Fraser's British advance corps rushed the bridge, to find the bridge guard in drunken stupor beside their silent guns.

Burgoyne reacted to the new situation with commendable energy. Sending Fraser's advance corps hot-footing it behind St. Clair, he ordered von Riedesel to back him up, and himself smashed the boom at Ticonderoga, sailed through, and bagged the

American baggage train at Skenesboro, its escorting regiment getting away to the south after a hot running fight. St. Clair's line of retreat had been cut.

22

Hubbardton
July 7, 1777

Reaching the hamlet of Hubbardton, where the Military Road joined the route to Castleton, St. Clair led his harried column on to Castleton, leaving Seth Warner's battalion of Green Mountain Boys from the New Hampshire Grants and Colonel Nathan Hale's* 2nd New Hampshire to await the arrival of Colonel Ebenezer Francis's 11th Massachusetts, the original rear guard. Warner would command this new rear guard, 760 strong, and his orders were to join the main body at Castleton by nightfall.

But Francis, whose orders were to gather before him "every living thing," didn't arrive until late afternoon, herding more than a hundred stragglers ahead of him, and Warner chose to stay until morning.

In early dawn Fraser's British advance corps sighted the bivouac and attacked at once. Hale's New Hampshire men dissolved. Warner and Francis, mustering between them about six hundred men, counterattacked not once but three times, stopping the British completely. Not until the pudgy von Riedesel, leading in person his own advance party of some two hundred men, turned the American right flank, was the match settled. Warner's troops melted into the woods.

* No relative of the martyred hero.

Hubbardton was a British victory. Ninety-six Americans were dead or wounded (Francis among the killed), 228 prisoners bagged, mostly from Hale's regiment, taken after the hour-and-forty-five-minute fight had ended. But the British had lost 50 men killed and more than 100 wounded, some 17 percent of the troops engaged. Brunswick losses were 10 killed and 14 wounded. Fraser, his troops completely exhausted, could make no further move for two days.

As one British participant put it later: "The Advanced Corps certainly discovered that neither were they invincible, nor were the Rebels all Poltroons." Looking at the big picture, St. Clair, marching rapidly toward Rutland, and bypassing the exhausted British at Hubbardton, had escaped. He would join Schuyler later at Fort Edward, twenty-five miles below Skenesboro on July 12. The Green Mountain Boys, flitting through the trees to safety, would have another rendezvous at Bennington, thirty-five days later. And Burgoyne, taking up the task of moving south through wilderness, still had two small American forces in the field against him. Gloomily he wrote: "The New Hampshire Grants . . . now abounds in the most active and rebellious race of the continent, and hangs like a gathering storm on my left."

23

Oriskany and Fort Stanwix
August 1777

Barry St. Leger owes his place in history primarily to his foundation in 1776 of the English horse-race classic bearing his name, which since has been run annually at Doncaster. His mission the following year was to make a 150-mile march down the Mohawk Valley from Oswego on Lake Ontario to Albany, rendezvousing there with Burgoyne. His means were 750 men—100 regulars each of the 8th and 34th Foot; contingents of two Tory militia regiments: Johnson's Royal Greens and Butler's Rangers; and one battalion of Hesse-Hanau jägers. About one thousand Indian auxiliaries led by Joseph Brant accompanied him. He carried with him four light field guns and four small mortars.

The route was over a well-defined trail cut by the so-called Grand Portage, key to the Mohawk Valley, where dilapidated Fort Stanwix stood. What St. Leger did not know was that Stanwix had been lately occupied and reconditioned by Colonel Peter Ganse-voort's 3rd New York Continentals, 550 strong. Nor did he expect much other resistance, for sparsely populated Tyron County was a fratricidal battleground, where local militia under elderly Brigadier General Nicholas Herkimer were continually bickering with Tory troops maintained by the wealthy Johnson family.

St. Leger, approaching Stanwix, arrived too late to intercept a two-hundred-man Massachusetts reinforcement with a convoy of supply, swelling Gansevoort's garrison. On August 3 the British settled down to a formal investment.

Meanwhile Herkimer was mustering his county militia at Fort Dayton, on the Mohawk, some thirty miles below Stanwix. On August 4 he marched to the relief of Fort Stanwix, with eight hundred men, a long train of oxcarts, and some sixty Oneida Indian scouts. A message to Colonel Gansevoort had gone ahead, asking for a supporting sortie, heralded by a three-gun signal, when Herkimer should come within striking distance.

St. Leger, warned of the approaching militia column, boldly denuded his investing force to ambush Herkimer with all of Brant's Indians and detachments of the Royal Greens and Rangers, with Colonel Sir John Johnson in command. As Her-kimer's long column was winding through a deep ravine near the settlement of Oriskany, six miles from Fort Stanwix, on August 6, the trap was sprung.

Herkimer went down, badly wounded, in the first burst of fire.

His rear guard fled, but the main body, assailed on all sides, stood and fought, while their general, propped against a saddle and smoking his long pipe, gave directions as he observed the fight swirl around him.

After forty-five minutes the hand-to-hand, kill-or-be-killed struggle was temporarily quelled by a rain squall that dampened all musket primings. When the sun again beamed out, fighting resumed. But at Herkimer's direction, his encircled men were fighting now in teams of two, one loading while the other fired. The result was sustained firepower. Brant's Indians lost interest and disappeared; a charge by a Royal Green detachment was repulsed, and the now outnumbered Tories called it a day.

Herkimer's men were only too glad to see them go. Forgetting all thought of their original objective, they gathered up their wounded, fifty in all, including their general (who would later die) and went home. No accurate statistics of the Battle of Oriskany exist. Somewhere between 150 and 200 Patriots lay dead, while Tory and Indian losses are estimated at about 150.

St. Leger's ambuscaders returned to their camp to meet another blow. Herkimer's message to Gansevoort had been received, the three-gun signal had been fired, and Lieutenant Colonel Marinus Willett, with a 240-man detachment of the 3rd New York and 9th Massachusetts, had sortied to spread destruction through the Tory and Indian camps. Arms, ammunition, and camp gear, including the Indians' deerskin sleeping wraps, had been destroyed or carried off. Even Colonel Johnson's portfolio of private papers was now in Gansevoort's hands.

Placating as best he could the enraged Indians and disgruntled Tories, St. Leger continued his siege of the fort in formal investment. He knew that the defenders' food and ammunition were dwindling. In fact, Willett and another American officer had sneaked through to the British lines to Fort Dayton, appealing for help.

And help was indeed on the way. Schuyler, at Stillwater, fearing that any formal relief operation would not only weaken his forces facing Burgoyne but also might invite open antagonism among his officers, called for a general officer to lead a volunteer expedition up the Mohawk. It was Schuyler's last order; on August 19 he was relieved of his command, General Horatio Gates succeeding him (Gates's lobbying in Philadelphia had paid off).

Benedict Arnold, who had just been sent up by Washington to the northern front, leaped at the opportunity to relieve Fort Stanwix, and volunteers rushed to his command. By August 21 he was at Fort Dayton with 1,100 men. On the 23rd he began a forced march toward Fort Stanwix. But ahead of him he had sent an odd individual with a peculiar mission: one Hon Yost Schuyler, Herkimer's nephew and a local half-wit, then under sentence of death at Stillwater for alleged treason. Arnold offered him complete pardon if he would seek out St. Leger's camp and spread the rumor of a relief column coming in great strength.

Hon Yost was not too half-witted to know on which side his bread was buttered. Shooting bullet holes in his coat, he safely gained the British camp, telling everyone he met—particularly the Indians, to whom he was one of the sacred of the great Manitou— of thousands of Patriot troops on the way, led by the one man most feared by both British and Indians in the North. To St. Leger he showed his riddled coat.

Brant's Indians, rioting, demanded immediate retreat. St. Leger, with his allies "more formidable than the enemy," decamped on August 22, leaving tentage, ammunition, cannon, and stores behind him.

One of the three converging British columns was disposed of. There were still two, however, and much more formidable: the armies of Burgoyne and Howe.

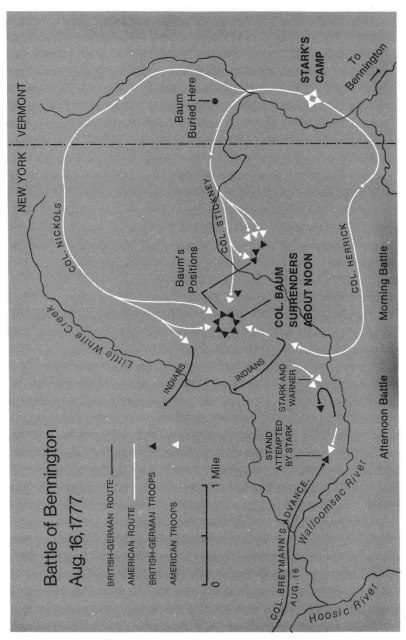

Battle of Bennington
Aug. 16, 1777

BRITISH-GERMAN ROUTE ——
AMERICAN ROUTE ——
BRITISH-GERMAN TROOPS ◄
AMERICAN TROOPS ◄

0 _____ 1 Mile

Map 8

24

Bennington
August 16, 1777

Burgoyne moved south from Skenesboro on July 25, making a mile a day over a wilderness road methodically sabotaged by Schuyler's men, with barricades of felled trees, demolished bridges, and dammed-up streams that turned the footing into bogs. Reaching Fort Edward on the Hudson on the 29th, Burgoyne found it deserted; Schuyler had decamped farther south, still wrecking the road behind him.

Burgoyne now received depressing news from Howe, a letter dated July 17 announcing initiation of his planned move from New York to Philadelphia. To Burgoyne, however, this increased the urgency of pressing on to Albany and his rendezvous with St. Leger. But he needed horses, both mounts for his jackbooted, foot-slogging Brunswick dragoons, and draft animals. He also needed wagons, cattle, and recruits. These his political adviser, Colonel Philip Skene, wealthy Tory landowner (Skenesboro was in his domain), assured him he would find in plenty east of the Hudson.

So, while Burgoyne waited at Fort Edward, Brunswicker Lieutenant Colonel Friedrich Baum, who didn't speak a word of English, moved with some eight hundred men up the Battenkill Valley into this promised land. His command included the dismounted dragoons, a hundred-man detachment of jägers and grenadiers, a handful of British "sharpshooters," and three hundred assorted Tories, Canadians, and Indians. Two light cannon trundled with them. Skene accompanied the raiders.

Both General Fraser and Baron von Riedesel had some qualms about the venture; doubtless the lessons of Hubbardton were remembered by two competent soldiers. Riedesel in particular warned Baum to avoid "the corps of Mr. Warner, now supposed to be at Manchester."

Baum, unsuccessful in garnering either horses or recruits, pushed on for Bennington, where it was known that large stocks of Patriot supplies were stored. Meanwhile, the New Hampshire legislature, alarmed by Burgoyne's invasion, had coaxed John Stark to raise a brigade of militia. Stark had accepted a Continental commission after Bunker's Hill, but had later resigned in disgust when younger and less experienced officers were promoted over his head. Patriotism now overcame pride, and with 1,500 men Stark marched to Bennington, while Warner and his Green Mountain Boys were—as Riedesel had assumed—at Manchester.

Baum, clashing with Stark's scouts, stopped and entrenched some four miles west of the present New York-Vermont border. He sent word to Burgoyne that he was opposed by a strong force. Stark, calling on Warner to join him, prepared for attack. On August 16, a hot, rainy morning, he fell on the Brunswickers in a double envelopment. Baum's Indians and Tories fled, his regulars were rushed simultaneously from left, right, and rear. Then an ammunition cart, his only reserve, blew up. The Brunswick dragoons attempted to hack their way out of the melee with their long swords. But when Baum went down, mortally wounded, they surrendered, apparently ending the brief but bloody battle.

Flushed by victory, Stark's men momentarily relaxed. They were galvanized into action when, at 4:30 P.M., a new enemy force came on the field. It was the remainder of the Brunswick advance corps, under Lieutenant Colonel Heinrich von Breymann, hurried by Burgoyne to reinforce Baum: seven hundred infantrymen and two fieldpieces.

Hot and muddy, tired and water-soaked in their heavy uniforms, von Breymann's disciplined jägers and grenadiers were nevertheless formidable. Advancing in close formation, they brushed off three quickly assembled elements of Stark's men, also tired. At this moment Warner and his Green Mountain Boys arrived from Manchester. They, too, were hot and muddy after a tough forced march. But they had gained their second wind in a brief pause at Bennington, aided by a rum ration swilled as they dropped their packs. And, also remembering Hubbardton, they had a score to settle.

Half of Warner's men outflanked Breymann's right. The remainder—about 150 men—with Stark's rallied troops held the center and overlapped the Brunswick left. Breymann, his troops still in hand, attempted to withdraw after a short fire fight; his ammunition was running low. The move didn't work; the Patriots were in their element now, open-order harassment of a slowly moving enemy. The Brunswick formations crumbled; Breymann was wounded. He ordered his drummers to beat a long roll to signal a parley, but that was merely noise to his attackers, and the Brunswickers reeled down the road in rout.

With dusk, Stark called off the pursuit and some two-thirds of Breymann's men got away.

In this amazing Patriot double victory, 207 Brunswickers had died; 700 more, including 30 officers, were prisoners. Four cannon, 250 broadswords, four ammunition wagons, and muskets and jäger rifles by the hundreds had fallen into Patriot hands. Stark's losses were fewer than 20 men killed and about 40 more wounded. New England's spirits rose, while Burgoyne across the Hudson pondered on his increasing troubles. Nevertheless, he persisted in attempting to hurry down to Albany and to keep his rendezvous with St. Leger. He need not have hurried; St. Leger would never arrive.

25

Brandywine
September 11, 1777

In June 1777, after several weeks of inconclusive maneuvering against Washington, General Howe withdrew his troops from New Jersey across the river to New York. Washington knew that British General Burgoyne was pushing south through the Lake Champlain valley, and at first he assumed that Howe planned to advance up the Hudson and join Burgoyne. However, leaving about one-third of his army under Clinton, to garrison New York, Howe and sixteen thousand men put out to sea instead. Sixteen warships escorted 245 transports and supply ships.

Howe recognized that the way to defeat the Americans was to destroy Washington's army, but he had been unable to entice the American general into battle in eastern New Jersey. So he decided to threaten Philadelphia from the south, advancing from the northernmost tip of Chesapeake Bay at Head of Elk. Howe felt certain that Washington would have to stand and fight to protect the seat of Congress. He confidently expected that he could destroy Washington's army and seize the rebel capital in one campaign.

When Howe sailed from New York on July 23, Washington realized that the British objective might be Philadelphia. Yet he could not believe that Howe would go away and leave Burgoyne unsupported and isolated in upper New York State. Until Howe actually made his way into Chesapeake Bay, Washington felt he was probably feinting to the south and would reappear at New York to support Burgoyne.

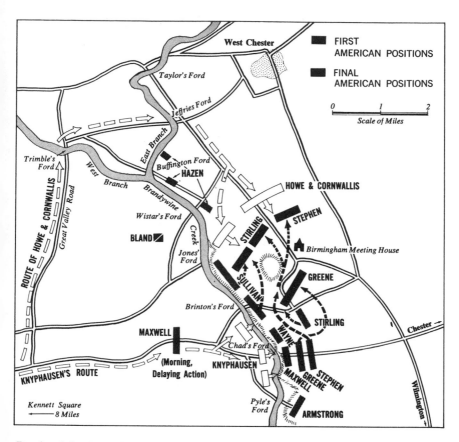

Battle of the Brandywine, September 11, 1777.

Map 9

Meanwhile, he shifted his army to central New Jersey, so as to be able to defend the capital, if need be, while he could still move back promptly to block a British move up the Hudson. At the same time, as Burgoyne advanced farther and farther into upper New York from Canada, Washington detached some of his most reliable troops and most capable commanders to reinforce the Northern Army. He could ill afford to detach units like Morgan's rifle brigade, and commanders like generals Arnold and Lincoln, but he knew that Burgoyne must be stopped at all costs. Furthermore, he reasoned that the opportunity to destroy a British army that was inland and isolated from British sea power was worth risking a possible defeat near the Atlantic coast.

Once Howe sailed into Chesapeake Bay, his intentions were clear. Washington had ample time to move southward to take up defensive positions to protect Philadelphia. By September 1 he had about fifteen thousand men between Wilmington and Philadelphia, but of these more than one-third were unreliable militiamen. His Continental troops were organized in five divisions, commanded by Generals Greene, Sullivan, Stephen, Stirling, and William Maxwell.

Washington selected a defensive position behind Brandywine Creek, a tributary which ran into the Delaware River just north of Wilmington. Howe's logical route from Head of Elk to Philadelphia would lead him to cross Chad's Ford (now Chadds Ford) on the Brandywine. The creek valley was deep and narrow, and made a good obstacle, although the stream was fordable in several places.

Washington posted Greene's division and Brigadier General Anthony Wayne's brigade of Maxwell's division at Chad's Ford. Farther south Brigadier General John Armstrong's Pennsylvania militia held the easily defended cliffs overlooking Pyle's Ford. Sullivan's division was responsible for protecting the army's right flank, and was deployed to the north between Brinton's and Jones's fords. Sullivan sent Colonel Moses Hazen's so-called Canadian Regiment to cover Wister's and Buffington's fords, still farther north. Stephen's and Stirling's divisions were held in reserve behind Chad's Ford.

Washington sent Maxwell's light infantry brigade to form an outpost line covering the expected British route toward Brandywine Creek. He stationed Colonel Theodorick Bland's 1st Dragoons west of Jones's Ford to screen all of the northern approaches to the creek up to Buffington's Ford. A body of Pennsylvania militia was to screen the approaches to the creek north of Buffington's Ford.

Pennsylvania officers told Washington that there were no more fords for twelve miles north of Buffington's. He did not reconnoiter the area himself, nor did he send a trustworthy officer to do the job. This was possibly the most serious mistake of his military career, because the information was wrong. The Great Valley Road, that ran west of the Brandywine, swung east, crossing both the West Branch and the East Branch of the creek before they joined just south of Buffington's Ford. Washington knew nothing of these crossings, but Howe had learned about them from his scouts. On September 10 the British general and his two corps commanders, Lord Cornwallis and General Wilhelm von Knyphausen, personally explored the area with the aid of local Loyalists. They knew the American dispositions and they knew of the open road to the north. Howe decided on the strategy that had worked so well at the Battle of Long Island—a frontal diversion, with a wide-sweeping envelopment as his main effort. Knyphausen, with five thousand troops, would make the frontal diversion; Cornwallis, with eight thousand, would make the main attack.

At dawn on September 11 the British left their camp near Kennett Square. About 8:00 A.M. Knyphausen's advance guard struck Maxwell's brigade about three miles west of Chad's Ford. Maxwell withdrew slowly, fighting a commendable delaying action. Two hours later he brought his men across the creek and into position between Wayne's brigade and Greene's division. Knyphausen followed, deploying his men on the west bank of the valley, between Chad's and Brinton's fords. His Hessian and British troops kept up a fire just lively enough to hold the attention of the Americans, and to cause them to expect a frontal attack across the creek. Meanwhile, Cornwallis and his men were marching north, then east, along the Great Valley Road.

Late in the morning Washington received a report from Colonel Hazen, through Sullivan, that a large body of British was moving north on the Great Valley Road. This was surprising, since there had been no report from Colonel Bland, whose cavalry was covering the area west of the creek. He immediately sent a message to Bland, ordering him to investigate. Bland's reply was vague and unsatisfactory, but meanwhile Washington had received a very clear report from Pennsylvania Lieutenant Colonel James Ross, who had been scouting in the enemy rear. Ross said that at 11:00

A.M. he had seen about five thousand British troops, with sixteen or eighteen guns, on the Great Valley Road.

Washington was now convinced that Howe had divided his army, and he believed this would give the Americans a chance to defeat the British in detail. He ordered a counterattack across the Brandywine by Greene, Wayne, Maxwell, and Sullivan. Stirling and Stephen were to remain in reserve, between Chad's Ford and Birmingham Meeting House, about two miles behind the creek.

Then, just as the counterattacking force was beginning to move, Sullivan sent another report, stating that the Pennsylvania militia had seen no British near the northern fords. Sullivan commented that the reports from Hazen and Ross were probably wrong.

While Washington was puzzling over this confusing and contradictory information, a little after 2:00 P.M., an excited local farmer ran into the headquarters claiming that the British had crossed the Brandywine and were marching south toward Birmingham Meeting House. It did not seem possible to Washington that the enemy had gotten so far, but he called off his counterattack.

Another message from Sullivan soon confirmed the farmer's report. Washington immediately deployed his troops for defense against the envelopment. Sullivan was to swing his division into a new position facing north, at right angles to the line of the Brandywine. Stirling and Stephen were to move to the right of Sullivan's new position, near Birmingham Meeting House.

Between four and four-thirty, Washington heard heavy artillery and musket fire from the right rear and realized that the British attack was in greater force than he had anticipated. He pulled Greene back from Chad's Ford, leaving only Wayne's and Maxwell's brigades to hold the ford. Accompanying Greene, Washington hastened to the sound of the battle.

Sullivan, Stephen, and Stirling were still deploying into their new positions when the British struck. Sullivan's division was hit hard, and after a brief, intense fight, gave way. However, Brigadier General George Weedon's Virginia brigade, of Greene's division, arrived behind Sullivan's left and was able to hold the threatened position. Sullivan's troops fell back through Weedon's ranks.

Stephen's and Stirling's divisions held fast, and Cornwallis decided to stop for the night. The day had been hot, and his men were exhausted after their sixteen-mile march and two-hour fight.

At Chad's Ford, meanwhile, Knyphausen had quickly taken advantage of the removal of Greene's division. Covered by an intense artillery bombardment, his troops crossed the creek valley and gained the east bank. Wayne and Maxwell delayed the Hessians, slowly withdrawing their badly outnumbered men in good order, although eight guns were lost.

It was now clear to Washington that he could not possibly regain his lost ground, or re-establish a good defensive position. So he pulled his army back to Chester under cover of darkness. He had been defeated, mainly because he had failed to have the countryside properly reconnoitered. He had fought the battle skillfully, however, once the true tactical situation became clear, and the morale of the American troops remained good. They lost about 200 killed, 700 or 800 wounded, and almost 400 prisoners. British casualties were reported as 89 killed, 488 wounded, and 6 missing.

26

Freeman's Farm (First Saratoga)
September 19, 1777

Burgoyne in early September 1777 faced a difficult decision. He knew now that Howe was not coming from New York to meet him; he also had learned of St. Leger's dismal failure. His inadequate Canadian supply line would literally freeze up in the winter. Already his communications were being threatened by Patriot

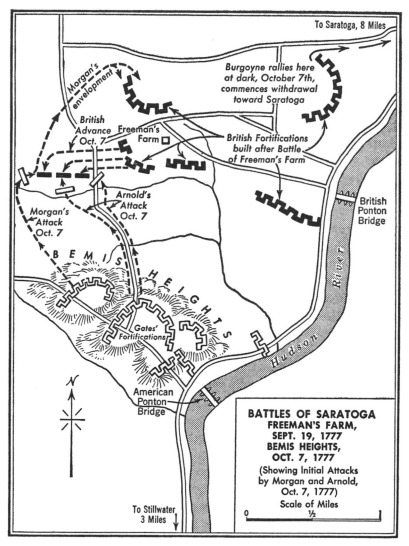

Map 10

nibbles at Fort Ticonderoga, now garrisoned by a Brunswick regiment.

Should he retreat or should he go ahead? If the latter, on which side of the Hudson River? The east bank route was easier, and would facilitate communications with Canada. But he would have to cross sometime to reach Albany, and Gates's army lay on the west side, ready to oppose such a crossing. The decision must be made quickly, since he now had barely thirty days' provisions on hand for his 6,500 men, and local supplies were almost non-existent. Choosing Albany and the west bank, he threw a bridge of boats across the Hudson, crossed on September 13, and then dismantled it.

His Rubicon was crossed; his connection with Canada ended.

Inching down the west bank, his boats dragging behind him in the river, Burgoyne groped for Gates. He had been blinded by the desertion of his Indian auxiliaries. One of his foraging parties, ambushed between Stillwater and Saratoga, disclosed that Gates lay heavily entrenched on Bemis Heights, three miles north of Stillwater. Burgoyne decided to attack.

Cautious "Granny" Gates, reinforced now by Washington's generous donation of Morgan's rifle corps and Henry Dearborn's light infantry, lay close to the river behind fortifications carefully designed by Kosciusko.

The American works extended along three sides of a quadrangle three-quarters of a mile long on each face. The river façade, over which Gates himself took charge, was held by the Massachusetts brigades of John Glover, John Paterson, and John Nixon. Below it a bridge of boats spanned the Hudson. Learned's Massachusetts brigade and James Livingston's New York regiment manned the northern face. On the western side, under Arnold, were Morgan's brigade, most of Poor's New Hampshire–New York brigade, and some Connecticut militia. Except for the Connecticut contingent all these troops were Continentals. They numbered some seven thousand men, with an adequate assortment of artillery.

Burgoyne's plan was to envelop the American left and drive the defenders down into the river. Fraser's advance corps, reinforced by Breymann's jägers and grenadiers—some two thousand men and eight guns—would circle wide to high ground on the west, then drive southeast, making the main effort.

Hamilton's brigade, the 9th, 20th, 21st, and 62nd Foot—eleven hundred men and six guns—would hit the northern face of the American works. Burgoyne would accompany this contingent. Down the river road would come Riedesel's Brunswick brigade, the regiments of Riedesel, Specht, and Rhetz, with the eight guns of the Hesse-Hanau artillery. Back at Burgoyne's headquarters just south of Saratoga lay the train, the stores, and the boats nestling at the riverbank, guarded by the Hesse-Hanau regiment and six companies of the 47th Foot.

Patriot reconnaissance that sunny morning of September 19 disclosed the British advance. Gates, despite Arnold's vehement protests, decided to await the assault behind his fortifications. He was induced, however, to permit Morgan's brigade to develop Burgoyne's intentions, and protect the left flank.

Near Freeman's Farm, a mile north of the American position, Morgan's riflemen flushed a British picket and drove it in. Their hot pursuit brought them, badly extended, against Hamilton's brigade. The British volley fire scattered the riflemen. Arnold pushed in Cilley's 1st and Scammell's 3rd New Hampshire regiments, who fell foul of Fraser's light infantry encircling force, and were thrown back. Arnold threw the rest of Poor's brigade between Fraser and Hamilton. Fraser, while assisting Hamilton's right, with the 24th Foot and Breymann's command, continued his encircling move with his grenadiers and light infantry, only to be halted by Morgan's reorganized riflemen.

For the rest of the day a confused fire fight ensued, surging back and forth on the fifteen-acre clearing of Freeman's Farm. The focal point was Burgoyne's artillery. Morgan's riflemen picked off the gunners, but Poor's men, attempting to capture the guns, were thrown back by bayonet charges.

Burgoyne, in a serious situation, called on Riedesel for guns and men, while Arnold imperiously demanded reinforcements. But

Gates, back at headquarters, refused, and a violent quarrel broke out between the two American generals.

Meanwhile Riedesel was saving the situation for Burgoyne. He had already begun movement toward the sound of the cannonade when Burgoyne's message reached him late in the afternoon. Rushing his guns forward, he preceded them at the head of an advance party and charged into the battle, driving in Arnold's right flank. The Brunswick guns came rolling in, quickly dropped trails, opening with grape at pistol range. Behind them the Brunswick infantry plodded stolidly into line. With dusk, the fire died away, the Continentals withdrew, and Burgoyne's troops bivouacked on the field.

British losses were some 600 men killed, wounded, or captured; Hamilton's brigade alone suffered casualties of 350 men, most in the 62nd Foot, which entered the fight 350 strong, and emerged with but 60 men and five officers. American losses were 65 killed, 218 wounded, and 33 missing.

Tactically, the British attack at Freeman's Farm had been turned into a stubborn and successful defense. Strategically, Burgoyne had gained nothing; he had squandered irreplaceable manpower while Gates was still solidly entrenched on Bemis Heights, opposing further advance. On the American side, the elation of stopping the British regulars in open battle was offset by the frustration of an opportunity lost, while the quarrel between Arnold and Gates weakened morale. The casualties had been light, replacements obtainable. Only a shortage of ammunition—most of it had been shot away—was cause for anxiety.

27

Philadelphia and Germantown
October 4, 1777

Following the Battle of the Brandywine, Washington and Howe maneuvered for a fortnight south of Philadelphia. Washington hoped to defeat Howe by striking as the British crossed the Schuylkill River, but he was misled by a British feint. On September 26 the redcoats marched easily into the American capital. Congress and many of the citizens of Philadelphia had fled a week earlier.

Howe put Cornwallis and about three thousand troops in Philadelphia, while the main body, eight thousand men, bivouacked at Germantown, about five miles to the northwest. Another three thousand were deployed along the Delaware, cooperating with the British fleet in operations against American forts blockading the river.

Howe prepared no defensive fortifications, and Washington, who knew the area well, saw an opportunity for a decisive surprise attack. He now had about eleven thousand men—eight thousand Continentals and three thousand militia. Thus he knew that he outnumbered the Germantown contingent of Howe's divided force.

Washington and his staff planned a complicated surprise predawn attack on October 4, calling for the coordination of four separate columns in the dark after a long night march.

On the far right, Brigadier General John Armstrong's Pennsylvania militia was to turn the British left flank near the Schuylkill River. To Armstrong's left, along the main north-south road from

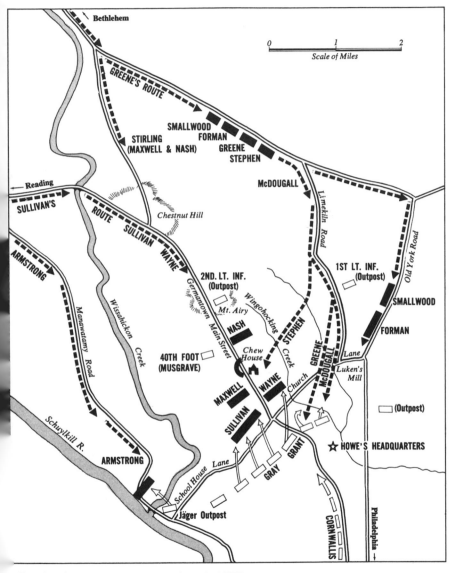

Battle of Germantown, October 4, 1777

Map 11

Reading into Germantown, came General Sullivan with Wayne's brigade attached to his division. Washington accompanied Sullivan.

The main attack was to be made by the American left-center under General Greene, with his own division and that of General Stephen, plus Brigadier General Alexander McDougall's brigade. Greene's mission was to envelop Howe's right and force the British back against the Schuylkill.

To the extreme left, Brigadier General William Smallwood and Brigadier General David Forman led their Maryland and New Jersey militia to get behind the right rear of the British by way of the old York Road. In reserve was Stirling's division, to move to Chestnut Hill, ready to support either Greene's or Sullivan's wing.

Washington's plan allowed time for almost two hours' rest after the troops reached their preattack positions. Then they were to move out at 4:00 A.M., striking the British outposts silently, with bayonet only, at five, still an hour before dawn. The schedule did not go according to plan. Everyone was late. To make things worse, General Greene's guide lost his way on the dark roads, and Greene was almost an hour further behind schedule than Sullivan's force.

Sullivan's lead brigade finally deployed for attack on the British Mount Airy outpost at 6:00 A.M., in a misty dawn. The Americans didn't know that they had been sighted on the march almost three hours earlier, and that the outpost was alerted. On the other hand, the British thought that this was only a small raid.

As Sullivan's troops approached, the alert British outposts fired, then withdrew slowly in good order, to where a battalion of British light infantry was waiting. It delivered a volley and then counterattacked. The 40th Foot was brought up beside the light infantry to form a line of battle across the road.

The Americans, themselves surprised, still did not panic. Their superior numbers soon carried them into the northern outskirts of Germantown. Now it was the turn of the British to be surprised, because of the weight of the attack. Howe went forward to rally the light infantry, shaming them for fleeing from a few rebels. But when grapeshot from the American artillery knocked leaves and branches onto his shoulder, Howe, convinced that the Americans were in great force, hastily withdrew to prepare for a real battle.

The morning mist now became a heavy fog, confusing British and Americans alike. It was especially handicapping to Washington and his commanders, however, since they were now on unfamiliar ground, with many separate forces to concentrate.

Washington was worried when he realized that there was no firing on Sullivan's left, where Greene should have been making the main effort. Because of this, Sullivan shifted Wayne's brigade east of the main road, to protect his left flank. Reducing the weight of Sullivan's attack, and shifting it somewhat eastward, Washington decided to commit his reserve—Stirling's division—to make up for Greene's absence, and further to protect Sullivan's open left flank.

Nevertheless, Sullivan was pushing back the 40th Foot and the light infantry, driving them in considerable disorder into Germantown. As they withdrew past the solid stone mansion of Judge Chew—just east of Germantown's main street and north of the center of town—Lieutenant Colonel Thomas Musgrave, commanding the 40th Foot, gathered about 120 of his soldiers into the house and made it into a fortress. As Maxwell's brigade, from Stirling's reserve division, was deploying under Washington's supervision, musket fire blazed from the Chew House.

Washington was undecided whether to bypass the Chew House or delay his attack while it was reduced. However, his able artillery officer, General Knox, strongly urged that the fortress must first be taken. American artillery banged away at it, but most of the shot bounced off its sturdy stone walls. The fog prevented accurate aiming at the shuttered windows, which Musgrave's men had loopholed for muskets.

After half an hour, Washington decided that the delay at the Chew House was too expensive. Both of Stirling's reserve brigades were being held up far behind the main battle, when they were badly needed to support Sullivan. The Chew House could be taken care of later.

It was at about this time that Washington learned that Greene had reached the British outposts on the Limekiln Road, and was now engaged on the outskirts of the British camp, to the left of Wayne. From the sound of the firing, it seemed possible that Greene might actually be in the camp. Thinking that victory was almost won, Washington rode forward to rejoin Sullivan.

The battle was far from over, however. The firing to the left front increased in intensity, as British counterattacks halted Greene's advance. Then came more firing from the left rear. The earlier sound of battle around the Chew House had worried Wayne, who slowed his attack and sent some of his force back to investigate. Stephen's division, which should have been attacking on the left of Greene, had also been drawn by the sound of firing far off course to the Chew House, where some of his men began a new effort to reduce the little fortress. This renewed noise led some of Wayne's men to believe that they were being attacked from the rear, and they began to panic.

It was now about 9:00 A.M., and the fog was beginning to lift. The British main army was fully engaged, having been given time to organize, thanks largely to the Chew House delays. British General Grant found the gap in the American line created by Stephen's prolonged detour to Chew House, and pushed through. Sullivan's and Wayne's men had wasted much ammunition in the early morning, firing through the fog at trees and fence posts. Now their cartridge boxes were empty. The panic in Wayne's brigade spread to adjacent units, and some of Greene's and Sullivan's troops also began to break.

At this time Cornwallis came up from Philadelphia with reinforcements. The pressure on Greene's division increased, his right flank now threatened by Grant's penetration. He reluctantly ordered a withdrawal, but was able to save his guns. Washington, realizing that nothing more could be done, ordered Sullivan and Wayne also to pull back to reorganize.

The two wide-circling attacks—Armstrong's on the right, and Smallwood's and Forman's on the left—also failed, because of delays and overcaution. Washington ordered a general withdrawal, and the battle of Germantown was over.

The American defeat was the result of an overcomplicated plan and bad luck. The confusion caused by the fog also had probably hurt them much more than it had affected the British, who were on the defensive on their own ground. The British lost about 70 killed, 450 wounded, and 14 missing, while the American losses were 152 killed, 521 wounded, and almost 400 missing. Fortunately for American morale, Washington's men thought they had inflicted more casualties than they had suffered.

Howe was impressed by the fact that Washington and his troops had fought so skillfully and aggressively less than a month after the defeat at the Brandywine. He gave no thought to pursuing the Americans. Instead, he withdrew to Philadelphia and fortified the city. He also opened a line of communications down the Delaware River, capturing several American forts on the riverbank.

28

Bemis Heights (Second Saratoga)
October 7, 1777

From September 21 until early October Burgoyne and Gates glowered at one another from behind fortifications. The Englishman had thrown up a well-organized entrenchment roughly two miles north of Gates's Bemis Heights position. "Gentleman Johnny's" earthworks extended west from the Hudson, in front of a depression called the Great Ravine. The right flank of this position was protected by a large horseshoe-shaped redoubt, its toe pointing west-southwest. The entire front had been cleared to afford fields of fire. Below the bluffs on the Hudson bank nestled the British rear echelon, while with his boats Burgoyne had fashioned a ponton-type footbridge to the east bank. Unfortunately for him, Burgoyne could muster now barely five thousand fighting men, rations were dwindling, and local foraging was checked by sharpshooting Patriot patrols.

On October 3, with rations cut by one-third, Burgoyne, Riedesel, Fraser, and Phillips went into a huddle. All they knew of Gates's situation was that his strength must be increasing; no British patrols could break through his sharpshooter screen. But an immediate decision was imperative. Burgoyne, always the gambler, decided to make a reconnaissance in force on October 7, to test Gates's strength. If circumstances warranted, he would throw in his entire army in one attack. If not, he would withdraw to the Battenkill and there await the arrival of Sir Henry Clinton, new British commander in New York, who had sent a message in mid-September that he would soon start up the Hudson.

The decision made, twelve barrels of rum were broken out that night, to hearten the troops.

Gates, for his part, was content to wait out Burgoyne's inevitable dissolution. Up north General Lincoln's militia were harassing the Brunswicker garrison of Fort Ticonderoga. Some two thousand New Hampshire militia occupied the Fort Edward area, and 1,300 Massachusetts militia, coming down the Battenkill, had been ordered to cross the Hudson and blocked the west bank road north of Saratoga.

Gates had eleven thousand men now, his largest reinforcement being a contingent of Lincoln's men from the Manchester-Bennington area. On September 29 they poured into Gates's position, 2,200 strong.

Inside the American camp, however, the quarrel between Gates and Arnold had become a scandal. Gates, who had made no mention of Arnold in his report on the battle of Freeman's Farm, relieved him from command, appointing Lincoln in his place, and barring the firebrand from his headquarters. A round-robin signed by every American general officer present—except Gates and Lincoln—urged Arnold's retention until the impending battle be resolved. Gates, oddly enough, acceded to the request but with strict injunction against any physical participation by Arnold.

On the morning of October 7 Burgoyne made his cast of the dice, moving out in three closely linked columns, but without any determined objective. They debouched from the right flank of his position. Fraser on the right led the light infantry of his advance corps. In the center was Riedesel, with the 24th Foot attached to his Brunswick units. The grenadier battalion, also detached from the advance corps, was on the left, followed by eight fieldpieces and two howitzers. The strength of this oddly assorted demonstration amounted to 1,600 men, with Burgoyne himself in command. As a diversion, far to the right roamed a detachment of rangers, Canadians, and a few Indians.

On discovery of the British advance, Morgan urged immediate attack, but Gates, always stingy in his dispositions, sent forward only two brigades: Morgan against the enemy right, Poor against its left. Poor, moving straight to his front, charged the grenadiers, who met him with the bayonet, but the sheer weight of the American attack rolled them up. Morgan's riflemen struck the British light infantry in flank. Trying to charge front to meet Morgan, this column was also hit by Dearborn's light infantry, attached to Morgan. The column broke, and Burgoyne's entire right wing, abandoning its guns, fell back behind its entrenchments. Riedesel, in the center, unsupported, for a few moments held the attack of Learned's brigade now moving slowly out from the Bemis Heights fortifications.

At this climactic moment Benedict Arnold, a little man on a big bay horse, raced across the field, seeking action, willy-nilly. Gates, who had seen him dash out, sent an aide to order him back, but the aide never caught him. Taking command of the attack, Arnold led Learned's men up to Riedesel's line. Repulsed, he tried again, while Morgan and Poor closed in on the flanks. Sullenly, the Brunswickers began withdrawing toward their entrenchments, mixed in with the light infantry.

Gallant Fraser tried to check the withdrawal, using his own 24th Foot, but one of Morgan's riflemen drew a bead on the Britisher, conspicuous on a gray charger, and Fraser went down mortally wounded. Fifty minutes from the time they started out, Burgoyne's troops were back behind their own earthworks.

By this time the word of Arnold's presence had spurred Gates's entire force to join the attack. Arnold, it seemed, was everywhere. Leading Paterson's and Glover's brigades against the western salient, he glimpsed Learned's men moving on his own left, and galloping across the field of fire, led them around the angle toward the horseshoe redoubt.

Breymann, holding the redoubt, now had but two hundred men still standing. Arnold led an impetuous charge into the sally-port, to be unhorsed, with a jäger bullet through a fractured thigh, but his cheering men swept in. Breymann was killed, and resistance ceased.

Burgoyne had lost his gamble, for the horseshoe dominated his entire position. Struggling against the inevitable, he withdrew in the night, leaving his wounded to American care. Gates, acting quickly for once, pursued and pinned Burgoyne down at Saratoga, seven miles north of the battlefield. On October 13 Burgoyne called for a parley. His bivouac was flooded by atrocious rains, his men were starving, and John Stark with his one thousand New Hampshire militia and a battery of artillery had crossed the Hudson, completely cutting off retreat.

Gates, fearing a possible advance up the Hudson by Clinton, agreed to a "convention," not a "capitulation," and Burgoyne's troops laid down their arms. The British army, marching to Boston—subsisting on American rations—was to go home in British ships; pledged not to serve again in North America unless exchanged by cartel.

American losses at Bemis Heights had been 150 men killed or wounded; British battle casualties 600. Seven general officers were among the 5,700 prisoners taken, together with 27 guns, 5,000 stands of small arms, and other matériel.

Thanks primarily to Benedict Arnold, an entire British army of well-disciplined troops had been lost to makeshift American forces. The outcome astounded Europe. France entered into alliance with the new republic; Spain and the Netherlands were nudged closer to a future war against England. The turning point of the American Revolution had been reached.

But for Burgoyne's "Convention Army," trudging on the way to Boston and their expected repatriation, heartbreak lay ahead. Congress repudiated Gates's agreement. Save for its officers and small number of men actually exchanged, the rank and file remained prisoner until the end of the war, herded from pillar to post. Many deserted, not a few died. In 1781 approximately half the surviving 2,500 were shipped home, while the others disappeared in the American melting pot.

29

Cruise of the *Ranger*
1777–1778

On June 14, 1777, the Continental Congress appointed Captain John Paul Jones to command of the new sloop of war *Ranger*.

Jones, a Scotsman by birth, went to sea at the age of thirteen and thereafter made his home in Virginia. He had served as a lieutenant on the *Alfred* during Esek Hopkins's expedition to the Bahamas the year before. After that he had commanded, in turn, the *Providence,* then the *Alfred.*

Cruises of the Ranger *and* Bonhomme Richard.

Map 12

The *Ranger* had been built in Portsmouth, New Hampshire, and named for the famous Rogers's Rangers.* Her hull was already in the water when Jones was appointed to command, but it took until late October to procure and rig the masts, spars, sails, eighteen guns, and all the other equipment for this 110-foot, square-rigged three-master, and to sign on a crew.

Just as the *Ranger* was ready to sail, Jones was assigned his first mission as her captain. He was given duplicate copies of the dispatches from Congress informing the American commissioners in Paris about the great victory at Saratoga. (The original copies were carried on a French merchant vessel.) Jones also carried with him a letter from the marine committee of Congress to the commissioners, instructing them to give Jones command of a new frigate, to be built or bought in Europe.

On November 1, 1777, the *Ranger* headed to sea. She arrived at Nantes, France, on December 2, having captured two prizes on the way. The messages were sent to Paris, and Jones was summoned there two weeks later by the commissioners: Benjamin Franklin, Arthur Lee, and Silas Deane.

At Paris, Jones learned that the commissioners were unable to get him a new and larger ship, as he had hoped. However, they did approve his suggestion for orders to take the *Ranger* to sea and "proceed with her in the manner you shall judge best for distressing the Enemies of the United States, by sea or otherwise, consistent with the laws of war, and the terms of your commission." If he should make "an attempt on the coast of Great Britain," however, he was warned that he should not return immediately to France, which was still neutral. As a matter of fact, an attempt on the coast of Great Britain was exactly what John Paul Jones had in mind.

Jones returned to Nantes to begin preparation for the coming cruise. He made many changes in her rigging to improve the *Ranger*'s sailing qualities. He also recruited more men for his crew

---

* Ironically, Robert Rogers and his Rangers had remained loyal soldiers of King George.

from the polyglot riffraff of the Nantes waterfront, and laid in a large supply of provisions and ammunition.

Early on February 13, 1778, Jones sailed from Nantes for Quiberon Bay. He then worked his way up the coast of Brittany to Camaret, where he had further changes made in the *Ranger*'s masts and rigging, to get the most in speed and easy handling from his ship. Satisfied at last, he put to sea on April 10.

Jones's plan was to raid an English seaport and take some important Englishmen hostage, to be exchanged for imprisoned American sailors. On the way north he captured two English merchant ships. He sank one of these, but put a prize crew aboard the other and sent her back to Brest.

Jones was reluctant to weaken the crew of the *Ranger* by detaching a prize crew, but he did this for the sake of his men. The crew had been unhappy when he sank captured vessels, instead of keeping them as prizes, and they resented his firm and unrelenting discipline. Although refusing to loosen the discipline, Jones felt that by sending a valuable prize back to Brest he would reduce the discontent of his men.

Jones headed for the ports on the northern shore of the Irish Sea, where he knew that a number of British merchant vessels were gathered. On the way he captured two more small merchant ships and sank them. Then he sailed into the North Channel between Ireland and Scotland.

Off Carrickfergus, on Belfast Lough, Jones found HMS *Drake* (20), a British sloop of war, riding at anchor. Disguising his vessel as a merchantman, Jones sailed boldly into the harbor. He planned to capture the British ship in a surprise night attack, but the plan miscarried when, because of the clumsiness of a drunken quartermaster, the *Ranger*'s anchor was not lowered until the ship had drifted past the *Drake*. Fortunately the disguise as a merchantman fooled the British sailors, but they had become alerted by the near collision. So Jones cut his anchor cable and headed off and out of the lough. Before he had gone far a gale came up, and the *Ranger* sought refuge under the southern shore of Scotland.

Jones had grown up in that part of Scotland, and had shipped out of Whitehaven when he first went to sea. He decided to create a scare by slipping into the harbor, burning what he could, and then running away. It was a daring plan, and certainly unexpected. His crew, however, had little interest in a hit-and-run raid on a coastal town. Jones heard rumors of a plan for mutiny, as they lay off the Scottish coast. He promptly nipped the scheme in the bud by putting the ringleaders in irons, and continued his plan to raid Whitehaven.

Whitehaven Harbor was divided in two parts by a stone pier; a battery of guns defended each part. Jones personally led the raid, during the night of April 22–23, 1778. He and his men went ashore in three ship's boats. They spiked the guns of the two batteries guarding the harbor and set fire to a ship moored at a wharf. Hastily the local militia swarmed toward the beach, in search of the invaders. Jones captured three prisoners, then embarked his men on their boats, and rowed back to the *Ranger*.

Little serious damage had actually been done in Whitehaven, and the fire was soon put out. But the psychological effect of the raid was enormous. Word spread up and down the coast. The inhabitants armed themselves and organized for local defense, outraged at the failure of the great Royal Navy to protect them. The name of John Paul Jones struck fear in British hearts.

Jones, disappointed by the results of the Whitehaven raid, decided to land on the nearby estate of the Earl of Selkirk, the most eminent nobleman in the area. Jones planned to kidnap him, in order to arrange an exchange of prisoners with the British government in return for Selkirk's release.

The *Ranger* reached the vicinity of the Earl of Selkirk's mansion, on Kirkcudbright Bay, at ten o'clock on the morning after the raid on Whitehaven. Jones, with two officers and a dozen well-armed sailors, rowed the ship's cutter to shore. He left a few men to guard the boat on the beach and approached the mansion. When Jones learned that the earl was not at home he was about to abandon the whole mission, but his officers insisted that they should be allowed to loot the mansion, in retaliation for the burning of houses by the British in New England. Jones gave permission to go to the house and demand the family silver, but in no other way molest the family. The men carried out his instructions to the letter. The countess turned over the silver to them, and the party returned to the *Ranger* and sailed away.

Jones was disturbed by the outcome of this adventure, which was too close to piracy for his taste. Later he had the silver appraised in Brest and paid his officers and men their share of the $510 value out of his own pocket. After the war he sent the silver back to the earl.

Jones decided that it was time now to deal with the *Drake*. He headed from Kirkcudbright Bay back toward Belfast Lough. At daybreak the following morning, April 24, 1778, near Carrickfergus, he sighted the *Drake,* under sail. The *Ranger*'s disguise as a merchantman was so successful that the *Drake*'s captain sent an officer in his gig to find out what manner of ship this really was. As the gig came alongside the *Ranger,* the officer in charge was invited aboard. When he climbed on deck he was informed that he was a prisoner of Captain John Paul Jones, of the United States Navy.

Jones's men had no desire to fight, and had again been on the point of mutiny. However, they were pleased by this trick, and decided to support their captain. Jones, unaware of the plot, was already maneuvering to entice the *Drake* into open water. When the ships were within hailing distance of one another, about an hour before sunset, Jones hoisted the American colors and the fight was on.

Jones started the action with a broadside that raked the *Drake*'s deck as the *Ranger* sailed across her bow. Then he concentrated his fire on masts, sails, and rigging, in order to spare the *Drake*'s hull and take her as a prize. Because of these tactics, after an hour and five minutes of fighting the *Drake* had lost only four men dead and nineteen wounded, but she had become completely unmanageable. Her captain had been killed and her first lieutenant mortally wounded. As the vessel drifted helplessly, the third in command called, "Quarter!" and the gunfire ceased. Jones sent a boarding party to the *Drake* in her own gig. They found the ship's decks a mess of spars and rigging. The *Ranger* had not been seriously damaged, although she had lost four men dead and five wounded.

Jones took the *Drake* in tow, since she could not sail. A small crew was put aboard the battered ship, and they worked all night to put up jury rigging so that she could sail. The next day, a short distance south of Belfast Lough, Jones cast her off long enough to capture the brigantine *Patience*.

Later that day Jones put the three prisoners he had taken in Whitehaven ashore in one of the *Ranger*'s boats. He also gave the released men some pocket money. They returned to their homes full of praise for the gallant American captain.

By this time the *Drake* was in condition to sail. Jones sailed his two ships north through the North Channel, around the top of Ireland, and then back to France. On May 4 the two vessels sailed into Brest, twenty-eight days after the *Ranger* had left.

Franklin and the French Minister of Marine now promised Jones a larger ship, and possibly a squadron. Sending the *Ranger* back to the United States, he awaited the promised larger command.

30

Valley Forge and von Steuben
1777–1778

Soon after the defeat at Germantown Washington went into winter quarters near Valley Forge on the slopes of a ridge overlooking the Schuylkill River. Close to Philadelphia and a constant threat to Howe, it was yet a position that was readily defensible against either British raids or a full-scale attack.

It was about this time, late fall of 1777, that Washington

became aware of unrest within the army, and of serious efforts by some of his subordinates, and some members of the Continental Congress, to have him removed from command. Despite defeats, long marches, inadequate pay, and shortages of food, clothing, and weapons, the bulk of Washington's Continentals, and their officers, were totally loyal to the quiet, strong-willed commander. The unrest and intrigue centered in a few senior officers, many of whom were foreign soldiers of fortune.

Chief among these intriguers was Brigadier General Thomas Conway, a French soldier of fortune of Irish descent, who was disappointed that he had not been given a top command. Conway and the other intriguers wanted Congress to dismiss Washington from command, and replace him with Major General Horatio Gates, whose fame and reputation were great, because of his recent victories at Saratoga. Conway and other conspirators apparently felt that they could influence and control Gates in a way that was impossible with Washington. There has never been any conclusive evidence that cautious, careful Gates was personally involved in this intriguing, and historians are divided in their conclusions on the subject. It is clear, however, that his closest military associates, and his good friends in Congress, were very much involved. The increasing arrogance of Gates's words and actions, and his attitude toward Washington, make it practically certain that he was, at the very least, kept fully informed.

Whispered slanders about Washington's personal responsibility for the loss of Philadelphia, his poor leadership in battle, and his general incompetence, spread through the army and through Congress in late October and November. At the same time the ability of Gates received increasing praise. Congress appointed him president of the Board of War, and promoted Conway to major general and appointed him Inspector General. To the dismay of Washington's loyal officers, the General at first refused to recognize the barbs of faceless accusers, and devoted himself exclusively to efforts to provide adequate food, shelter, and clothing to his cold, tired, sick, and hungry soldiers in their windswept encampment at Valley Forge.

Washington's enemies were misled by his initial attitude toward their criticisms. He did not reply, since, as he pointed out to some understanding members of Congress, this would reveal to the British exactly how weak his army was. The schemers evidently concluded that if Washington were criticized sufficiently, and were insulted enough, he would resign in disgust.

In private correspondence then and later, Washington made it clear that if Congress and the American people thought someone else could do a better job than he as leader of the American armies, he would accept that decision. But until relieved by Congress, he was determined to allow no discouragement, no insult, no hardship to interfere with performance of his duty as he saw it. Furthermore, he was aware of his honor and his rights as a man and as Commander-in-Chief. He had no intention of allowing his enemies to defeat him by default.

The conspirators also misjudged the attitude of the army. They had not realized the fierce loyalty to Washington among the officer corps—led by Greene, Lafayette, and Hamilton, who made clear to everyone their utter contempt for the conspirators.

Without impairing his dignity, without in any way resorting to deceit or intrigue, in early February Washington seized the initiative to defeat his enemies at their own game. Gates wrote a letter to Washington complaining that he and Conway were being slandered by members of the Commander-in-Chief's own staff. Ostentatiously displaying his supposedly clear conscience, and at the same time attempting to establish himself as Washington's coequal, Gates had sent copies of this and other letters to Congress.

This was too much for Washington. He sent a response to Gates—with a copy to Congress—revealing his complete understanding of, and contempt for Conway. The letter made it clear, also, that the General knew all of the details of the intrigue against him, as well as the identity of the intriguers. If, therefore, Gates persisted in his efforts to justify such a palpably contemptible individual as Conway, and his own relationship with such an individual and other intriguers, then—said Washington—fair-minded men would be forced to draw the obvious conclusion.

Neither Gates nor his supporters in the army or in Congress had a response to Washington's powerful counterattack. Most of the senior officers in the army were delighted. The fair-minded members of Congress—to whom Washington was really addressing his letter—were either shocked or ashamed to learn (or to realize) the implications of what had been going on. The so-called Conway Cabal suddenly collapsed. Gates, never one to take military or personal chances, wrote Washington a craven letter of apology. Although by this time Washington had no illusions about Gates, he magnanimously accepted the apology.

Meanwhile the condition of the army grew worse. The winter was cold. Food was short. There were not enough blankets. The men were inadequately clothed—the general lack of shoes was tragically demonstrated in bloodstains on the snowy trails of the fortified encampment. Most serious, however, were the ravages of disease, particularly typhus. During that terrible winter nearly three thousand soldiers died of starvation, exposure, or disease. It is amazing that the army held together at all under these dreadful conditions. That it did was due solely to the influence of Washington's strength of character, will, and determination, and the affection that bound officers and soldiers to this austere man.

Remarkably, by the end of February, despite deaths and desertions, Washington still had six thousand troops in the Valley Forge encampment. Of these some four thousand were fit for duty, and were sent off on frequent foraging expeditions into the neighboring regions of Pennsylvania, New Jersey, and Delaware. Although Washington insisted upon paying for all food that could be found, the farmers were not happy to receive payment in Continental dollars, which had become the standard of worthlessness: "Not worth a Continental." And so they tried to hide their choicest produce and livestock from Washington's men, saving it for British foragers, who paid in good sterling.

This was the situation that existed at Valley Forge when, in late January, another foreign soldier of fortune joined the army. Since he came with the highest recommendations of Ambassador Benjamin Franklin, Washington received the new arrival courteously.

But he feared that this Prussian Baron Friedrich von Steuben might be another troublemaking foreigner like Conway.

Surprisingly, however, Washington found that his first reaction to von Steuben was favorable. Since the Baron spoke no English, Washington loaned him two of his own French-speaking aides-de-camp, John Laurens and Alexander Hamilton, and asked him to look over the army in its miserable encampment and to give his opinion as to how its deficiencies could be corrected.

Washington was as much impressed by von Steuben's frank reports and cogent recommendations as by his growing friendship with Hamilton and Laurens, and with General Greene. Finally, von Steuben's martial bearing, superb horsemanship, gracious manner, keen sense of humor, and incisive observations won the liking and respect of both officers and men. Washington appointed von Steuben his Acting Inspector General, and authorized him to initiate measures to train the army.

This was a formidable task. There were no drill regulations, there was no uniform procedure for handling weapons, nor even a commonly accepted method of marching.

Von Steuben decided to devise a new system of drill which could be formulated into clear regulations understandable to inexperienced officers and men. Also, a group of qualified instructors must be trained who could do the drilling.

Nothing reveals the true genius of von Steuben better than his realization that the drill regulations of the Prussian Army could not be translated bodily to America, and that American soldiers could not be trained by the methods then in vogue in Europe. As he later wrote:

"The genius of this nation is not in the least to be compared to that of the Prussians, Austrians, or French. You say to your soldier 'Do this,' and he does it; but I am obliged to say, 'This is the reason why you ought to do that'; and then he does it."

Von Steuben's program was based on a simple series of movements intended to appeal to Americans, suspicious all of rigid military pedantry. His first great victory with American officers and men was in demonstration that a perfectly satisfactory and efficient manual of the musket could be performed with only ten commands, half the number used in the English, French, and Prussian armies.

Von Steuben wrote out new drill regulations, in French. As soon as he had written one day's lesson, it was translated by a French assistant, then the Baron memorized the commands in English, as taught to him by Laurens and Hamilton. Night after night this continued, following a full day's labor on the parade ground.

It was on the drill field that the sturdy, jovial, and shiny-domed soldier won the hearts of the men, and—despite initial reluctance—the enthusiastic support of the officers. Washington authorized him to select 120 men from different regiments, to comprise the Commander-in-Chief's bodyguard, and also to become von Steuben's model drill company. He also selected a brigade inspector from each brigade. These men—the bodyguard and the brigade inspectors—von Steuben drilled personally, giving his commands "in a curious mixture of German, French, and English."

After a week the brigade inspectors were sent back to their commands, to carry the new system of training to the entire army. Infected by the Baron's enthusiasm, these officers became able instructors. The example of a general officer personally drilling troops had been enough to show the junior American officers that there was no reason why this should be beneath their dignity. They threw themselves into the task with the same enthusiasm which the Baron had already imparted to the brigade inspectors.

Von Steuben did not limit his introduction of regularity, precision, and efficiency to external training and disciplinary drill. He introduced a system of inspections which he was to develop and improve during the course of the war. Every man had to be accounted for, and so did his equipment. Above all, he stressed the responsibility of officers for the well-being of their men.

During the weeks of late winter and early spring Washington paid close and favorable attention to everything the Baron was doing. This, he knew, was the answer to the most serious combat problem of the new American Army: discipline and efficiency to match that of the British regulars. Furthermore, the arrival of von

Steuben, and his ability to organize the training of the army, gave Washington time to devote more attention to administration, to supply, and to the recruitment of new troops for the coming campaign.

By late March a thin stream of new men was flowing into Valley Forge. So too were adequate food, clothing, and weapons for the slowly growing army, thanks to Washington's efforts, and thanks also to the efficiency of his newly appointed Quartermaster General, Nathanael Greene. By early May, under the efficient teamwork of Washington, von Steuben, and Greene, the Continental Army had grown to more than eleven thousand men, fit, trained, and equipped for battle.

At this time, also, came the electrifying news that France had recognized the newly independent nation, and had joined the United States in an alliance against Great Britain. The road ahead would be long, hard, and often terribly discouraging. Valley Forge, however, had seen the transformation of an army and of a cause, both rising from the depths of disaster and despair to the promise of victory.

31

Monmouth Courthouse
June 28, 1778

In May 1778, General Sir Henry Clinton arrived in Philadelphia to replace General Howe as British commander-in-chief in North America. Clinton had been ordered to evacuate Philadelphia, to withdraw to New York, and go on the defensive in the north. Because of the treaty of alliance between France and the rebel

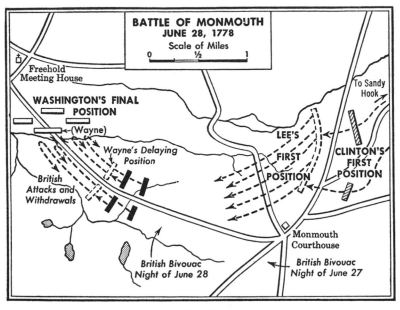

Map 13

government, the British decided to concentrate their efforts in 1778 on operations to regain control of the southern colonies, while the Royal Navy conducted a naval campaign against France in the West Indies.

At about this same time, arrangements were made to exchange a captured British major general for American Major General Charles Lee, who had been a prisoner of war since December 1776. Lee, who had been a professional British soldier before the Revolution, had been second in rank only to George Washington during 1775 and 1776. In the early days of the war he had performed capably, and was honored by Washington and most of the American Army as an outstanding professional officer. He had begun to behave strangely, however, during the fall of 1776. Several times he had ignored or disobeyed orders from Washington, and during the dark days of November he had stayed east of the Hudson after Washington had withdrawn to New Jersey. After he finally did come to New Jersey at Washington's insistence, Lee was captured by the British. As a prisoner, he had had many conversations with General Howe. There is no conclusive proof, however, that he committed treason. Lee's talks with Howe were not known to the Americans, and Washington warmly welcomed him when he was exchanged.

By late May of 1778 it was clear to Washington at Valley Forge that Clinton was preparing to leave Philadelphia. Shiploads of supplies and baggage went down the river every day. Washington heard rumors that the British were planning to go to New York. He decided to follow them closely and harass them constantly, but not to attack unless an especially good opportunity presented itself.

Washington now had about 14,500 well-trained men, of whom nearly 12,000 were Continental troops. He knew that Clinton probably had about 16,000.

Another foreign volunteer, the young Marquis de Lafayette, was now serving as a major general with the American forces at his own expense. Washington put Lafayette in command of an advance guard, and told him that if Clinton left Philadelphia he was to be ready to pursue. Anthony Wayne was second-in-command of this advanced guard, consisting of about two thousand men in six brigades.

On June 18 the British crossed the Delaware from Philadelphia and began marching northeastward. Lafayette's brigades moved out immediately. A few hours later the remainder of Washington's army followed.

The Americans made faster progress in the intense summer heat than the British, who were encumbered by a flock of Tory refugees. By June 27, when Clinton reached Monmouth Courthouse (now Freehold), Washington's army, to the north, was closer to New York. Up to this time Clinton's route had been so selected as to give him the choice of going overland all the way to New York or going to Sandy Hook, where he could then embark on ships to reach the city. The overland movement was simpler, but the area just west of the Hudson was cut by many streams, and Clinton realized that if he were forced to fight there he might be defeated in detail. Now, with Washington ahead of him on the land route, there could be only one choice; Clinton determined to push east to Sandy Hook. First, however, he rested his hot and tired men all day at Monmouth Courthouse. Washington had already guessed that Clinton would take the water route, and he knew that there was only one road running from Monmouth Courthouse toward Sandy Hook. He was determined to seize the opportunity for a decisive victory.

On June 26 Washington more than doubled the strength of his advance guard to over six thousand men, in anticipation of striking Clinton's army quickly, as soon as it was stretched out on the single road to Sandy Hook. General Lee asked for the honor of commanding this force. Washington was a little reluctant to assign Lee to this important command, because up to this time Lee had opposed aggressive action, arguing that American troops could not stand up to British regulars. But it was traditional that the officer second in seniority should command an army's major detachment, and Washington could see no reason for denying Lee's request.

On June 27, while Clinton's army was resting, Washington ordered Lee to attack as soon as the British were on the road the next morning. Washington promised to join him quickly with the main army. The order was clear, and was given to Lee in the presence of several other American generals. Lee's advance guard was at Englishtown, northwest of Monmouth, while the main army was farther west, between Englishtown and Cranbury.

Clinton, recognizing the danger of an American attack, had divided his army into two portions. The leading division, about six thousand strong, was under German General von Knyphausen, and it would be followed by the army's supply train of 1,500 wagons. The main body of the army, probably slightly fewer than ten thousand men, would follow under General Cornwallis.

Knyphausen's leading contingent moved out at 4:00 A.M., on June 28. An hour later Washington got the news. He immediately sent an order to Lee to attack. He again promised Lee that he would bring up the main body of the American army to support him as soon as possible.

Despite Washington's orders of the day before, and this renewed and specific order to attack, Lee issued no battle instructions to his brigade commanders. He merely started his troops on a slow march toward Monmouth Courthouse. His leading units arrived there somewhat after 10:00 A.M., as the last British were leaving. Lee still issued no orders, but Lafayette and several other brigade commanders had heard Washington's instructions the previous day. They attacked without orders. Clinton promptly ordered Cornwallis to turn around to deal with these uncoordinated efforts.

There is no clear record of Lee's actions at that time. He certainly issued no attack orders. Apparently he personally told one or two of his brigadiers to withdraw. In any event, some of the advanced guard units were still attacking while others were withdrawing, and the majority stood by useless under the broiling sun, waiting for orders.

Clinton at once perceived this indecision. He ordered Cornwallis to counterattack, and sent orders to Knyphausen to halt and send back three thousand troops. In the face of Cornwallis's determined attack, most of the outnumbered Americans broke and ran. Wayne's brigade, alone, firing and falling back in good order, prevented disaster.

By this time it was about noon. Washington, passing Freehold Meeting House with the main body of the army, was disturbed to hear only sparse sounds of battle; he had expected a steady roar of cannon and musketry as soon as Lee and Lafayette engaged the enemy decisively. Then the Commander-in-Chief was amazed to meet fleeing troops. He at once galloped forward, accompanied by his staff. Soon he met Lee riding to the rear, apparently unconcerned about this turn of events.

"What, Sir, is the meaning of this? Whence come this disorder and confusion?" demanded Washington.

The scene has been described by several witnesses and depicted by artists, but no one can be sure now just what was said. Some witnesses later said that Washington, in an unusual burst of temper, cursed Lee; others denied this. All agree, however, that Washington clearly communicated to Lee his scorn and indignation. Then, wasting no more time, he rode forward to rally his men and salvage what he could of the situation. He soon met Wayne's hard-pressed brigade, still falling back in good order.

Just two hundred yards in front of the leading British, Washington gathered and reorganized two more regiments to reinforce Wayne's delaying line. The General then rode back a few hundred yards, where he found a good battle position on a low ridge overlooking a shallow depression. He and his staff began rallying stragglers. As often in the past, Washington's commanding physical presence and determined personal leadership made the difference between success and rout.

Soon General Greene appeared, at the head of the main body of the army. Washington promptly put him in command of the right wing of the line he was building up, and assisted by Greene and Lafayette, deployed the arriving troops in battle line. Wayne then fell back into the center of that line. The closely pursuing British found themselves met by a determined counterattack. Astonished at the calm, professional fighting of the Americans, the leading British elements withdrew from the valley, and back out of range.

It was now after 5:00 P.M. Clinton's troops were exhausted from heat as much as from the battle. He broke off the infantry engagement, but the artillery on both sides continued firing. It was at this time that the legendary Molly Pitcher (Mary Ludwig Hays), after bringing water to the thirsty American gunners, took her wounded husband's place at his cannon.

Finally the cannonade ended; the Battle of Monmouth was over. The Americans reported that they had suffered 360 casualties, killed, wounded, and missing, of whom 40 were deaths from sunstroke in the 100-degree heat. The British reported 358 casualties, including 59 deaths from sunstroke. Actual losses on both sides were probably twice as high as reported.

At midnight the British broke camp and were safely away before the Americans awoke. They reached Sandy Hook, and made good their escape to New York by ship.

For Washington the battle was heartening in its demonstration of the value of the Valley Forge training program. But the failure to gain a decisive victory because of Lee's inexplicable behavior was a bitter disappointment.

Lee, offering no explanation, had the effrontery to demand either a court-martial or an apology from Washington because of the public tongue-lashing he had received from the Commander-in-Chief near Freehold Meeting House. He received the court-martial, and suspension from his command. He was eventually dismissed from the army by Congress.

32

Stalemate at Newport
August 1778

Relations between France and England had grown more and more strained during the early years of the Revolution, mainly because of British indignation over French economic and material assistance to the colonies. On July 10, 1778, France formally declared war. In March 1778, in anticipation of this declaration, Admiral Charles Henri Theodat, Comte d'Estaing, had sailed from Toulon with twelve ships of the line and four frigates, carrying four thousand troops. His objective was to surprise the British fleet and army at Philadelphia. When he arrived off the Delaware Capes, however, he found that the British Army had left Philadelphia and was already in New York. He had just missed Admiral Viscount Richard Howe's fleet, which had sailed for New York only ten days before.

D'Estaing headed for New York, seeking a battle with Howe's fleet, over which he had an advantage of three ships and three hundred guns. Arriving off Sandy Hook, the French began sound-

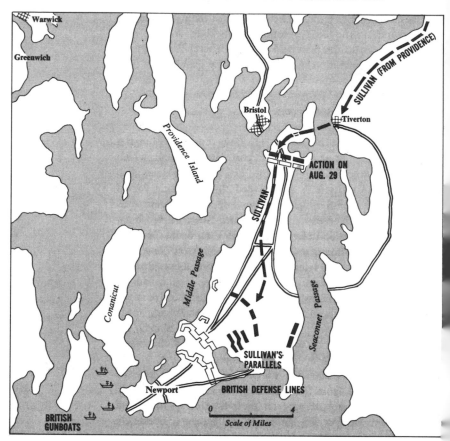

The Siege of Newport.

Map 14

ing, searching for a way across the bar; their larger ships drew more water than those of the British, which could easily pass the bar at high tide. After eleven days d'Estaing, afraid that his deep-draft ships might ground on the bar, abandoned the idea. This was a great disappointment to Washington, who had hoped for a joint operation against the British in New York.

Since there could be no attack on New York, Washington suggested a joint attack on British-held Newport, Rhode Island. As d'Estaing's fleet sailed through Long Island Sound, General John

Sullivan, commanding at Providence, was put in charge of a land expedition to attack Newport. Washington sent the Marquis de Lafayette and two Continental brigades to reinforce Sullivan, and militiamen flocked to Tiverton from all over New England. This gave Sullivan ten thousand men, of whom four thousand were Continentals.

The 3,500-man British garrison was concentrated above the village of Newport, in the southwestern tip of the island. To the west, in the Middle Passage, between Newport and Conanicut islands, lay four small British frigates and some smaller craft.

The French and American commanders planned a joint attack for August 9. D'Estaing would land his four thousand troops on the west side of the island while Sullivan ferried his across to land on the east shore. On August 5, two French ships of the line were sent to reconnoiter the western channel; at the same time two frigates sailed up the eastern channel. This French reconnaissance accomplished more than d'Estaing expected. The British ships, trying to take refuge in the harbor at Newport, ran aground and were destroyed by their own crews. This turned out to be the most successful part of the whole operation.

On August 8, without consulting d'Estaing, Sullivan suddenly decided to take his troops across the channel to land on the island a day ahead of schedule. D'Estaing was furious. He considered this independent action a personal affront and an insult to France. While Lafayette was trying to re-establish a cordial relationship between the touchy French admiral and the bullheaded American general, the situation changed completely.

Admiral Howe had received reinforcements, including four more ships of the line. Confident that he could now take the French, he had sailed from New York in search of d'Estaing. When the British appeared off Newport, d'Estaing promptly sailed out, also eager for battle. For two days the fleets maneuvered for position, seeking the advantage of wind and water. But just as the antagonists were apparently finally about to close for battle, a gale scattered the ships of both fleets, severely damaging spars and rigging.

The condition of his ships gave d'Estaing an excuse not to return to Newport. Despite the appeals of Lafayette and an apology from Sullivan, d'Estaing reassembled his fleet and sailed around Cape Cod to Boston for repairs. Sullivan briefly besieged the British at Newport; then he withdrew, to avoid being cut off by Admiral Howe's ships.

33

George Rogers Clark and the West 1778–1779

For the first two and a half years of the war, American frontier settlements in the Ohio Valley suffered terribly from Indian depredations instigated and directed from Detroit by British Lieutenant Colonel Henry Hamilton, Lieutenant Governor of Quebec. Hamilton was nicknamed "Hair-Buyer" because he paid cash to the Indians for American scalps.

During these years a youthful surveyor and landowner, not yet twenty-eight years old in late 1777, emerged as one of the principal leaders of the frontiersmen in their desperate defense of their homes in the "Dark and Bloody Ground." His name was George Rogers Clark.

Clark believed that the Americans should try to take the initiative away from the British and their Indian allies. He set his sights on three former French settlements in Illinois: Vincennes on the Wabash, and Cahokia and Kaskaskia on the Mississippi (Cahokia lay a few miles south of, and across from, Spanish-held St. Louis; Kaskaskia, about fifty miles south, was at the junction of the Kaskaskia and Mississippi rivers). The support of the scattered

French inhabitants could be enlisted against the British, Clark believed, and from this Illinois base an offensive against Detroit could then be mounted.

Clark persuaded his fellow Kentuckians to elect him to go back to Williamsburg as their representative in order to secure support and military assistance from the Virginia government—which claimed all the Northwest Territory. In late 1777 Governor Patrick Henry and the Virginia legislature approved his plan. Kentucky was recognized as a county of Virginia. Patrick Henry commissioned Clark a lieutenant colonel of Virginia militia, authorized him to recruit 350 men for his expedition, and provided more than $6,000 for ammunition and supplies.

Early in 1778 Clark returned by way of Fort Pitt, where he recruited 150 men—mostly tough Indian fighters—for his expedition. He embarked his small command on four boats on the Monongahela, and then went down the Ohio River to Corn Island, at the Falls of the Ohio (modern Louisville). There, in late May, he established a base. A few local frontier recruits brought his total strength up to 175.

On June 26 Clark's party started down the Ohio, Kaskaskia his first objective. A few miles beyond the mouth of the Tennessee River, they hid their boats on the north bank of the Ohio, and began a 120-mile hike northwestward through the wilderness. Traveling light and fast, they approached the settlement and its stone fort during the night of July 4–5 and captured it in complete surprise; not a shot was fired.

The townsfolk, mostly French, were at first apprehensive, but they became enthusiastic when they learned that France had joined America in the war against England. Clark sent a detachment fifty miles north to Cahokia, where they were received with equal enthusiasm. With the assistance of the local French parish priest, Father Pierre Gibault, Clark sent another detachment to seize Vincennes, where the French militia was called out and placed under the command of Captain Leonard Helm, to garrison the wooden fort—Fort Sackville—the British had built there a few years earlier.

By now, however, Clark had run out of funds. He could neither pay nor supply his men. However, while the expedition was being fed through the help and charity of Father Gibault, Clark got in touch with Oliver Pollock, a patriotic American merchant in New Orleans, who received covert support from Bernardo Gálvez, the governor of Spanish Louisiana. Pollock went into debt to send supplies up the Mississippi River; Clark pledged his own small fortune and extensive landholdings to get more credit from other New Orleans merchants.

Meanwhile, British Colonel Hamilton had responded promptly to Clark's actions. Leading a force of 175 British troops and 300 Indians from Detroit, he reached Vincennes on December 17, 1778. The French militia refused to fight, and Helms and his one American soldier were forced to surrender Fort Sackville without a struggle. Hamilton decided to advance on Kaskaskia the following spring. Staying with a garrison of eighty men at Vincennes, he sent the remainder of his troops back to Detroit to gather supplies. The Indians scattered to their villages, promising to be back for the fun in the springtime.

By this time Clark's command had dwindled to fewer than eighty men. However, he made the amazing, and apparently foolhardy, decision to go by river and overland 180 miles in the dead of winter, to recapture Vincennes. He recruited fifty French volunteers, and on February 6, 1779, set out from Kaskaskia with 127 men. They could carry little food with them; so Clark pushed his men to the edge of exhaustion, in order to avoid starvation. Nonetheless, by February 23 his tired, frostbitten men were gnawing on elm bark to reduce the pangs of hunger.

That afternoon they arrived in sight of Vincennes. There was a brief rest until dark. Then Clark and his men dashed into town, surrounded Fort Sackville, then boldly dug shallow trenches thirty yards from the fort, so that the cannon, high on the ramparts, could not be depressed to reach them. As day broke, the frontier riflemen picked off any British soldier who showed himself on the ramparts, or at the embrasures in the wooden walls. Hamilton refused Clark's first surrender demand. Later in the day, when he realized that he and his men were helpless, and would soon be starved, he tried to negotiate. Clark refused; it was surrender or starvation. Hamilton surrendered.

Clark then sent a detachment to ambush the supply train marching from Detroit to join Hamilton. All of the supplies, and the forty British soldiers with the train, were captured and brought to Vincennes. Clark hoped to use these supplies to help support an expedition against Detroit, but only a handful of the five hundred men promised him from Virginia ever arrived.

In the following years Clark vainly tried to get enough men and supplies to mount an offensive to drive the British out of Detroit. He knew that a large force would be required, because the British recognized the threat, and had reinforced and strengthened Detroit. He had to be satisfied, therefore, with using the few men and supplies which he had to subdue and pacify the Shawnee Indians, the fierce allies of the British.

When the war ended the Americans firmly held the Ohio Valley and most of the rest of the Northwest Territory, except for the scattered British forts along the Great Lakes. This was due mainly to the dynamic leadership and physical and financial efforts of one man: George Rogers Clark. Thus, the American negotiators in Paris were able to demand, and receive, American sovereignty over the vast territory.

Sad to relate, his contemporaries never properly recognized what Clark had done. He had been moderately wealthy until he pledged his property and land to pay and supply his men. Neither the Continental Congress nor Virginia reimbursed him, and he lost his property and land to his creditors. He had been appointed Indian Commissioner in the Northwest Territory, but thanks to the efforts of James Wilkinson, a subordinate of Gates who had figured in the Conway Cabal (and who would gain greater infamy in coming years) Clark was dismissed from that post. Not surprisingly, Clark spent most of the years until his death in 1818 in Louisiana, preferring the company of the French and the Spanish to that of his countrymen who had treated him so badly.

34

Stony Point
July 15–16, 1779

After the Battle of Monmouth, Washington continued northeast to the Hudson River north of New York. Two years after the disastrous 1776 campaign, he was back near Manhattan Island. This time, however, it was the British who were defending the island, and the Americans who were the besiegers.

Washington disposed his forces in a wide arc around the blockaded city, along the west bank of the Hudson, and then across Westchester to Long Island Sound. The American positions also protected the vital communications line between New England and the states to the south.

Numerous raids. by both sides and skirmishes between patrols took place in 1778 and early 1779. Then in May 1779 Clinton decided to capture two American forts on the Hudson, to weaken the American blockade, and to serve as bases for possible operations up the Hudson Valley. On June 1, with a picked force of five thousand men, Clinton went up the river by ship, and landed at the south end of the Hudson Highlands. Quickly they seized Stony Point on the west bank and Verplanck's Point on the east bank. At Fort Lafayette on Verplanck's Point, the seventy-man American garrison resisted but was soon overwhelmed.

Possession of these two forts gave the British control of both ends of King's Ferry, where the main north-south highway crossed the Hudson. Clinton moved swiftly to make Stony Point a virtually impregnable fortress.

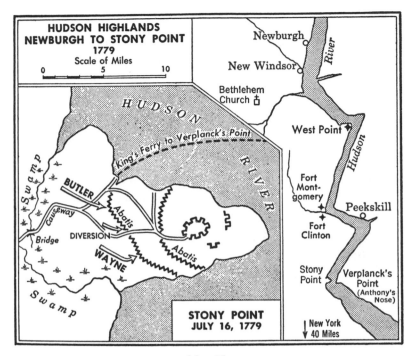

Map 15

Stony Point projects like an arrowhead out into the river, surrounded by water on three sides. Its steep sides of bare rock rise 150 feet above the river. Clinton had a citadel built, surrounded by artillery batteries that were connected by trenches. To protect the land approaches to the fort, two successive arcs of abatis were constructed. At high tide the fortified area was an island that could be reached only by a causeway across the surrounding marsh. Clinton left about seven hundred men at Stony Point under the command of Lieutenant Colonel Henry Johnson. There was a smaller garrison at Fort Lafayette. The sloop of war HMS *Vulture* was at anchor in the river to provide gun support to both forts.

One of Washington's most able and experienced commanders, Brigadier General Anthony Wayne, proposed to capture the seemingly invulnerable Stony Point fort with brashness that amazed his fellow officers. Although Washington approved Wayne's plan, other Americans began to call him "Mad Anthony."

Wayne and his hand-picked, well-trained brigade of 1,300 set out on the morning of July 15, 1779. They marched thirteen miles to their jump-off point, about a mile from Stony Point, and then Wayne gave them their orders.

Each man was to keep his unloaded musket on his shoulder throughout the march and up to the moment of attack. No word was to be spoken. They would approach the fort in two columns, with Wayne leading one group through the swamp to strike from the right and Colonel Richard Butler leading the other group farther north along the causeway to strike from the left. Between these two forces was a smaller group with loaded muskets which were to be fired on the fort as soon as the assault began, to create a diversion.

Ahead of each attack column were 150 men with axes, who were to chop a way through the abatis. Behind them were twenty men and an officer, volunteers who were to rush immediately through the openings and attack with the bayonet. Cash awards were promised to the first men inside the fort.

It was impossible to move through the mud and water of the swamp in complete silence. However, the British pickets did not detect the attackers until the leading axemen were almost ready to go into action. Gaps began to appear in the outer abatis, and then the inner; the eager troops worked their way in, undeterred by British musket fire. In response a blaze of American musket fire broke out in the center as the little demonstration force carried out its mission.

British Colonel Johnson responded as Wayne had hoped, rushing half his garrison down to the abatis in the area of the American fire, while on both sides of him the silent bayonet forces moved through the first abatis, then the second, and then over the parapet and into the citadel itself. A French volunteer, Lieutenant Colonel François Teissedre de Fleury, won the $500 reward as the first man in.

Once within the outer abatis the hitherto silent Americans began shouting incessantly and at the tops of their voices, "The fort's our own." This final touch of Wayne's was effective psychological warfare. Confused and panic-stricken British began surrendering wholesale, and by the time Colonel Johnson realized what was happening it was too late to get his center force into action. The battle was over in thirty minutes, with 63 British dead, more than 70 wounded, 543 captured, and the fort in American hands. The captors promptly turned the Stony Point guns on the *Vulture,* and the ship quickly moved downstream.

The American losses had been surprisingly light—15 killed and 80 wounded. The victory was greeted by the American Army and public with incredulous joy. Congress awarded Wayne a gold medal, and gave each man in his command a share of the cash value of the supplies captured.

Despite the victory, Wayne continued to be known as "Mad Anthony." Boldness and imagination he certainly had, but "mad" was an ironic nickname for an officer whose striking success came, above all, from careful planning and the firm leadership of thoroughly trained and disciplined troops.

35

Fiasco at Penobscot
July–August 1779

By 1779 Britain was suffering economically from the loss of trade with the American colonies. One of the most serious results was the inability to get tall masts for British ships. For many years most of the masts of Royal Navy vessels had been cut from the white pine forests of Maine. It had been Admiralty practice to keep on hand enough masts for three years. But the supply had been allowed to run low, and by 1779 it was almost exhausted.

In order to improve the source of supply, in June 1779 Brigadier General Francis MacLean was sent from Halifax to Penobscot Bay. There he built a fort near modern Castine and established a colony, where he could both control the cutting of the timber and protect the shipments to England from American privateersmen.

The Patriots were anxious to prevent the British from solving their mast problem, and an expedition to attack the British in Penobscot Bay was formed jointly by Massachusetts and the Continental Congress. With Brigadier General Solomon Lovell in command, a contingent of nearly a thousand troops, including a militia artillery unit under Colonel Paul Revere, left Boston by ship on July 21, 1779, convoyed by a squadron under Continental Commodore Dudley Saltonstall: three vessels of the Continental Navy, three Massachusetts ships, one from New Hampshire, and twelve privateers. Saltonstall's command was stronger on paper than in fact, because the different contingents were jealous of their independence, and he was not strong enough to whip them into line.

The expedition reached Penobscot Bay on July 24. Three small British vessels lay at anchor there, and six hundred men were ashore, in unfinished Fort George. The American troops landed and made some half-hearted attack gestures, but Lovell was no stronger than Saltonstall. For forty-seven days there were small skirmishes near the fort. Saltonstall's fleet, despite its three hundred guns, provided little support. The Americans should have taken the fort with little difficulty, and MacLean knew he was outnumbered. But neither Lovell nor Saltonstall could make any firm plans, and the British were allowed time and opportunity to strengthen their fort.

MacLean sent a message about the American threat to British authorities in New York. Admiral Sir George Collier set sail at once in the HMS *Asia* (64) accompanied by five frigates and a sloop of war. The appearance of the British vessels at the entrance to Penobscot Bay created a panic among the Americans. The troops rushed back to their transports, and Saltonstall fled, with all his ships, up the Penobscot River. There the vessels were destroyed, some by British naval guns, others by their own crews. The Americans—soldiers and sailors—started on foot back to Boston, leaving about five hundred dead or missing behind.

Saltonstall was court-martialed and dismissed from the Continental Navy. Paul Revere was convicted of negligence by one court-martial, but was later cleared by a second. So ended the fiasco of Penobscot Bay, for the Americans. The British quickly built up their reserves of masts in English shipyards.

36

Cruise of the *Bonhomme Richard*
August–September 1779

After giving up command of the *Ranger,* John Paul Jones remained in France, waiting for the new and larger ship that had been promised him. Months of disappointment followed. Not until February 1779 was an old India merchantman, *Le Duc de Duras,* made available to him for conversion into a frigate. He promptly renamed the vessel *Bonhomme Richard,* in honor of Benjamin Franklin, whose famous *Poor Richard's Almanack* had been published in Paris as *Les Maximes du Bonhomme Richard.*

By early summer conversion of the Indiaman to a ship of war was complete. She was a forty-gun frigate, carrying six 9-pounders on her forecastle and quarterdeck, sixteen new and twelve old 12-pounders on her gun deck, and six old 18-pounders aft on the deck below.

During these months Jones built up a squadron of ships to

accompany the *Bonhomme Richard* on a proposed foray into British waters. Newest and strongest of these was the American frigate *Alliance* (36), commanded by a Frenchman in American service, Pierre Landais. Jones also had three French ships under his command: the frigate *Pallas* (32), the brig *Vengeance* (12), and a fast cutter, *Le Cerf* (18).

Having finally equipped his ships and manned them with a polyglot assortment of men, Jones and his squadron put to sea from Lorient on July 19, 1779, to escort some French merchantmen to various ports on the Bay of Biscay. To Jones's disappointment he found that the *Bonhomme Richard* was too slow to catch several small British warships that were sighted. He also learned more about the arrogance and incompetence of Captain Landais of the *Alliance*.

Back in Lorient, Jones found orders (which he had requested) to proceed with his squadron west of Ireland, north to the Orkney Islands, then down through the North Sea to the Naze and the Dogger Bank, attacking such enemy vessels as he might find. He was to return via Holland, in order to escort a Baltic merchant fleet, carrying naval supplies to Brest.

The small American squadron finally sailed on August 14. A few days later Jones took two British merchant vessels as prizes, and sent them back to France.

As they worked their way northward, the ships of the squadron separated. Landais defiantly took the *Alliance* off on his own; the *Pallas* stopped to repair her tiller; the *Cerf* never tried to rejoin after an unsuccessful attempt to retrieve two boatloads of deserters who had headed for the Irish coast. Accompanied only by the *Vengeance,* Jones continued on his way.

Off northern Scotland in early September, the *Alliance* and *Pallas* rejoined. On September 3 the squadron turned, to head south along the eastern coast of Scotland. Again Landais, after refusing to confer with the commodore, took the *Alliance* off on her own.

A daring plan to capture Leith, the seaport of Edinburgh, was foiled by a sudden gale. Since the countryside had been alerted by the approach of the American warships, Jones abandoned the project.

The squadron proceeded down the coast, its next objective a raid on Newcastle-on-Tyne, source of London's coal. As they neared Newcastle, however, the French captains of the *Pallas* and the *Vengeance* refused to cooperate, and Jones decided not to risk the attack with the *Bonhomme Richard* alone. Word of his approach spread down the coast. Civil defense and militia were alerted in all of eastern England to repel a landing.

On September 23, while Jones was hovering off the Humber estuary, waiting for a favorable wind that would enable him to sail in and terrorize the seaport of Hull, the squadron was rejoined by the *Alliance*. In midafternoon, as the four ships were sailing slowly with the wind toward Flamborough Head, they sighted numerous sails heading toward them out of the north-northeast. From two captured Humber pilots Jones learned that this was a convoy from the Baltic, escorted by HM frigate *Serapis* (44) and the sloop of war *Countess of Scarborough* (20). Jones decided to fight the British warships, and then to take as many prizes as possible from the convoy.

At almost the same time Captain Richard Pearson, commander of the *Serapis,* sighted the *Bonhomme Richard.* He sent his convoy close to shore toward the protection of Scarborough Castle, while the *Serapis* and *Countess of Scarborough* put on all sail and moved to cut off the American squadron from the rich merchant prizes. Jones crammed all possible sail on the *Bonhomme Richard,* called his men to general quarters, and hoisted the signal for his other ships to form line of battle. The signal was ignored.

Shortly after six-thirty the *Bonhomme Richard* and the *Serapis* drew in close to each other, both on the port tack, heading west, side by side. The *Bonhomme Richard,* flying the British flag, was on the windward side. As Jones watched from the quarterdeck, and his gunners stood ready to fire, the *Serapis* opened her gunports.

As Captain Pearson of the *Serapis* hailed him, Jones ordered the British colors hauled down. Up went the red, white, and blue

American colors. Almost at the same instant, both ships opened fire.

The results of a brief exchange of broadsides were disastrous to the *Bonhomme Richard*. One of the old 18-pounders exploded, killing many gunners, ruining all the other 18-pounders, and blowing a hole in the deck above. This quickly gave the *Serapis* a 44–34 advantage—with heavier guns. Jones decided to try to grapple his foe and board, before enemy broadsides caused more damage. He suddenly backed his sails and dropped astern. Raking the British frigate as he crossed her stern, he moved in on the *Serapis*'s starboard side and attempted to board. The gunners on both ships continued to fire as fast as they could reload.

By superior speed Pearson evaded Jones's attempt to board, and tried to cross the bow of the *Bonhomme Richard* to get in raking position. Jones skillfully avoided being raked by running the *Richard*'s bowsprit into the stern of the enemy ship. But his situation was desperate. He was still being hammered by several *Serapis* guns, while he, bow-on as he was, could not aim a gun at his opponent. Pearson, looking down from his quarterdeck to the *Richard*'s deck, could see a shambles of rigging, splinters, and blasted bodies. Not seeing the *Richard*'s flag, he called out: "Has your ship struck?"

From the *Richard*'s quarterdeck came Jones's immortal response: "I have not yet begun to fight!"

Jones pulled away, and for a short time the two ships again sailed on a parallel course. Then, skillfully taking advantage of a fresh puff of wind, Jones pulled ahead and turned, as though to cross the bow of the *Serapis*. However, so many of his guns had been silenced that a raking position would do him little good. He was seeking another chance to board.

As Jones hoped, the *Serapis* collided with the stern of his ship, her bowsprit tangled in the shrouds of the *Richard*'s mizzenmast. Swung round by the wind, the two ships soon lay side by side, bow to stern, a fluke of the *Serapis*'s starboard anchor hooked to the *Richard*'s side, attaching them securely. Jones's men quickly attached lines to hold the two ships closer together.

The *Serapis,* despite the handicap of having her guns almost aboard the *Bonhomme Richard,* could continue to fire her 18-pounders, with deadly results. But from the decks and the yards of the *Bonhomme Richard,* Jones's marines placed such a rain of accurate musket fire that few men survived on the *Serapis's* exposed deck. Several Americans leaped into the rigging of the *Serapis* and fired almost straight down upon her deck from above. The Americans also threw hand grenades and burning matches upon her deck, setting several fires. But the British gunners on the deck below continued their murderous fire into *Richard.* It was now dark, but the opponents had little difficulty seeing each other. Battle lanterns were lit, guns were blazing, and fires were raging on both ships.

Meanwhile Jones's other ships were less than helpful. The *Vengeance* stood off and did nothing. The *Pallas* was fighting the *Countess of Scarborough.* Landais sailed the *Alliance* back and forth and fired several broadsides, not at the *Serapis* but at the *Bonhomme Richard.* This extraordinary performance came close to finishing Jones and his ship—as Landais undoubtedly expected.

By this time Jones knew his ship was sinking. There was so much water in the hold that the master-at-arms released the prisoners, who willingly helped man the pumps to save their skins. But Jones did not falter. His few remaining guns were aimed at the *Serapis's* mainmast, and her deck was strewn with dead and wounded from the deadly, incessant fire of muskets and grenades. With the mainmast trembling and about to fall, Pearson himself hauled down his flag. It was just after 10:00 P.M.

A boarding party from the *Bonhomme Richard* stepped across to the deck of the *Serapis* to take possession. Captain Pearson was escorted across to the *Bonhomme Richard's* quarterdeck to hand his sword to Jones, just as the mainmast of the *Serapis* fell. Jones issued orders for emergency repair of the damage on both ships. He had lost some 150 men killed and wounded; Pearson's crew had suffered about 120 casualties.

The efforts of her crew could not save the *Bonhomme Richard.* On the morning after the battle John Paul Jones moved his flag to the *Serapis*. Damaged though she was, she was still afloat, she could still sail with a jury rig, and much of the destruction could be repaired. The *Bonhomme Richard* went to a watery grave on the morning of September 25.

Followed by the other ships of his squadron, Jones was soon on his way to Holland. Though disappointed by the failure of his subordinates to make any attempt to seize prizes from the rich convoy, nonetheless Jones had been victorious in one of the most remarkable and most bitterly contested engagements in naval history. The battle off Flamborough Head is the only recorded naval action won by a sinking ship, with the victorious crew sailing away in the defeated vessel.

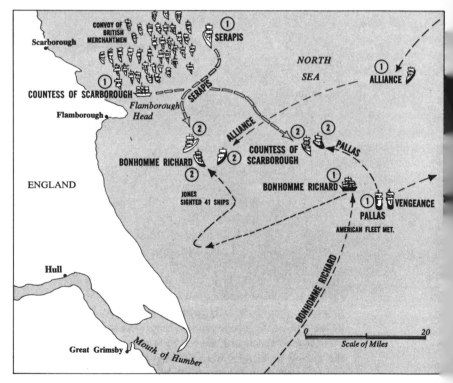

Battle off Flamborough Head—U.S.S. Bonhomme Richard *v. H.M.S.* Serapis.

Map 16

37

Savannah
September–October 1779

Sir Henry Clinton, commanding British forces in North America in
1778, turned his attention southward. In late November he sent
Lieutenant Colonel Archibald Campbell by sea from New York to
Georgia, with 3,500 men, convoyed by Commodore Hyde Parker's
squadron.

Disembarking at the mouth of the Savannah River, Campbell's
force started toward Savannah. Patriot Major General Robert
Howe, hurrying up from Fort Sunbury, thirty miles southwest of
the city with seven hundred Continentals and three hundred militia,
attempted on December 29 to check the British, but Campbell in a
double envelopment shattered the American troops and occupied
Savannah. American losses were 83 men killed and 433 others
captured; the British lost but 3 men killed and 18 more wounded.
Campbell then captured Augusta, on January 29.

Major General Augustine Prevost, commanding British forces in
East Florida, marched overland into Georgia with a small force.
He captured Fort Sunbury, then joined Campbell, assuming com-
mand.

Major General Benjamin Lincoln, commanding the American
Southern Department, responded to the British seizure of Georgia
by advancing from Charleston with 1,000 Continentals and 1,500
militiamen to Purysburg, on the east bank of the Savannah River,
north of Savannah. One of Lincoln's Continental units was

Pulaski's Legion, a mixed infantry-cavalry unit commanded by Colonel Casimir Pulaski, a foreign volunteer from Poland.

Prevost, with three hundred men, moved opposite Lincoln on the west bank of the river. Receiving reinforcements, Lincoln evaded Prevost, crossed the river, and despite the defeat of one of his detachments at Briar Creek, on March 3, threatened Augusta. Prevost then advanced to make a counterthreat against Charleston, and Lincoln was forced to return to South Carolina. By summer the two armies were back where they started, facing each other across the Savannah River.

Meanwhile, French Admiral d'Estaing, in the West Indies, accepted an invitation from Governor Rutledge and General Moultrie at Charleston to assist in the capture of Savannah. Anxious to retrieve his fiasco at Newport in 1778, d'Estaing appeared off the mouth of the Savannah River on September 8, with an imposing naval armada and a host of transports carrying some five thousand French troops.

Prevost, commandeering slave labor, ringed Savannah with an elaborate fortification. Having only 2,500 troops—including Tories and a Hessian detachment—he also called in the garrison of his outpost at Port Royal Island, eight hundred regulars, under Lieutenant Colonel John Maitland, to join him. Meanwhile, the British garrison at Fort Sunbury also joined.

D'Estaing, slow in debarkation and overdeliberate in advance, did not approach the city until early October.

On the 16th he demanded surrender of the city. Prevost, whose Port Royal Island contingent had not yet joined, asked for a twenty-four-hour delay to consider terms. Foolishly, d'Estaing complied. But by next day Maitland arrived by boat from Port Royal Island after a difficult trek through inside passages, and Prevost rejected the demand for surrender. British forces now amounted to some 3,200 men.

That same day Lincoln, with 600 Continentals and 750 militia also arrived, following Pulaski's Legion, 200 strong, which had already joined the French forces. Subsequent arrivals of Patriot militia units soon brought the besieging force up to approximately ten thousand men.

D'Estaing, enraged by delays in mounting siege batteries, and fearful both of the coming hurricane season and the probable approach of a British fleet, insisted on an immediate assault.

Badly coordinated, the assault was a dismal failure. On the left a French attack was repulsed at Sailor's Battery. Pulaski, charging gallantly but stupidly against entrenchments, was mortally wounded and his mounted legion shattered. Lincoln's Continentals and the main French infantry assault pierced the British defenses near Spring Hill, but after an hour of bitter fighting had to retire when General Isaac Huger's South Carolina militia failed against the earthworks on the right.

Allied losses were 244 killed and 584 wounded; the British reported 40 killed, 63 wounded, and 62 missing; these figures do not include considerable Tory and Hessian losses.

After nine more days, during which Lincoln and d'Estaing squabbled, the erratic Frenchman decided he would stay no longer. Displaying considerably more alacrity than they had during their landing, the French re-embarked in forty-eight hours, sailing on October 20. Lincoln's troops retired north of the Savannah River. The entire area of Georgia—including a valuable naval base—was still under British control.

38

Charleston
April–May 1780

General Clinton was dissatisfied with the results of the 1779 southern campaign. When he learned of the Franco-American siege of Savannah, he decided to take matters firmly into his own hands. On December 26, 1779, he and General Cornwallis sailed southward from New York with 8,500 picked troops, leaving General Knyphausen with a like number to hold New York.

Clinton had learned before he embarked that the American and French besiegers had failed in their efforts to take Savannah. But he knew that London was becoming impatient with his lack of progress in the south. He was determined to get some results.

Clinton's troops were convoyed by five ships of the line and nine frigates under Admiral Marriot Arbuthnot. The ships were buffeted by winter storms of exceptional severity; several small transports were lost, and the others were scattered all over the western Atlantic. Finally, after stopovers on the Virginia and Georgia coasts, on February 11 Clinton began to land his troops on Johns Island, thirty miles south of Charleston.

General Lincoln, commanding American forces in the south, immediately began intensive efforts to improve the fortifications of Charleston. He also gathered all available Continentals—fewer than a thousand—and local militia to garrison the city.

Clinton advanced very slowly. Not until March 7 did the first British troops reach the Ashley River, across from Charleston. It was the 29th before Clinton pushed his first troops across the river north of the city. Thus, Lincoln's soldiers, and six hundred slaves furnished by Governor Rutledge, had plenty of time to strengthen the earthworks across the isthmus north of the city, to construct a stone redoubt in the center of the line, to build a series of small forts along the entire waterfront, and to repair and rearm forts Moultrie and Johnson covering the entrance to the harbor.

Meanwhile both sides were receiving reinforcements. By mid-April Clinton's army had grown to about ten thousand men. Admiral Arbuthnot had about five thousand seamen in his fleet, just off Charleston bar.

Washington sent all of the Virginia and North Carolina Continentals from his army to join Lincoln. By early April Lincoln had 2,650 Continentals, 380 Pulaski Legionnaires, or dragoons (now commanded by French volunteer Colonel Charles Armand), and 2,500 militia. About five hundred of these, including all of the cavalry, were under General Huger about thirty miles north of Charleston at Monck's Corner, near the headwaters of the Cooper River, protecting the line of communications to the north. The remainder held Charleston and the two forts at the harbor mouth.

A small American flotilla of six frigates and three sloops of war was pulled back up the Cooper River. The guns were removed from five of these vessels, and they were sunk to form an obstacle between the town and Shute's Folly Island. The remainder of the warships would help keep open the Cooper River line of communications to the north, past the British lines across the peninsula north of the city.

Lincoln felt that he had an adequate line of retreat up the Cooper River. In case of necessity he could move his troops directly eastward across the Cooper River into the swampy lowlands and islands, and thence to the mainland to the north. He persuaded Governor Rutledge and part of his council to leave in early April, in order to continue the administration of the state outside the beleaguered city.

On April 8 the British fleet boldly sailed into the harbor, past the two forts in a violent but relatively harmless exchange of fire. On the 10th General Clinton and Admiral Arbuthnot called upon the garrison to surrender. Lincoln refused. On April 13 the British siege artillery north of the city opened up on the defenders with shell and red-hot shot, causing much damage in the town.

That same day a mixed force of British infantry and cavalry was able to block Lincoln's Cooper River line of communications. Lieutenant Colonel Banastre Tarleton, with the 550 Tories of his British Legion (mixed cavalry, mounted infantry) and the hundred men of Major Patrick Ferguson's American Volunteer Rifle Corps, struck before dawn against Huger's five hundred men at Biggin's Bridge, near Monck's Corner. About a hundred Americans were captured, and most of the remainder lost their horses. Tarleton, joined by two British infantry regiments, then proceeded to occupy the area east of the Cooper River, northeast of Charleston, completely blocking Lincoln's escape route.

On April 20 Lincoln and his generals held a council of war. At first they decided to try to get away from Charleston, to the east through the swamps, south of the region now occupied by Tarleton. This plan was objected to by the Charleston city fathers, sitting in on the council of war. One civilian threatened that the citizens of Charleston would cut up the army's boats and open the gates to the British if the troops attempted to leave. In the face of this threat, Lincoln weakly gave in, and agreed to stay on in the city.

On the 21st Clinton refused Lincoln's proposal that his troops be allowed to evacuate Charleston with the honors of war, and without limitation on their further activities. On April 24 the Americans made a sortie, but did little damage. The British captured Fort Moultrie on May 6, and British troops now stretched along the entire east bank of the Cooper River.

By May 8 the British siege lines had reached to within musket range of the American defenses, and Clinton again demanded the city's surrender. In reply, Lincoln agreed to surrender but demanded full honors for his troops. Clinton and Arbuthnot refused to allow full honors, and at 8:00 P.M. on May 9 hostilities resumed. A furious artillery duel that lasted through the night, with British shells and roundshot, created severe damage in the city. The terrorized townspeople became much more docile. After they petitioned Lincoln to surrender, the American general finally accepted the British terms.

On May 12 the Continentals marched out, not allowed by the British to display their colors. When the British saw how few regular troops had been holding the three-mile perimeter of Charleston, they praised the Americans' gallant defense. Nevertheless, the capitulation of Charleston was the most serious defeat the Americans had suffered during the war. In addition to 2,500 Continentals, some 2,000 militia surrendered, and the British captured substantial stores and great quantities of weapons. American casualties during the siege amounted to almost 100 killed and 150 wounded (about 90 percent among the Continentals). The British lost 76 killed and 189 wounded.

Clinton occupied Charleston, then on May 18 sent three columns into the interior to pacify the entire State of South Carolina. Two of these were small and went to the northwest, one to seize the post at Ninety-six and the other to occupy the region east of Augusta. The third column of 2,500 men, under Cornwallis, advanced northward toward Camden. Cornwallis sent Tarleton's cavalry raiding ahead of him.

Late in May, as the British were approaching Camden, Cornwallis and Tarleton learned that Colonel Abraham Buford with a force of approximately 350 Virginia Continentals, and a handful of cavalry under Colonel William Washington, was withdrawing toward North Carolina.

Tarleton, with 270 of his green-coated dragoons and mounted infantry, immediately pursued. After a sharp engagement on May 29, in the region known as the Waxhaws, just east of the Catawba River, Buford surrendered to a force which he thought outnumbered his. Tarleton's dragoons, on the pretext that some of the Americans had fired after the surrender, gave no quarter. In an orgy of ruthless butchery, all save a handful of the Americans were cut down.

Word of this "massacre of the Waxhaws" spread like wildfire among the Patriots of North and South Carolina. While it unquestionably inspired considerable dread of Tarleton and of the green-coated Tory troopers of his British Legion, it also stimulated widespread determination for revenge.

Two days later, on May 31, Cornwallis occupied Camden. The British reconquest of South Carolina seemed to be virtually complete.

39

Camden
August 15, 1780

Satisfied that South Carolina was restored to royal control, Clinton returned to New York. He left Cornwallis with eight thousand troops to complete the job, and to extend British control to North Carolina. Cornwallis, setting up his headquarters in Charleston, scattered garrisons across the colony. He decided to wait for cooler weather before moving into North Carolina.

British assumptions about the reconquest of South Carolina, however, proved to be premature. Latent, but widespread, anti-British sentiment was ignited by the "massacre of the Waxhaws." Local militia leaders called their men out in vicious guerrilla opposition to the British. Outstanding among these leaders were Francis Marion, Thomas Sumter, and Andrew Pickens.

Unknown to the guerrilla leaders at the time, Washington had already taken steps to send reinforcements to the Southern Army. A division of one thousand Continentals, commanded by Major General Johann de Kalb—one of the most skillful and reliable of the foreign volunteers—had been sent south as soon as Washington learned of the siege of Charleston. When news of Lincoln's surrender reached him, Washington prepared to send his most able

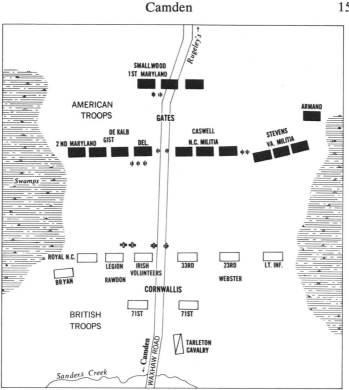

Battle of Camden.

Map 17

subordinate, Major General Nathanael Greene, to take command in the South. However, the Continental Congress suddenly intervened in military affairs.

Although carefully avoiding any censure of Washington, many delegates in Congress held him responsible for the loss of Charleston and the destruction of Lincoln's Southern Army. Ignoring Washington's plans, Congress named Major General Horatio Gates, who had gained the somewhat dubious title "hero of Saratoga," as the new commander of the Southern Army. Gates was to report directly to Congress, and not through Washington. He thus became an independent commander, virtually coequal with Washington.

In July Gates rode south from Philadelphia with a small staff. On the 25th he joined de Kalb, and some contingents of Virginia and North Carolina militia on the Deep River, in North Carolina. Two days later he began a leisurely march south toward Camden, with an army of slightly more than 3,000 men, including de Kalb's 1,000 Continentals and 120 regulars in Armand's Legion; the rest were militiamen. The weakness of his army was pointed out to him at Rugeley's Mill on August 15, when Gates ordered a night march of twenty miles to make a surprise dawn attack on the British at Camden. "Sir," replied Gates to Colonel Otho Williams, his doubtful adjutant general, "there are enough for our purpose."

Had Gates's soldierly abilities matched his choice of words, that statement would be among the quotations to be memorized by every American schoolboy. Unfortunately, the fact was that Gates's dilatoriness had already permitted Cornwallis to rush northward from Charleston to reinforce the garrison at Camden. Gates had failed to coordinate his activities with those of guerrilla leader Sumter, operating nearby, who had asked help in harassing Cornwallis's column. And now Gates not only failed to make use of Sumter in the expected battle at Camden, he completely disregarded the advice of his two senior, experienced subordinates, de Kalb and Armand. In the previous two weeks both had urged him to move more rapidly to Camden. Now they were appalled that Gates was attempting a long, difficult night march, in humid summer heat, to be followed by a major battle, with an army made up mainly of inexperienced militiamen.

By coincidence, Cornwallis had also decided upon a night approach march, planning a surprise dawn attack against the Americans the next morning. The British set out from Camden at 10:00 P.M., the same time the Americans left Rugeley's Mill.

At 2:00 A.M. Tarleton's British Legion and Armand's American Legion ran into each other on the road, opening fire simultaneously. After a brief skirmish, the two advanced guards hastily entrenched. Both generals ordered their armies to deploy in the sultry darkness.

The armies were in an open, sparsely wooded pine forest, with firm ground for a few hundred yards on each side of the main road. Beyond, the land became swampy in both directions. Thus the flanks of each army were protected. The Americans were on slightly higher ground; the British had a creek to their backs.

At dawn the British began to advance, while the artillery of both sides opened fire. There was no wind, and gunsmoke hung close to the ground, adding to the slight morning haze. Cornwallis decided to make his main effort on his right, against the Virginia militia, apparently the weakest part of the American line, and ordered an immediate attack. As the British light infantry, bayonets fixed, bore down upon them, Stevens's Virginians began to waver. At about fifty yards the British halted, fired a volley, and then charged. This was too much for the Virginians. A few men fired generally southward, but most simply dropped their loaded muskets and ran.

The panic spread to the North Carolina units on their right. Suddenly the entire left flank and the center of the American army melted away. Most historians report that Gates was then "swept off the field" by the fleeing men. Smallwood's Continental Maryland Brigade, in the second line, was also thrown into considerable disorder, as the militiamen ran blindly through their ranks. Smallwood, too, seemed to have been "swept off the field," but his regiments rallied and quickly reformed.

Colonel Otho Williams, the army's adjutant general, somehow avoided being "swept off the field." Personally assuming command of the brigade, he ordered it forward in response to an order from de Kalb, who held the right of the first line with Gist's Maryland-Delaware Brigade.

It was too late. The British right had advanced to where the Virginians and North Carolinians had stood, and were now preparing to attack the left flank of Gist's brigade. Williams's advance with Smallwood's brigade caused the British again to shift front to the north, but they now occupied a position between the two American brigades, and repulsed Williams's efforts to join de Kalb and Gist. Cornwallis ordered his reserve into the fight, and Tarleton's cavalry galloped up to take Smallwood's brigade on the right flank. This development, combined with repeated charges by the reinforced British regulars, soon broke the already shaken Marylanders. Despite the efforts of Williams and the other officers, they fell apart under the terrific pressure from a force at least twice their numbers.

Meanwhile, Gist's brigade, under the inspirational leadership of de Kalb, was fighting one of the most glorious actions of the war. Not only had they repulsed the first Tory charge, but de Kalb had advanced, and in repeated attacks had driven the Tories back behind their starting position. At this point, the victorious troops of the British right swung against his left flank. The giant general, exposing himself courageously, reorganized his troops to face in two directions, then ordered still another bayonet charge. The uneven battle continued for about half an hour.

His horse was shot from under him, but de Kalb got up, bleeding from numerous wounds, and led his men forward on foot. Now for a few minutes took place what was probably the most violent hand-to-hand bayonet clash of the war. The result was a foregone conclusion; the Continentals were hemmed in by forces outnumbering them nearly four-to-one. Tarleton's dragoons, smashing into their rear, ended the battle. Gallant de Kalb sank down, mortally stricken with eleven wounds. Cornwallis ordered the giant hero taken back to camp and given the best of medical care, but he died a few hours later.

British casualties were reported as 79 killed and 245 wounded; they were probably about twice this number. American losses are not known, but there were probably 600 dead; about 1,000 men were captured, and more than half of these were wounded. Tarleton pursued until his horses were exhausted, killing and wounding fleeing American troops, and capturing considerable booty.

Gates himself arrived at Charlotte, sixty miles away, that night. He reached Hillsboro, 180 miles from the battlefield, early on the 18th. In commenting on this, Alexander Hamilton bitterly wrote, "One hundred and eighty miles in three days and a half. It does admirable credit to the activity of a man at his time of life."

Cornwallis did not move after the routed Americans for three weeks. Meanwhile, Tarleton surprised and defeated Sumter at Fishing Creek on the 18th.

Two days later, however, "Swamp Fox" Marion gained partial revenge by a successful dawn attack on a British-Tory column escorting prisoners from Camden to Charleston. Some 160 American captives were released, and fled to Marion's swamp refuge.

Meanwhile a chastened Congress humbly asked General Washington to appoint a new Southern Army commander. He again recommended Major General Nathanael Greene, who was promptly appointed to replace Gates.

40

The Treason of Benedict Arnold
September 1780

On September 23, 1780, three "skinners"—American irregulars—prowling for loot along the river road just north of Tarrytown on the eastern bank of the Hudson stopped a lone traveler in civilian clothing, bound south. He gave his name as John Anderson. Searching him, they discovered military papers hidden in his boot; so despite his safe conduct pass, signed by Continental Major General Benedict Arnold, commanding the fortress of West Point, they turned their captive over to the local Patriot authorities.

Two days later General Arnold was fleeing to New York on board a British warship. On October 2, the intercepted traveler on the river road, Major John André, Clinton's adjutant general, swung on a gibbet at Tappan on the Hudson, executed as a spy.

Arnold, hero of the long march on Quebec, of Valcour Island

on Lake Champlain, of the relief of Fort Stanwix, and of the victory at Saratoga, was also a conscienceless egotist and spendthrift. His traitorous correspondence with General Clinton began in 1779, when Arnold commanded the Philadelphia area. At the time he was involved in financial irregularities for which he was court-martialed and reprimanded by Washington. He was also burning to avenge an accumulated series of slights and injustices suffered at the hands of Congress.

On receiving command of West Point, the guardian of the Hudson Valley—a signal mark of Washington's confidence—Arnold bluntly advised Clinton that for £20,000 in gold and a major generalcy in the British Army he would turn over his post to the British. Gallant Major André, who handled Clinton's correspondence with the traitor, was sent to arrange the details.

Dropped ashore at Haverstraw by HMS *Vulture,* the British station ship on the Hudson, André in full uniform—Clinton's orders—was hurried by an intermediary to Arnold at the home of Tory William Smith at King's Ferry.

The details were arranged on Arnold's terms, including a failsafe proviso that should the scheme fail Arnold would be paid his expenses, plus a brigadier generalcy in the British Army. Meanwhile, having been fired on by a Patriot battery nearby, the *Vulture* slipped her cable and dropped downstream, leaving André in the lurch. Much to his horror, he would have to make his way to New York overland, in civilian clothing; if captured within Patriot lines he would face a spy's fate.

When the "skinners" turned over their prisoner and his papers to Lieutenant Colonel John Jameson, Patriot commander at North Castle, several things happened. Jameson sent the prisoner to Arnold at West Point, but sent the papers to General Washington, then in the vicinity of Danbury, en route to West Point. Colonel Benjamin Tallmadge, heading Washington's secret service, happened to drop in at North Castle, and learned of the André incident. At once he persuaded Jameson to call the prisoner back. André, the soul of honor, was questioned by Tallmadge. On finding out that his incriminating documents were on the way to General Washington, he at once revealed his identity, but without mentioning Arnold's name; vehemently he insisted that he had been betrayed "into the vile condition of an enemy in disguise within your lines."*

On Monday morning, September 25, Arnold, his aides, and two officers of General Washington's staff had breakfast together in the Robinson home, Arnold's quarters across the river from West Point. They were awaiting the expected arrival of Washington on a routine inspection visit. While they were still at the table, Colonel Jameson's messenger arrived with word of "John Anderson's" capture and the forwarding of his documents to General Washington. Imperturbable Arnold finished his breakfast, calmly excused himself, and strolled out of the room. He then went quickly upstairs to tell his Tory wife, Peggy Shippen, that their plot had been discovered. He came back downstairs and informed his visitors that he had urgent business over at West Point. Having ordered out his barge, he jumped aboard, but instead of crossing to the west bank, he ordered his boatmen to row downriver to find the *Vulture*.

Washington arrived at the Robinson house shortly after this, accompanied by Lafayette, Henry Knox, and Alexander Hamilton. He went over to West Point, and though surprised not to find Arnold, made an inspection of the post and returned to the Robinson house. There he found Jameson's second messenger, bearing the incriminating papers, and another with a letter from André acknowledging his identity. At the same time Mrs. Arnold went into a realistic fit, accusing an aide of attempting to murder her child. In the midst of the excitement came word that the still-absent Arnold had last been seen in his barge going downriver.

Washington acted with his usual vigor. The garrison of West Point was alerted, Hamilton was sent posthaste to try to intercept Arnold, and André was ordered brought to trial before a court of officers headed by General Greene. An arrogant letter from Arnold, sent ashore from the *Vulture* under a flag of truce, further ruffled Washington's feelings.

* Boatner, *Encyclopedia of the American Revolution,* p. 38.

The court of thirteen officers—including, besides Greene, Generals Lafayette, Knox, von Steuben, and St. Clair—regretfully found that André, who refused to quibble, was a spy and deserved a spy's fate. Washington approved. André's plea that he be given a soldier's death by shooting, rather than the noose, was refused.

On October 2, 1780, John André, in full regimentals—his soldier servant had been allowed to cross the river with the uniform—was hanged by the neck at Tappan. Mourned by both friend and foe at the time, his remains rest today in Westminster Abbey. The traitor Arnold, after a short but sanguinary career as a British brigadier general, died in England in 1801—"unwept, unhonored and unsung."

41

King's Mountain
October 7, 1780

Some three weeks after his crushing defeat of Gates at Camden, Cornwallis resumed the offensive, North Carolina-bound. His front and right were screened by Tarleton's British Legion, while well to the west Major Patrick Ferguson, British regular with a flair for partisan warfare, covered the British left flank. Ferguson's force consisted of a hundred Tory rangers (his own unit which he had personally raised and trained in the North) and some thousand Tory riflemen from South Carolina, whom he had recruited and trained following his arrival with Cornwallis in the southern theater.

Almost spontaneously, North Carolina's Patriot militia—the men of Colonels Isaac Shelby, Charles McDowell, John Sevier,

William Campbell, Benjamin Cleveland, and others—began mus-
tering in the Rocky Mount area to meet the threat posed by
Cornwallis. The Patriots, well over one thousand strong, found
Ferguson—whom they had learned to hate as much as they did
Tarleton—in the vicinity of Gilbert Town. Buzzing like angry
hornets, they moved toward him, gathering strength every day.

Ferguson, calling for reinforcements from Cornwallis, seventy
miles away, withdrew eastward. The Patriots, who had elected
Campbell as their leader, hastened to cut him off. Fearing his
escape, some nine hundred of the best-mounted men—all these
militiamen rode horses—went scurrying eastward. They found
him at King's Mountain early on October 7, 1780.

King's Mountain was a bare ridge about three hundred yards
wide and about a mile long, on the east bank of King's Creek; its
boulder-strewn slopes were covered by dense woods. Ferguson,
determined to make a stand, bivouacked on the easterly end of the
ridge. Oddly, perhaps unaware of Campbell's pursuit, he had
posted no outguards nor made any attempt to improve the position.
He had sent out two hundred of his men to forage.

About a mile from their objective the pursuers dismounted,
picketed their mounts, and advanced on the ridge in four columns.
Undetected, they ringed the ridge and started a coordinated infil-
trating assault through the woods. Actually, their advance was not
discovered until their leading fringes were within a quarter-mile of
the top. Ferguson's people never had a chance. As the leading
Patriots broke out onto the bare ridge, Ferguson met them with
several bayonet charges, but the mountaineers mowed his men
down by skillful rifle fire from the trees. Ferguson, conspicuous,
with a crippled arm, and a gaudy shirt over his uniform, for a few
minutes galloped from side to side in the open, rallying his followers. Then he toppled from his charger with eight sharpshooters'
bullets in his body.

White flags began to flutter. But the Patriots, with Tarleton's
massacre at the Waxhaws to avenge, were in no mood to give
quarter. Before the firing could be stopped, 157 of Ferguson's
troops were dead and 163 others so badly wounded they could not

be evacuated. The victors bagged 698 prisoners, and 1,400 stands of arms. Patriot losses were 28 killed and 64 others wounded.

The action at King's Mountain has been well called the turning point of the war in the South. Sir Henry Clinton commented it was "the first link of a chain of evils that followed each other in regular succession until they at last ended in the total loss of America."*

42

The Cowpens
January 17, 1781

Major General Nathanael Greene, engaged in a Fabian effort to check Cornwallis's superior force in the Carolinas in October 1780, made the dangerous decision to divide his forces. With the major portion of his little army he began moving from Charlotte toward Cheraw. The remainder, under Brigadier General Daniel Morgan, he sent across the Broad River into western South Carolina, to rally local militia forces and threaten the fortified British post at Ninety-six.

Morgan, shabbily refused promotion by Congress, had resigned in 1779. But following the disaster of Camden, ignoring crippling arthritis (a legacy of the Canada campaign), he hurried from his Virginia home to offer his services to Gates. After renewed appeals from Gates and Washington, Congress commissioned him a brigadier general, just in time for him to become the right-hand man of Nathanael Greene.

* As quoted by Boatner, *Encyclopedia of the American Revolution*, p. 582.

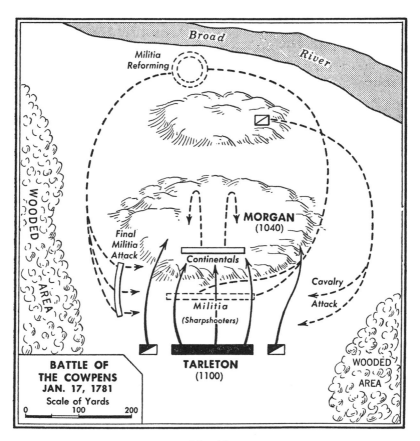

Map 18

Morgan's command included 320 Maryland and Delaware Continentals, veterans of de Kalb's division, under Lieutenant Colonel John E. Howard. He also had some two hundred expert and reliable Virginia riflemen—discharged Continental veterans organized as a volunteer militia unit—and eighty Continental Light Dragoons under Colonel William Washington.

Morgan was joined by an additional 140 North Carolina militiamen, about two hundred North Carolina and Georgia riflemen under Major Charles McDowell, nearly a half-hundred militia horse under Lieutenant Colonel James McCall, and by Colonel Andrew Pickens with one hundred of his partisan fighters. Thus by mid-January Morgan's total strength was nearly 1,100 men.

Cornwallis, also dividing his forces, sent Lieutenant Colonel Banastre Tarleton after Morgan, to destroy him and protect Ninety-six. They met on January 17, 1781, in what was known as the "Cowpens," a wide clearing in the great bend of the Broad River, just south of the North Carolina–South Carolina border; a site deliberately chosen by Morgan.

Tarleton had his Legion of two hundred horse and as many foot, a troop of the 17th Light Dragoons, one battalion each of the 17th Foot and the 71st (Fraser's Highlanders) and two small 3-pounder guns, known as "grasshoppers" because of their tripod mounts; some 1,200 men in all. Numerically the two forces were almost equal in size, but Tarleton had the advantage of a cohesive force of trained veteran troops; Morgan's men were fighters, too, but barely half of them were disciplined soldiers.

Morgan's force occupied a gently rising hill, with the unfordable Broad River about three miles to its rear and Thicketty Creek, easily fordable, skirting the woods to the front, a mile away. Howard's Continentals lay just below the hillcrest, flanked on the right by the veteran Virginia riflemen and on the left by the most reliable of the Georgia militia. Two hundred yards in front of and below them the North and South Carolina militia, under Pickens, were drawn up, while the remainder of the militia, most of them expert riflemen, under Majors John Cunningham of Georgia and Charles McDowell of North Carolina, lay below. Behind the hill, to the rear, Washington's dragoons and McCall's mounted militia waited in reserve. A thin line of pickets guarded the front and flanks to prevent surprise attack.

Morgan's instructions, given in person as he hobbled about the bivouac before the battle, were precise.

Tarleton, he told them, was but eight miles away that night; he would attack next day. They would await him. When the British assault was fifty yards away—not more—the first militia line would fire three volleys—"Three shots only, boys!"—then scamper back around the hill to shelter. The second line would repeat the procedure. He didn't tell them how far to run; the unfordable Broad River would take care of that.

Tarleton, moving out shortly after midnight, reached the Cowpens at daybreak. Deploying for immediate attack, he sent his dragoons forward to probe the position. Alert militia riflemen promptly emptied fifteen saddles, and the horsemen turned back.

Meanwhile the British infantry moved to the assault, the 7th Foot on the left, the Legion infantry in the center, and the light companies of the 7th and 71st on the right. The two grasshopper guns flanked the Legion infantry, and on each flank a platoon of the 17th Dragoons kept pace. The remainder of Fraser's 71st Highlanders followed in reserve, with the Legion's green-coated dragoons beside them.

The first militia line fired two volleys, checking the advance. Then the twinkling British bayonets came through the smoke and the militiamen broke and fled. Three volleys from Pickens's men in the second line again checked but didn't halt the British advance, and Pickens's men, too, fled around the hillside.

Tarleton loosed his 17th Light Dragoons at the running mob, but they were met by Washington's dragoons. Broken up, the surprised British horsemen galloped to the rear, pursued by the Patriot troopers.

Tarleton, his first line momentarily halted by Howard's Continentals and Virginia veterans, threw in the Highlanders on his left to turn Howard's right flank.

While this was going on, Morgan and Pickens, meeting the militia fugitives swarming back, rallied them, and Pickens started forward around the west side of the hill. Howard, on the crest, attempted to refuse his right flank, and momentary confusion followed. Tarleton, seeing this, ordered a final charge, at the same time alerting his Legion dragoons for the *coup de grâce*.

Then three things happened at the same time. Howard's troops, their line dressed, charged the British with the bayonet, throwing them back; Pickens's rallied militia came around the hill on the British left to envelop the Highlanders; Washington's dragoons, returning from their original chase of the 17th Dragoons, came slashing up from the British right rear into Tarleton's light infantry and Legion foot.

Tarleton, shocked to see his foot soldiers tumbling back from the hillcrest, ordered his only remaining reserve, his Legion cavalry, into the melee. But they, too, saw what he was witnessing and they had had enough. Turning tail, they galloped off the field. Tarleton, with a handful of men, for a few minutes opposed Washington's dragoons. He and Washington for a moment engaged in a cut-and-slash personal encounter. Then Tarleton drew rein and followed his fleeing horsemen. Save for these few, most of the British force was captured or killed. First to surrender were the Legion, the light infantry, and the 7th Foot. Five minutes later the Highlanders threw down their arms. Gallantly resisting, the few cannoneers serving the grasshoppers died beside their pieces.

Within a two-hour period the British had lost 110 men killed, 229 more wounded, and more than 800 made prisoner. Morgan, whose losses were only 12 killed and 61 wounded, bagged Tarleton's entire baggage train, 100 horses, 800 muskets, and a considerable supply of powder.

Perhaps the most remarkable thing about this battle was that Morgan, whether or not he had ever heard of Hannibal, had planned and won a complete double envelopment remarkably reminiscent of Hannibal's victory over the Romans at Cannae in 216 B.C.

43

Guilford Courthouse
March 15, 1781

Shortly after the battle of Cowpens, Greene learned that Daniel Morgan's arthritis was severely handicapping him. Greene left his own command in the hands of Brigadier General Isaac Huger and joined Morgan early in the retreat. By February 6, when the two segments of the American Southern Army rejoined at Guilford Courthouse, Morgan could no longer sit his horse. Greene sent him back to his Virginia home.

Greene now had 1,400 Continental troops and 600 much less reliable militiamen. He briefly considered standing and fighting, but realized that he had no hope of victory against Cornwallis's army of almost three thousand regular troops. Greene withdrew toward the lower Dan River, where he had already ordered all available boats to be gathered in case of need. After a long and dramatic pursuit, Cornwallis arrived at the south bank of the river just in time to see the last Americans crossing, and all the boats for miles around gone with them.

Cornwallis, having failed in his effort to catch the retreating Americans, withdrew to Hillsboro for rest and supplies. He detached some units to protect his line of communications back to Camden and Charleston. Then he began a series of maneuvers in an attempt to lure Greene into battle.

Having received reinforcements, cautiously Greene returned southward. When he again arrived at Guilford Courthouse on March 14, he decided that he could risk a battle. He now had

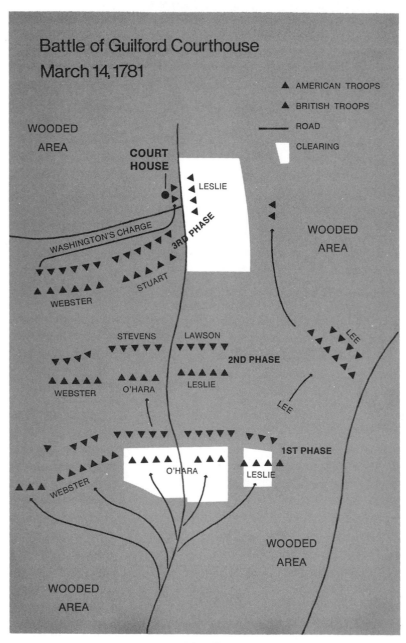

Battle of Guilford Courthouse
March 14, 1781

▲ AMERICAN TROOPS

▲ BRITISH TROOPS

── ROAD

☐ CLEARING

WOODED AREA

COURT HOUSE

LESLIE

WASHINGTON'S CHARGE

3RD PHASE

WOODED AREA

WEBSTER

STUART

STEVENS

LAWSON

2ND PHASE

LEE

WEBSTER

O'HARA

LESLIE

LEE

1ST PHASE

WEBSTER

O'HARA

LESLIE

WOODED AREA

WOODED AREA

Map 19

4,300 men, of whom 1,600 were Continental infantry and 160 were Continental cavalry. Cornwallis by this time probably had fewer than two thousand troops, but all first-class regulars.

Greene selected a favorable defensive position just south of Guilford Courthouse, and astride the main north-south road through central North Carolina. The courthouse was located near the top of a commanding ridge, and Greene emplaced his troops in a thinly wooded area on the southern slopes. He adopted a plan very similar to the one Morgan had used at the Cowpens. There were to be three battle lines, with the least reliable troops—bolstered by a few regulars—in the front line, and the most reliable—the bulk of his Continentals—in the third and main line of defense. He had his riflemen on the flanks, where, according to advice written him by Daniel Morgan, they could direct enfilade fire against the flanks of the advancing enemy. The cavalry of Colonel Henry ("Light-Horse Harry") Lee's Legion covered the front as an outpost line.

Greene's three lines were considerably farther apart than Morgan's had been at the Cowpens. The Virginia militiamen of the second line could barely see the front line through the trees. Coordinated action would therefore be difficult. Greene himself planned to take position behind the third line, at the courthouse.

While waiting for the British to arrive, Greene spent most of his time with the North Carolina militia in the first line. He followed Morgan's psychological approach. Since he felt sure the militia would break and run sooner or later, he tried to make it later by giving them a definite and limited task to perform. "Three rounds, my boys, and then you may fall back," he told them again and again, using Morgan's battle-proven formula.

When Cornwallis learned of Greene's approach, late on March 14, his small army was about twelve miles south of Guilford Courthouse. He got his troops on the march early the following morning. A cavalry screen of Lee's Legion fell back before them.

As Lee's Legion pulled back, to take position on the left of the first American line, the British moved up until they reached the southern edge of the clearing in front of the North Carolina militia.

Two American cannon, stationed in the road, in the center of the line, immediately opened fire.

Two British artillery pieces were quickly unlimbered to reply to this fire, while Cornwallis deployed his troops. He placed Major General Alexander Leslie's brigade on the right, with Colonel von Bose's Hessian regiment farthest right, a battalion of the 71st Highlanders left of it, and the 1st Battalion of the Guards centered behind them. Left of the main road that bisected the battlefield was the brigade of Lieutenant Colonel James Webster, including the 23rd Foot (Royal Welsh Fusiliers) next to the road, the 33rd Regiment to the far left, and placed behind them, a company of Hessian jägers and the light infantry companies of the rest of the army. Lieutenant Colonel Charles O'Hara was in command of a small reserve contingent including the Guards 2nd Battalion and all the grenadier companies.

As the British and Hessian troops advanced into the clearing at about 1:30 P.M., the North Carolina militiamen fired their first volley, and then a second. Gaps appeared in the advancing lines. The British halted briefly to fire a return volley; then Webster ordered his men to charge. When the flashing British bayonets approached, the North Carolina militia ran.

As the British surged forward into the wooded area beyond the fence where the American first line had been, they still saw their comrades falling, and realized that accurate American fire was coming from their flanks. It was from the Virginia riflemen Greene had placed in the woods to the right and left of his first line. Leslie's and Webster's flank battalions wheeled to face the flanking fire. The Virginia riflemen, Kirkwood's Continental light infantry, and Washington's horsemen on the American right flank fell back in good order in front of Webster's men, taking prearranged positions on the right flank of the American second line. The American riflemen and Lee's troops on the left flank, however, were pushed to the northeast and isolated from the rest of the American force. Leslie left his Hessian troops to deal with this pocket and led the rest of his troops forward against the left wing of the American second line.

On the British left, Webster's vigorous advance was halted only briefly by Stevens's brigade of Virginia militiamen in the second line. Repulsing a counterattack by Washington's horsemen and Kirkwood's light infantry, Webster smashed Stevens's brigade. The Virginians fled. On the British right, however, Leslie was still held up by Lawson's brigade.

While Leslie dealt with the remaining Virginians, Webster advanced toward the third American line, the solid Continentals on the hillside. As the British stormed up the hill, they met heavy fire from the waiting Continentals. The British and Hessians hesitated, then were struck by a bayonet counterattack of the Virginia Continentals and driven back to the left rear, across a ravine, away from the main body of the British force.

Greene's battle plan had worked well. Despite the expected flight of the North Carolina militia, an American victory seemed certain. The British right had been stopped and the left was now thrown back. An all-out counterattack would undoubtedly have carried the day. Greene, however, was too cautious to risk it, and the opportunity passed.

Lawson's brigade of Virginians finally gave way under Leslie's repeated assaults, with support from O'Hara's reserve, which moved into the center of the line after Webster's repulse. The British right wing swept forward to envelop the left of the American third line, while Webster re-formed his men and moved back against the American right. As Colonel Otho Williams shifted his Maryland brigade to meet the threatened envelopment of his left flank, the 5th Maryland Continentals became disorganized. This was a new unit that was not yet steady enough to meet the terror of a well-coordinated British musket volley followed by a bayonet charge. The Marylanders ran.

In the earlier fighting Colonel O'Hara had been wounded, but Lieutenant Colonel Duncan Stuart took his place in command of the center of the British line. Seeing the gap created in the third American line as the 5th Maryland fled, Stuart led a charge toward the courthouse. But just as the American line seemed to be cut in two, Colonel Washington's little cavalry force counterattacked.

Stuart was killed, and the wounded O'Hara resumed command as the British center withdrew in confusion.

Then the 1st Maryland Regiment, under veteran Colonel John E. Howard of the Cowpens fame, counterattacked O'Hara's shattered regiments, which were saved only by the arrival of Leslie's units. A fire fight between Leslie's brigade and Howard's Marylanders raged around the courthouse. At the same time the Virginia Continentals began to drive Webster's brigade back down the hill. Again the tide of battle swung in favor of the Americans.

At this point Cornwallis made a decision that saved the day for the British. Over O'Hara's protests he ordered his artillery to fire grapeshot into the struggling mass of soldiery on the hill. He knew that some British troops would be killed and wounded, but he believed that this was the only way to turn back the Americans. He was relying on disciplined British regulars to stand firm despite casualties from their own guns.

The tactic worked. The Americans fell back to regroup. But Cornwallis gave his tired and hungry men no respite. He ordered one final assault. As the British again moved forward, Greene, afraid that his own troops might not hold their positions, ordered a withdrawal. Firing as they pulled back, the Virginia Continentals again repulsed an attack by Webster's brigade; Webster himself fell, fatally wounded.

Guilford was a hard-fought battle. As often when two sides are evenly matched, casualties were high. British losses were about twice as great as those of the Americans, which was to be expected, since they were the attackers. Cornwallis lost at least 25 percent of his entire army. Official admitted losses were 93 British killed and 439 wounded; 78 Americans were reported killed and 183 wounded. Losses among British officers, easy to pick out by their epaulets, gold braid, and sword belts, were particularly high.

Cornwallis had driven Greene from the field and could rightly claim to have won the fight at Guilford Courthouse. But the battle left the British in a far worse situation than the Americans. Cornwallis knew he could not afford to fight another such battle, and he was isolated in a hostile countryside. He was forced to withdraw eastward all the way to the British-controlled port of Wilmington, North Carolina.

Although Greene and his men could be proud of their performance, he had been outgeneraled. His units had not been well coordinated, and because of overcaution he had missed two opportunities to destroy Cornwallis's army.

The rest of Greene's Carolina campaign followed the theme set at Guilford Courthouse. He fought three more battles—Hobkirk's Hill, Ninety-six, and Eutaw Springs—and the British had slightly the better of each encounter. Yet at the close of each battle, cautious Greene was in better shape than the victorious British commanders. By the end of the year he had pushed the British back into Charleston, where he blockaded them. '

44

Preliminaries in Virginia
May–August 1781

In early 1781 the Revolutionary cause was in trouble in Virginia. British Brigadier General Benedict Arnold was ravaging the eastern and central regions of the state, while Cornwallis was marching northward from Wilmington, North Carolina.

In May and June Washington sent Major General Lafayette to Virginia with about 2,200 Continentals, including the brigade of General "Mad Anthony" Wayne. Lafayette was soon joined by about 1,800 Virginia militia, but when Cornwallis joined Arnold at Petersburg, the British strength in Virginia was over seven thousand men. For several weeks the armies maneuvered in central Virginia, but Lafayette, with the able assistance of Wayne and von

Steuben, was able to avoid a decisive battle with the larger and better British Army.

Aggressive Cornwallis meanwhile was engaged in a debate by letter with cautious Clinton, his superior. Cornwallis felt sure that with reinforcements he could overwhelm all resistance in Virginia, and so wrote to Clinton, the British commander-in-chief, who was still in New York. Instead of receiving reinforcements, however, Cornwallis was ordered by Clinton to send three thousand men to reinforce New York, where Clinton feared a combined French-American attack. Cornwallis regretfully but obediently marched from Williamsburg down the Virginia Peninsula (between the York and James rivers), to cross Hampton Roads to Portsmouth, where he would embark the three thousand men for New York. On the way he ambushed Wayne's brigade at Jamestown Ford, on July 6, but the skillful American escaped from the trap with light losses.

Just as Cornwallis was embarking the three thousand men at Portsmouth, he received another message from Clinton, telling him that he could keep the men if he still felt he had to have them. Clinton, however, still refused to send reinforcements, and ordered Cornwallis to establish himself in a strong position on Chesapeake Bay. He suggested Yorktown, then called York. Cornwallis kept the three thousand men and moved by ship to Yorktown on August 4. He also occupied Gloucester Point, across the York River.

Cornwallis's move to Yorktown was promptly reported by Lafayette to Washington, who—with the assistance of a French army under Count Jean Baptiste de Rochambeau—was still blockading Clinton in New York. About the same time Washington received a letter from French Admiral Count François Joseph Paul de Grasse, who was sailing from the West Indies for Chesapeake Bay with a large French fleet. De Grasse wrote that he could remain off the American coast until October 15.

Washington immediately understood the strategic possibilities opened to him. Control of the sea in a crucial area was now possible. The capture of Cornwallis's entire force was also pos-

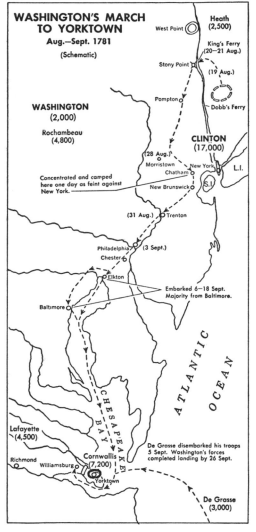

WASHINGTON'S MARCH
TO YORKTOWN
Aug.—Sept. 1781
(Schematic)

Heath
(2,500)

West Point

King's Ferry
(20—21 Aug.)

Stony Point

(19 Aug.)

Pompton

Dobb's Ferry

WASHINGTON
(2,000)

Rochambeau
(4,800)

CLINTON
(17,000)

(28 Aug.)
Morristown

New York

Chatham

L.I.

Concentrated and camped
here one day as feint against
New York.

New Brunswick

S.I.

(31 Aug.) Trenton

Philadelphia (3 Sept.)
Chester

Elkton

Embarked 6—18 Sept.
Majority from Baltimore.

Baltimore

ATLANTIC

OCEAN

CHESAPEAKE BAY

Lafayette
(4,500)

Richmond

Williamsburg

Cornwallis
(7,200)

Yorktown

De Grasse disembarked his troops
5 Sept. Washington's forces
completed landing by 26 Sept.

De Grasse
(3,000)

Map 20

sible. Washington—already considering a possible campaign in Virginia—decided to send all available French and American land forces to surround Yorktown by land, while de Grasse held off the British Navy and kept Cornwallis from escaping by sea. However, there were two big problems.

Clinton, who had more than ten thousand troops in New York, might learn of Washington's plan and attack the smaller American army as it moved down through New Jersey. And either de Grasse's fleet or the smaller fleet of Admiral Louis de Barras, which was sailing from Newport with needed French troops, guns, and supplies, might be intercepted and defeated by the British fleet of Admiral Thomas Graves.

To deal with the first of these problems, Washington prepared elaborate deceptions. The arrangements for the move south were planned to make the British expect an attack from New Jersey on Manhattan or Staten Island. The plan worked perfectly. The Americans, along with Rochambeau's French army, moved south through New Jersey on August 25, while a few troops created a diversion opposite Staten Island. Clinton did not realize that the French and American armies had continued south until September 2, too late to catch them.

There was nothing Washington could do, however, about the safety of the French fleets. On September 5, while at Chester, Pennsylvania, he learned that de Grasse, with three thousand troops, had arrived safely in Chesapeake Bay. Nevertheless, Washington was still concerned about de Barras, and worried lest Graves might drive de Grasse out of Chesapeake Bay.

45

Battle of the Capes
September 5–9, 1781

Late in August of 1781 the focus of the Revolution beamed sharply on Chesapeake Bay and the exercise of sea power. Cornwallis had holed himself up at Yorktown, expecting that the Royal Navy would keep open his one means of communication with New York—the sea lanes. He was loosely blockaded by Lafayette's small army of Continentals and militia. Washington's Continentals and Rochambeau's French regulars were hurrying south overland; de Grasse's French fleet was bowling up from the West Indies to close the trap.

Admiral Samuel Hood, also from the West Indies, was boldly hunting de Grasse, even though his fleet was seriously outnumbered by the French. Meanwhile, de Barras's small French squadron had already left Newport for Chesapeake Bay, carrying Rochambeau's heavy artillery, and British Rear Admiral Thomas Graves, with a small British squadron out of New York, was seeking to intercept de Barras.

Hood, with fourteen ships of the line, was the first to reach the Virginia Capes. Entering Chesapeake Bay on August 21, he found it empty of French ships and sailed for New York, where he joined Graves. Graves, the senior, assumed command, and the combined fleet—now nineteen ships of the line—sped back, searching for both de Barras and de Grasse. The British knew that de Barras had eight ships of the line, and thought that de Grasse had twelve.

Meanwhile, de Grasse—actually with twenty-eight ships of the line and a covey of transports carrying 3,500 French troops to reinforce Rochambeau—had made his landfall on August 26. Anchoring in Lynnhaven Bay, just inside Cape Henry, he landed his troops, contacted Washington, who was then passing through Chester, and disposed four of his ships across the James and York rivers to blockade Cornwallis tightly at Yorktown.

Early on September 5, while some two thousand of de Grasse's seamen were ashore gathering wood and water for the fleet, a French picket boat off the Capes reported a large fleet in the offing. The wind was unfavorable and de Grasse, not waiting for his shore parties, at once made sail with his remaining twenty-four large warships.

Clawing off a lee shore—the wind was blowing hard from the

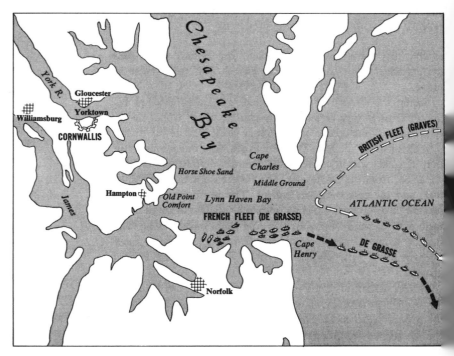

Battle of Chesapeake Bay.

Map 21

east—the French fleet moved out from the Capes by noon in three successive widely separated and somewhat ragged groups of eight ships each.

Graves, with the weather gauge, could have thrown his entire fleet on the leading French group, and then destroyed his enemy in detail. Instead, obsessed by the Royal Navy's stilted predilection for "the Line" as the approved formation for a sea battle, he changed course, heading eastward in an attempt to parallel the straggling French line.

Consequently, only eight or nine of the British fleet were at first engaged, against the eight leading French ships. In a two-hour running fight, all vessels involved suffered heavy damage, although superior French long-range gunnery and weight of metal had a bit the better of the fight. At dusk, de Grasse, with sea room under his feet now, sheered off to correct his line. The leading Britishers lost contact; the others were unable to catch up.

For four long days and nights the opposing fleets jockeyed up and down the coast in parallel columns, just out of gun range, while damages were hastily repaired. Cannily, de Grasse so maneuvered as to keep his ships between Graves and the shoreline, to cover de Barras should he appear. And appear he did, having made a long easting to avoid Graves's pursuit. He slipped inside the Capes just before a violent storm broke along the coast on September 9, dispersing both major fleets. One British ship, HMS *Terrible* (80), badly damaged in the initial clash, was so battered that she had to be abandoned and blown up. That night Graves gave up and shepherded his crippled fleet for New York to refit. De Grasse returned to Chesapeake Bay, where he found and captured two British frigates engaged in destroying his mooring buoys off Lynnhaven.

Rochambeau had received his siege artillery, de Grasse had corked up Chesapeake Bay, and Cornwallis's fate was sealed.

46

Yorktown
September 28–October 19, 1781

At Yorktown Cornwallis was only dimly aware of the momentous naval battle off the Virginia Capes that settled the fate of his army. He was well prepared for the siege he expected. He had built extensive fortifications, making full use of creeks and marshes that provided natural protection. The only open land approach to Yorktown was over a flat area less than half a mile wide, called the Pigeon Quarter. Three British redoubts had been built. The area was also swept by guns in the main Yorktown fortifications.

On September 28 the investment of Yorktown began. Washington assumed overall command; the Americans held the right side of the line, the French the left. Washington also sent a strong Franco-American contingent to contain the British force across the York River at Gloucester.

On September 29 Cornwallis received news that Clinton was sending him a relief expedition. Deciding to shorten his lines and conserve his strength while awaiting help, on September 30 he abandoned some outer fortifications, making the task of the besiegers easier.

During the night of October 6–7 French and American engineers began to dig a trench parallel to the enemy's fortifications. When this "first parallel" was completed, siege artillery was moved into it, and the bombardment began on October 9. Under the cover of this fire, allied troops dug approach trenches closer to Yorktown.

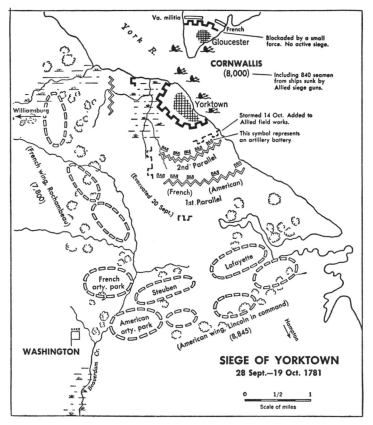

Map 22

The allies began their "second parallel" during the night of October 11–12. This was less than three hundred yards from the British fortifications in some places, but could not be completed down to the river because of two powerful British redoubts, designated No. 9 and No. 10, near it. Washington decided to take these. Redoubt No. 10, closest to the river, was to be assaulted by Americans, and No. 9 by French troops, in surprise nighttime bayonet attacks.

Shortly after dark on October 14, French Colonel Guillamme Deux-Ponts and four hundred men struck No. 9 and took it after a sharp struggle. The Americans at No. 10, commanded by Lieutenant Colonel Alexander Hamilton, had an easier time, since the big siege guns had broken down much of the abatis. Both redoubts were captured before 10:00 P.M. The second parallel was completed that night, and the artillery fire grew heavier as the big guns were emplaced there to begin hammering at the Yorktown defenses at short range. British casualties mounted.

To end or reduce this punishment, Cornwallis ordered a sortie for October 16. A band of 350 picked troops struck the second parallel before dawn. The British succeeded in spiking seven French and American guns, but were driven back by a determined French counterattack. By daylight the spikes had been removed from the touchholes, and the big guns were all in action again.

As the punishing allied bombardment continued, smashing the remains of the town and inflicting many more casualties on the defenders, Cornwallis decided to try to escape. The night of the 16th he had some of his men embarked for Gloucester, where he thought he might be able to break through the relatively weak allied lines and then race northward to safety. The rest of the garrison would be ready to leave when the boats returned.

This last British hope was frustrated by the weather. Gale winds prevented the return of the boats. The next morning the wind died, but the allies had been alerted; escape was now impossible.

Surrender, therefore, was inevitable. Cornwallis sent a message to Washington requesting talks on surrender terms. Washington would allow the British garrison only the limited honors of war that Clinton had granted General Lincoln at the surrender of Charleston. Cornwallis had no choice but to accept. On October 19 the British garrison marched out, colors cased, the bands not being allowed to play any American or French marches, as was permitted when full honors of war were granted. According to tradition, one of the marches played was an English tune called "The World Turned Upside Down."

The British casualties during the siege were 156 killed, 326 wounded, and 70 missing. Cornwallis surrendered 7,247 soldiers and 840 seamen. Allied losses were 53 Americans killed and 65 wounded; 60 Frenchmen killed and 193 wounded.

The very morning of Cornwallis's surrender Clinton sailed from New York with a relief army of seven thousand men, convoyed by Graves's reinforced fleet of twenty-seven ships of the line. They arrived off Chesapeake Bay on October 24, and Clinton learned of the surrender. Wisely he and Graves decided to avoid a dangerous battle with de Grasse's superior fleet, now thirty-six ships of the line, and they returned to New York.

Yorktown was the decisive event of the war. The struggle did not end at once, but there was little more serious fighting. There could no longer be doubt of the outcome. America had won independence from Britain.

French assistance had been crucial, particularly at sea. But Washington had been the man who realized how to make the most of the alliance. It was his quick grasp of the strategic situation, his decisiveness, his excellent planning, and the smoothness of American coordination and communications that assured the victory.

PART THREE

The
Participants

47

The Patriot Forces

The Thirteen United Colonies began their fight for freedom without any professional troops. Each colony, however, had its own independent militia organization—on a common basis of universal obligatory service in emergency dating back to 1636.* Since 1774 these militias—particularly in the New England colonies—had been pruned of Loyalist officers and prepared for immediate alert.

That is why on April 19, 1775, the Massachusetts militia came buzzing out with such remarkable alacrity; why the neighbors from New Hampshire, Rhode Island, and Connecticut scurried in to help; why, within forty-eight hours, British General Gage and his regulars in Boston found themselves penned in by a collection of some fourteen thousand armed men who knew how to shoot.†

On June 15, 1775, Congress selected Colonel George Washington of the Virginia militia to be General and Commander-in-Chief to lead "all the continental forces, raised or to be raised, for the defense of American Liberty." It had earlier that day authorized the enrollment of twelve companies of riflemen: eight from Pennsylvania, two from Virginia, and two from Maryland.

Washington arrived in Cambridge on July 3 to find, in his own words, ". . . a mixed multitude of People here, under very little discipline [or] order of government. . . . Confusion and disorder reigned in every Department."

* Arthur Volmer, *Military Obligations; A Compilation of the Enactments of Compulsion from the Earliest Settlements of the Original Thirteen Colonies in 1607 Through the Articles of Confederation, 1789.* Washington, D.C., U.S. Government Printing Office, 1947, *passim.*

† For a detailed survey of this militia mobilization see Galvin, *The Minute Men.* New York, 1967, *passim.*

He systematized the mass into twenty-six one-battalion regiments of infantry, added both a rifle regiment and an artillery regiment, and created rudimentary staff departments. The Continental Army thus tailored was reorganized, in 1777, to include four regiments of cavalry and sixteen additional regiments of infantry.

By 1779 the army's paper strength was eighty regiments, including several so-called Legions (mixed detachments of horse and foot). By 1781 its strength dwindled to fifty-eight regiments. Through its ranks passed 230,887 men. Yet never did its field strength muster at any one time more than 29,340. In fact, during the most crucial period of the Revolution—the Trenton-Princeton campaign of 1776—the Continental Army's strength was less than four thousand men.

Manpower—or its lack—was always one of Washington's major preoccupations. Ill-advised congressional policies of short-term voluntary enlistments and the pernicious bonus inducements, where both the states and the Congress vied to coax recruits into the militia or the Continental Army, fostered "repeaters," men who enlisted, drew their bonuses, and then promptly deserted to reenlist. Such things, added to the normal attrition of war and disease, created an ebb and flow highly detrimental to training and troop leading.

Time-expired men were always going out, recruits were always joining. In emergency serious gaps were filled by drafts of untrained militia, brought into service for periods ranging from sixty days to six months.

The official breakdown of men and sources is as follows:*

Continental Army

Massachusetts	67,907
Connecticut	32,039
Virginia	26,672
Pennsylvania	25,608

* Knox Report, Report of the Secretary of War. 10 May, 1790, as published in *American State Papers—Military Affairs,* vol. 1, pp. 14–19.

New York	17,781
Maryland	13,912
New Hampshire	12,496
New Jersey	10,727
North Carolina	7,263
Rhode Island	5,908
South Carolina	5,508
Georgia	2,679
Delaware	2,387
Total	230,887

Militia

From Army returns	86,370
Conjectural estimate	105,330
Grand total	422,587

The numbers bear little relation to the actual number of individuals engaged; many served through several successive enlistments, many others enlisted only to desert and re-enlist in order to collect the bounties offered by Congress.

The Continental Line regiments were of either one or—infrequently—two battalions, each of ten-company strength, including flank companies. These latter, following eighteenth-century organization, were officially light infantry (there were no grenadier formations). However, there was little difference between line and flank companies. In essence all Patriot infantry fell in the "light" class; certainly few men were burdened with heavy equipment.

Firearms were a heterogeneous mixture—ranging from the British Tower muskets, or a European counterpart, to fowling pieces; but the men knew how to shoot and well appreciated the value of aimed fire. A favorite load of Patriot musketeers was "buck and ball"; two buckshot dropped in on top of the normal bullet—a murderous charge at close range, and bitterly complained of by their opponents.

Exceptions to this assortment of smooth-bore flintlocks were the long, so-called Kentucky rifles carried by the rifle companies,

Continental and militia. These were weapons of precision evolved by German gunmakers in Pennsylvania from the short, heavy, cumberous "jäger" rifle used by Swiss, Bavarian, and Rhineland huntsmen.*

The rifle's military drawback was that a bayonet could not be fitted to it, a matter of small importance in the Patriot forces, where bayonets, like all other specialized equipment, were scarce. The rifle's value lay in its range and precision; at two hundred yards it was deadly; the smooth-bores were inaccurate beyond fifty yards.

The discipline and precision of regular troops were sadly lacking in the Continental Army until the winter of 1777–1778, when Washington placed von Steuben (see p. 121) in charge of training. The later Battle of Monmouth proved the value of von Steuben's labors; from that time on the Continental met his enemy on equal footing.

When the war ended, Congress, motivated by the innate fear of the military always displayed by the American people, wiped this professional force from the boards. Its one link of continuous service with the modern United States Army is provided by Captain Alexander Hamilton's Company of New York Artillery, some eighty-odd men and three officers, organized in 1776. It fortuitously was held in service at West Point and Fort Pitt in 1784, to live today as an element of the 5th Field Artillery Regiment, U.S.A.

Any attempt to present an orderly list of Continental Army or militia units invites bewilderment. Regiments were formed, disbanded, reorganized, split, renamed, or renumbered in maddening confusion. Some Continental regiments, notably the "additional" regiments of 1777, never received numbers; they were known by the names of their commanders. For instance, Vermont's Green Mountain Boys were carried on official muster rolls as "Colonel Seth Warner's Battalion from the New Hampshire Grants."

Total casualties (again an estimate) included 4,044 men killed

---

* Dupuy and Dupuy, *The Compact History of the Revolutionary War,* p. 461.

in action and 6,004 more wounded.* There are no records of casualties caused by accident or disease, nor of civilian losses.

However, today's roster of U.S. Army National Guard units reveals several regiments which not only fought in the Revolutionary War, but some of them dating back to the mid-seventeenth century.† Let's look at them:

Today	Organized	Revolutionary War Service
182nd Inf. (5th Mass.)	October 7, 1636, as North Regt., Mass. Militia	Middlesex Regt. (its Lexington company, commanded by Capt. John Parker, on April 19, 1775, was the first Patriot unit to be engaged). Later, successively Gardner's Regt., Bond's Regt., 7th, 25th, and again, 7th Continental Regt.
176th Inf. (1st Va.)	1652, as Charles City-Henrico Cos. Militia; (George Washington commanded it in 1758)	1st Regt., Va. Regulars (Col. Patrick Henry); transferred to Continental Line November 1, 1775. Surrendered at Charleston, 1780; later reconstituted, furnished drafts to other Va. regts. of the Continental Line.
104th Inf. (2nd Mass.)	May 7, 1662, as Hampshire Regt., Mass. Militia	In 1763 the Berkshire Regt. Its "minute" companies were engaged in the opening encounters around Boston. Reorg. May 27, 1775 in four battalions: Danielson's, Fellows's, Paterson's, and Woodbridge's. Mustered out in Dec. 1775.
169th Inf. (1st Conn.)	1672, as Regt. of Hartford County	1st. Regt. of Militia, 1739. Elements served in New York area in 1776, at Saratoga, and during the Danbury Raid of 1777.
102nd Inf. (2nd Conn.)	1672 as Regt. of New Haven County	2nd Regt. of Militia in 1739. Elements served in New York area in 1776; Danbury Raid and New Haven Alarm in 1777.

* Total Continental Navy losses were estimated to be 342 killed in battle, with 114 wounded. The Marines lost 49 killed and 70 wounded. Total American combat casualties were 4,435 dead, 6,188 wounded.

† R. E. Dupuy, *The National Guard*, pp. 147–148. See also *U.S. Army Lineage Books*.

Today	Organized	Revolutionary War Service
111th Inf. (3d. Pa.—The Associators)	1747 by Benjamin Franklin as the Associated Regt. of Foot of Philadelphia	In 1775 the Associators of the City and Liberties of Philadelphia (5 bns.). Participated in Trenton-Princeton campaign.
Troop A, 1st Sqn., 223d Cav. (1st Tr. Phila. City Cav.)	1774, as Light Horse of the City of Philadelphia	This unit of volunteer militia escorted Washington to Cambridge in 1775 and served (apparently refusing pay) as a personal bodyguard to him throughout the war.
175th Inf. (5th Md.)	Dec. 3, 1774, as Baltimore Independent Cadets	Capt. Gish's Co. in 1775. Absorbed into Smallwood's Md. Regt. in 1776. Expanded into Smallwood's Md. Brig. of the Continental Line in 1777.
181st Inf. (6th Mass.)	1775, as Groton Artillery	On April 19, 1775, this unit and several others gathered in Col. William Prescott's minuteman battalion to harass the retreating British column.
109th FA Bn. (Pa.)	1775, as Wyoming Valley Militia of Conn.	Settlers from Connecticut, which disputed the area with Pennsylvania. Served at Cambridge in 1775. Later absorbed in the Continental Line, it was absent when Butler's raid devastated the Valley in 1778. Minute companies engaged during 1777.

Some other units must be mentioned.

Then senior regiment, the Pennsylvania Continentals, began as Colonel William Thompson's Pennsylvania Rifle Battalion, part of the original twelve rifle units established by the Continental Congress on June 14, 1775. It took part in the siege of Boston and two of its companies (under Daniel Morgan's command) trudged with Arnold on the amazing march to Quebec. On January 1, 1776, the unit became the 1st Continental Regiment. Renamed next year the 1st Pennsylvania, it served as such through the remainder of the war.

Baylor's 3rd Continental Light Dragoons, in distinctive white uniforms faced with light blue, was organized in 1777. For nearly two years it served as part of General Washington's escort, gaining the unofficial title of "Lady Washington's Horse." Almost demolished near Hackensack in September 1778 by a night attack upon its bivouac, it was reorganized to serve with distinction throughout Greene's southern campaign under Colonel William Washington.

Morgan's Rifle Corps. Organized in 1777; based on Morgan's rifle company (established by Congress, resolution of June 16, 1775) and expert riflemen picked from various units of the Continental Army to reinforce Gates. Under Colonel Daniel Morgan it served with distinction at Saratoga. On rejoining the main army, its personnel returned to their former units. Attached to Greene, it took part in most of the major southern operations both with the main army and with "Swamp Fox" Marion's guerrilla militia raids.

Pulaski's Legion

When Count Casimir Pulaski, Polish cavalry officer, resigned in 1778 from his brief—and, to all concerned, irritating—command of the corps of Continental Light Dragoons, he received authorization to enlist an independent mounted unit; three troops of cavalry (lancers), a company each of riflemen and grenadiers, and three of infantry. His badly disciplined command was surprised in its first engagement, at Little Egg Harbor, and some fifty of his infantrymen were killed. Pulaski drove off the invaders with his cavalry. Sent south, the legion was badly mauled in front of Savannah, October 9, 1779, where Pulaski led his lancers in a madcap charge against a British position, and died a hero's death.

Armand's Legion

On December 5, 1775, Congress commissioned Barron Ottendorf to command an independent corps of foreign mercenaries. Recruiting lagged; to its ranks was added another independent company raised in Pennsylvania by a Captain Paul Schott. Meanwhile General Washington, impressed by the ability of Colonel Armand (Armand-Charles Tuffin, Marquis de la Rouerie), a French cavalry officer, authorized him to raise an independent corps. Purchasing Ottendorf's corps, Armand led it as a unit in Pulaski's Legion. Following Pulaski's death, the remnants of the Legion were reorganized as Armand's Legion. Present at Yorktown, the Legion carried itself well in an encounter with Tarleton's Legion.

Glover's Marblehead Regiment

Organized on May 19, 1775, by John Glover, wealthy Massachusetts shipowner, merchant, and fisherman. Its personnel, one thousand strong, were local fishermen and merchant sailors. Engaged in the initial operations around Boston; assisted in capture of British ordnance brigantine *Nancy,* November 1775, with an enormous cargo of military stores; redesignated 14th Continental Regiment in early 1776; the regiment (with the 27th Mass.) manned the boats evacuating Washington's troops from Long Island August 29–30. Its most amazing accomplishment was the ferrying of Washington's army across the Delaware, participating in the battle of Trenton and then ferrying the army and more than nine hundred Hessian prisoners back, all within thirty-six hours. Its enlistments up, the regiment was then disbanded. Many of its personnel took up privateering.

Hazen's 2nd Canadian Regiment

Authorized by Congress on January 20, 1776; to be composed of French Canadian volunteers to the Patriot cause. Colonel Moses Hazen (see p. 266) commanded. Actually its personnel also included many Frenchmen and Germans. An extremely efficient fighting unit, the regiment became known as "Congress's Own," and also as "Hazen's Own."

Lee's Legion

Captain Henry (Light-Horse Harry) Lee's troop of Bland's Virginia gentleman volunteer cavalry militia (Bland's Regiment), which became the 1st Continental Light Dragoons. In 1778 became a separate corps; two other troops plus three independent companies of infantry. The legion became Lee's Partisan Corps; won fame in its victory at Paulus Hook, 1779, and later with Greene in the Carolinas.

48

The Foreign Volunteers

When the Revolutionary War broke out, Europe was enjoying relative peace and unemployed professional soldiers were a dime a dozen. The Continental Congress, seeking a professional leaven for the forces it was raising, actively sought experienced European officers through its agents and diplomats abroad. France's war ministry encouraged those of its serving officers who wished to taste the war in North America, by issuing them leaves of absence. George Washington welcomed the foreign volunteers, albeit with some reserve; he sought quality not quantity.

Having been given the nod, American agents—Silas Deane in particular—spread the tidings so lavishly, with extravagant promises of rank and pay, that soldiers of fortune flocked into North America like steel filings to a magnet. The result in a number of cases brought embarrassment to the commander-in-chief, aroused the rage of competent American officers, and became a detriment to the Patriot cause.

Head and shoulders above the mass stand, of course, France's Lafayette, the youthful nobleman who gave himself and his riches unstintingly to the cause; Prussian von Steuben, who, in exchange for his soldier building wished only that his personal expenses be reimbursed; shrewd, competent de Kalb from Bavaria (via the French army), whose service ended only with his death in battle at Camden; the gifted Polish engineer Kosciusko; and that other Polish soldier, Pulaski, whose headstrong gallantry made up for his equally headstrong obstinacy; and French engineer Louis le Beque de Presle Duportail, whom Douglas Southall Freeman ranks with Lafayette and von Steuben.*

At the bottom of the list come some obvious misfits, incompetents and troublemakers. One such was Thomas Conway, the Irish-Frenchman whose jealousy and political meddlings brought about the Conway Cabal. Then there was Mathias Alexis de Roche Fermoy, the pseudo colonel in the French Army, who hailed from Martinique, sporting a Croix de St. Louis on his chest. A drunken incompetent, Fermoy set his own quarters afire at Fort Ticonderoga, alerting Burgoyne to St. Clair's hasty flight. Another spoiled apple in the foreign volunteer barrel was brilliant but overambitious Tronson de Coudray. His arrogant demand for seniority status in the Continental Army created wide antagonism among both senior American and French officers, until settled by de Coudray himself when he recklessly spurred his horse on board a Schuylkill ferryboat in 1777. The animal bolted and jumped into the river, and the rider was drowned.

Far different was François Teissedre de Fleury, another French officer who accompanied de Coudray to America. Soon shaking himself free of de Coudray's coattails, Fleury accepted a lieutenant-colonelcy, distinguished himself at Piscataway and later at the Brandywine (Congress formally presented him with a horse to

* *George Washington,* vol. IV, following p. 571.

replace the mount shot under him there), became an assistant inspector general to von Steuben, and at the storming of Stony Point under Mad Anthony Wayne was the first man to scale the enemy parapet. Congress gave him a medal for that.

Returning to France on leave, Fleury came back with Rochambeau's army—a major in the Saintonge Regiment, to win at Yorktown the coveted French Croix de St. Louis for gallantry in action. Quite a soldier, this Fleury.

In sum, whatever their motives, the foreigners who took up arms in the American struggle for liberty were—save for a few rapscallions—true to their salt. They played an important part in the Continental Army. As for the rapscallions, it must not be forgotten that the greatest rapscallion of all in that army was a home product: Benedict Arnold from Norwich, Connecticut.

49

The British Army in North America

In April of 1775 British Army troops stationed in the thirteen colonies numbered approximately 3,500 officers and men: eleven one-battalion regiments of infantry, one two-battalion regiment of Royal Marines, and a detachment of Royal Artillery, all stationed in Boston. From 1776 until the end of the war the regular establishment in America maintained an annual average effective field strength of about twelve thousand men and fifty-two of the then existing seventy regiments of infantry—English, Irish, Scottish, and Welsh. In addition two regiments of cavalry and eight batteries of artillery had been engaged either wholly or in part. The peak strength of sixteen thousand men was reached in 1781.*

The terms "regiment" and "battalion" were almost synonymous in the British Army of that era. The great majority of regiments in the field consisted of one-battalion units of five-hundred-man strength, in ten companies; two of these, termed "flank" companies from their positions in the line on parade, were respectively grenadiers and light infantry. These elite units, detached from their "line" comrades, were usually brigaded for field duty in separate battalions.†

The British infantry hand arm was the Tower musket—"Brown Bess"—a flintlock, muzzle-loading, smooth-bore musket weighing over ten pounds, approximately .75 caliber, firing round lead bullets (eleven to the pound). It was four feet nine inches long, and the bayonet, when fixed, extended fourteen inches beyond the muzzle. Its extreme range was 400 yards, but beyond 125 yards it was ineffective; actually, the best of marksmen could not expect more than 30 percent of his bullets to hit a man 75 yards away. Theoretically, a well-drilled infantryman could fire five rounds per minute. Since the bullet fitted loosely into the bore, the British regular, after pouring the powder from his paper cartridge in the muzzle and dropping in the bullet, would strike the butt sharply on the ground, obviating the use of the ramrod, a practice frowned upon because in the excitement of battle a misfire could result in putting an additional round in the gun, rendering it useless. Not infrequently, after combat, muskets were found which contained five or more unfired rounds in their choked bores.

Aimed fire was unknown in the British line. The soldier raised his piece shoulder-high, held it as level as possible, and on command pulled the trigger.

* For discussions of German mercenaries in British service, and of Tory units, see pp. 205 and 211 respectively.

† The generic term "grenadier" bore no relationship to the famous Grenadier Guards, then the 1st Regiment of Foot Guards, but had its origin in the seventeenth and eighteenth century use of prototypes of modern hand grenades; big strong men were needed to throw the grenades to maximum distances.

British Regiments Serving in America

CAVALRY

16th and 17th Light Dragoons (later 16th Queen's Lancers and 17th Duke of Cambridge's Own Lancers). Total approximate strength of the two units was not more than five hundred men. The 16th was returned to Britain in 1778.

INFANTRY

Household Troops

A composite brigade (four battalions); one battalion each of 1st and 2nd Foot Guards (later respectively Grenadier and Coldstream Guards) and two battalions of the Royal Scots (later Scots Guards).

Line Regiments

3rd Foot (later the Buffs, East Kent). To America in 1781.

4th Foot (later King's Own Royal Lancaster). In Boston garrison in 1775, Lexington, Bunker's Hill, New York, Germantown. To West Indies in 1778.

5th Foot (later Northumberland Fusiliers). In Boston garrison in 1775; served at Bunker's Hill. To West Indies in 1778.

7th Foot (later Royal Fusiliers, City of London). Served in Canada.

8th Foot (later King's Liverpool). Served only in Canada.

9th Foot (later Norfolk). Burgoyne's army.

10th Foot (later Lincolnshire). In Boston garrison in 1775. Served at Lexington, Concord, Bunker's Hill, and northern campaigns.

14th Foot (later Prince of Wales' Own West Yorkshire). Southern area. Went home in 1778.

15th Foot (later East Yorkshire). From Long Island to Germantown. Went to West Indies in 1778.

16th Foot (later Bedfordshire). In garrison in Florida when Spain entered the war in 1779. Overcome by Gálvez's Spanish troops at Baton Rouge and Pensacola. Detachment later served in the Carolinas.

17th Foot (later Leicestershire). Captured by Wayne at Stony Point; exchanged, it was later captured at Yorktown, with Cornwallis.

18th Foot (later Prince of Wales' Own Yorkshire; known also as the Green Howards). Served in the Carolinas from 1781 to end.

20th Foot (later Lancashire). With Burgoyne's army.

21st Foot Royal North British (later Royal Scots Fusiliers). With Burgoyne's army.

22nd Foot Royal Welsh Fusiliers. In Boston garrison in 1775. Served at Bunker's Hill. Served through entire war, ending at Yorktown.

24th Foot (later South Wales Borderers). With Burgoyne's army.

26th Foot (later Cameronian). Served in Canada. Served with Clinton in Hudson River campaign, 1777. Went home in 1778.

27th Foot (later Royal Inniskilling Fusiliers). From Long Island to 1778, when transferred to West Indies.

28th Foot (later Gloucestershire). Long Island to Germantown. To West Indies in 1778.

29th Foot (later Worcestershire). Burgoyne's army.

30th Foot (later East Surrey; also Huntingtonshire). Served in Nova Scotia, but its flank companies were with Burgoyne's army.

33rd Foot (later Duke of Wellington's West Riding). Entire service under Cornwallis. Surrendered at Yorktown.

34th Foot (later the Border Regiment). Burgoyne's army.

35th Foot (later Royal Sussex). In Boston garrison. Served at Bunker's Hill. Later stationed in New York area until returned to England in 1778.

37th Foot (later Hampshire). Long Island, to end.

38th Foot (later South Staffordshire). In Boston garrison in 1775. Served at Bunker's Hill. Then sent home to reorganize.

40th Foot (later Prince of Wales' Volunteers; South Lancaster). Long Island, to end.

42nd Foot (Royal Highlanders; the Black Watch). Long Island to Yorktown.

43rd Foot   (later Oxfordshire Light Infantry). Boston garrison in 1774. Bunker's Hill. Northern area, to end.

44th Foot   (later Essex). In Boston in 1775. Bunker's Hill. New York area until 1780, when sent to Canada.

45th Foot   (later Sherwood Foresters). Long Island. Then sent to Cape of Good Hope.

46th Foot   (later a battalion in Duke of Cornwall's Light Infantry). Long Island. Later sent back home.

47th Foot   (later Loyal North Lancashire). Boston in 1775. Bunker's Hill. Later sent to Canada. Burgoyne's army.

49th Foot   (later Princess Charlotte of Wales' Berkshire). Bunker's Hill. To West Indies in 1778.

50th Foot   (later Queen's Own West Kent). To New York in 1776, broken up and personnel used for replacements.

52nd Foot   (later Oxfordshire Light Infantry). In Boston garrison in 1774. Bunker's Hill to Yorktown.

53rd Foot   (later King's Shropshire Light Infantry). Burgoyne's army.

54th Foot   (later West Norfolk). Long Island, to end.

57th Foot   (later Duke of Cambridge's Own Middlesex). Long Island to Yorktown.

59th Foot   (later East Lancashire). In Boston garrison in 1775. Bunker's Hill, then sent home to reorganize.

60th Foot   Royal American (later King's Royal Rifle Corps). Organized at Governors Island, N.Y., 1755 during the French and Indian (Seven Years') War; recruited mainly from German emigrants; first British regiment trained specially for wilderness fighting. Three flank companies from 3rd and 4th battalions engaged at Briar Creek, 1779; later both battalions were among the troops surrendered by General John Campbell to Gálvez's Spanish forces at Pensacola in 1781.

61st Foot   (later South Gloucestershire). Burgoyne's army.

62nd Foot   (later Duke of Edinburgh's Wiltshire). Burgoyne's army.

63rd Foot   (later Manchester). In Boston garrison in 1775. Bunker's Hill. At Charleston in 1780. Part of its personnel later served with Tarleton's British Legion as mounted riflemen.

64th Foot   (later Prince of Wales' North Staffordshire). Part of

Boston garrison, 1775; northern and Virginia campaigns to Yorktown.

65th Foot   (later Yorkshire and Lancaster). In Boston garrison in 1775. Bunker's Hill; then sent home to reorganize.

70th Foot   (later East Surrey). Originally a battalion of the 31th Foot. Service in Nova Scotia.

71st Foot   Fraser's Highlanders. Raised in Scotland in 1775, following the battle of Bunker's Hill, by Major General Simon Fraser (not the General Simon Fraser of Burgoyne's expedition, killed at Saratoga). Took part in the entire war, from Long Island to Yorktown. Fraser did not accompany the regiment to North America. Three battalions in all were organized. One of them served with Tarleton at the Cowpens. Disbanded in 1783; it should not be confused with the Highland Light Infantry, which later bore the same regimental number.

84th Foot   A Tory regiment bearing this number was organized by and commanded by Allen MacLane, a British officer, in Canada: the Royal Highland Emigrants. It wore the tartan of the 42nd Foot. (See p. 202.) Served in Canada against Montgomery and Arnold.

ARTILLERY

Royal Regiment of Artillery. Eight batteries in America: A-2, A-9, D-4 (manned guns afloat on Lake Champlain in 1776; Valcour Island), E-1, H-6, H-9, I-1, I-3.

MARINES

First and 2nd Battalion, Royal Marines; personnel came from British warships in Boston harbor. Bunker's Hill. Similarly improvised Royal Marine detachments took part in many actions, notably at Savannah and Charleston.

50

Britain's German Mercenaries

By late 1775 London realized that it was confronted by an extremely serious insurrection in the North American colonies. This was a military problem of unprecedented magnitude and King George III's government hurriedly assessed the requirement for trained and experienced manpower to stamp out the rebellion. The British Army alone could not provide sufficient troops, even after milking part of Gibraltar's garrison. (Five infantry battalions from King George's own Duchy of Hanover were rushed as replacements to Gibraltar.)

Lord North, Britain's premier, after an unsuccessful effort to obtain troops from the Netherlands, at once began negotiations with the smaller German states whose autocratic rulers were only too willing to barter the lives of their subjects in exchange for cold cash.

In consequence, General Howe's expeditionary force gathering on Staten Island in July 1776 included some twelve thousand troops from Hesse-Cassel (causing Americans forever after to speak of all the various contingents of German mercenaries as "Hessians"). The leaders of this increment were, at first, Major General Leopold von Heister, and later, General Baron Wilhelm von Knyphausen.

During this same period the first of some six thousand troops from the Duchy of Brunswick began to arrive in Canada, where they were commanded by Major General Friedrich Adolph von Riedesel. They served under Burgoyne.

Before the war ended, Hesse-Cassel had provided fifteen regiments of infantry, including four battalions of grenadiers. From Ansbach-Beyreuth came three additional infantry regiments. Brunswick furnished four regiment of infantry, one battalion of grenadiers, a jäger (rifle) battalion, as well as a regiment (approximately 350 men) of dismounted dragoons. There were also one infantry regiment and three companies of field artillery from Hesse-Hanau. An additional infantry regiment from Anhalt-Zerbst reached Canada only after active operations had ended.

These German regiments, actually battalions, consisted each of approximately 650 officers and men, organized in five companies. The grenadier units were bled from the regiments, one company from each.

The basic hand arm of most of the German mercenaries was a smooth-bore musket (similar to Britain's "Brown Bess") with effective range of 125 yards—an extremely inaccurate weapon. The jägers, however, were armed with the short, heavy, German-rifled hunting firearm, progenitor of the lighter, longer, American "Kentucky" rifle.

The line infantry uniform was blue for most contingents. Jäger units sported green jackets, while the grenadier units were topped off in the mitrelike headdress common to all European grenadiers of the period. The unfortunate Brunswick dragoons, foot-slogging it in clumsy high jackboots totally unfitted for long marches, not only carried heavy muskets, but dragged behind them long cavalry sabers. (It was to provide these men with horses that Burgoyne finally sent them to their fate at Bennington.)

In all, 29,867 German soldiers came to America during the Revolution. They participated in practically every major engagement on American soil from Long Island to Yorktown. Only 17,313 of them ever returned to their homeland; 1,200 died in combat, 6,354 succumbed to illness and accident. And some five thousand of them deserted, to be swallowed up in the anonymity of the North American melting pot.*

For this reinforcement Britain paid through the nose. The

---

* Statistics abstracted from Lowell, *The Hessians*, pp. 296–301.

several treaties with the German princelets were cold-blooded butcher bills. Differing in detail, their basic provisions were similar. For each soldier furnished, Britain paid £7/4/4½ (approximately $22.50). Replacements for combat deaths were furnished at the same price; three seriously wounded men counted as one dead man, one-third the base price.

The agreements called for complete units, uniformed, armed, and equipped (except for the small Brunswick dragoon unit, furnished without horses). Officers were to be "of high caliber." Soldiers dying of disease, and deserters, were to be replaced at the seller's expense. However, should an entire unit be wiped out—in battle or through shipwreck—Britain was to foot the bill for recruiting a replacement unit, besides paying the basic £7/4/4½ head money per man. Rations, pay, hospitalization and evacuation to the homeland were responsibilities of the buyer, at rates comparable to British army rates and facilities.

The canny Duke of Brunswick, however, stipulated that his men should not be paid by British paymasters; their pay, *in toto,* was to be turned over to him for distribution. Whether or not any of this pay stuck to the duke's hands is a matter for speculation.

The Brunswick agreement also called for immediate payment by Britain—on signature—of a subsidy of £11,517/17, to be doubled annually until two years after the end of the war.

The following tabulation* gives the amounts actually voted by the British Parliament to the German princelets:

Brunswick	£	750,000
Hesse-Cassel		2,959,800
Hesse-Hanau		343,130
Ansbach-Beyreuth		282,400
Waldeck		140,000
Anhalt-Zerbst		109,120
	Total	£4,584,450

The use of these mercenary troops brought a worldwide flood of opprobrium upon King George's government. In Britain the

* Lowell, *op. cit.*

powerful antiwar Whig opposition, led by William Pitt and Charles James Fox, continuously denounced it, both in Parliament and through popular protests. On the Continent anti-British sentiment chimed in, ignoring the fact that for centuries past mercenaries had played major roles in European wars. Prussia's Frederick the Great was openly contemptuous of the petty German princes who rented out their subjects' lives. In the colonies, Patriot propagandists unceasingly stirred public opinion, picturing the Hessians as bloodthirsty savages.

What the British army received was a force in being, whose conscript soldiery had been trained in the rigid formalism of European eighteenth-century warfare, but were entirely ignorant of wilderness campaigning. Its officers were every whit as capable as their British opposite numbers, and its high commanders, Brunswicker von Riedesel and Hessians von Heister and von Knyphausen, were experienced professionals.

Fortunately for the Patriot cause the talents of these German leaders were disregarded by the British. The War Office, fearful lest through mischance a senior German general officer might become commander-in-chief in America, provided Clinton with a "dormant" commission of full general, effective immediately should Howe become incapacitated. When Clinton later became commander-in-chief, Cornwallis carried a similar "dormant" commission in his pocket.

In the field, Howe made good use of von Heister at Long Island, but later picked him as the scapegoat for the Hessian defeat at Trenton, and the old man went home in disgrace. Howe also used Heister's successor, von Knyphausen, to good effect in the strategic planning prior to Brandywine, and Knyphausen's attack across Chad's Ford assured British victory. Later, however, Clinton, though making use of Hessian troops, usually relegated von Knyphausen to a relatively minor role. For instance, he left the Hessian general in command in the New York City area when he made his up-Hudson demonstration in 1777. Knyphausen did, however, command in some independent forays from New York, notably the one culminating in the Battle of Springfield, in New Jersey, June 23, 1790.

Burgoyne went out of his way to treat von Riedesel as a hired hand during his invasion from Canada. Although officially the pudgy Brunswicker was "Gentleman Johnny's" second-in-command, he was markedly excluded from planning councils. At Freeman's Farm (first Battle of Saratoga), von Riedesel's first intimation of the British attack was the sound of cannonry.

The rank and file of the Hessian troops became Ishmaels from the beginning, despised by their allies and hated by enemies who likened them to mad dogs. Most of them spoke no English. Snatched willy-nilly from homes and families, the unhappy mass of cannon fodder had been marched halfway across northern Europe, then crammed like cattle into overcrowded transports. The terrors of an angry ocean ended when they landed on alien shores to fight in comparative wilderness in a cause incomprehensible to most of them.

No wonder, then, that they deserted in droves. The wonder is that this army without a soul, which lost nearly one-sixth of its total strength from desertion, fought at all. But fight they did, and their steadfastness in battle is a credit to the leadership of their own officers.

Even the deserters fought again—some of them, at least. In 1778 many of these masterless men volunteered for service in Armand's Legion, while others permitted themselves to be caught up by overeager Patriot muster masters seeking to fill Continental Army draft quotas. George Washington became so incensed over this practice that he issued strict orders to end it.*

German units in America were:

HESSE-CASSEL

Grenadier battalions (companies bled from the line regiments)

Von Linsingen
Von Block

* Upton, *Military Policy,* p. 35; quoting Jared Sparks, *Writings,* vol. 5, pp. 287–288.

Von Minnigerode
Von Koehler

Regiments

Lieb
Landgraf
Erbprinz
Prinz Carl
Von Dittforth
Von Donop
Fusilier Regiment von Lossberg, surrendered at Trenton; later reconstituted.
Grenadier Regiment Rall, surrendered at Trenton, later reconstituted as Wiellwarth, Trumbach, and d'Angelli in turn.
Von Mirbach (later Jung von Lossberg)
Von Trumbach, later Bose
Garrison Regiment von Stein
Garrison Regiment von Wissenbach
Garrison Regiment von Huyn (later von Benning)
Garrison Regiment von Bunau
Feld Jäger Corps von Wurm (light infantry, bled from line regiments)

BRUNSWICK (all with Burgoyne)

Regiment of Dragoons (dismounted)
Battalion of Grenadiers (companies bled from the line regiments)
Regiment Prinz Friedrich
Regiment von Riedesel
Regiment von Rhetz
Regiment von Specht
Jäger Battalion Barner

From Other German States Came:

Regiment Waldeck
Regiment Ansbach
Regiment Beyreuth

Regiment Hanau (together with the Hanau artillery, this unit served with Burgoyne)

A part at least of the Hanau jägers (light infantry) served with St. Leger's force. The Anhalt-Zerbst regiment reached Canada late in the war; saw no combat south of the border.

51

The Tories

A possible one-third of the total white population of the thirteen colonies stood firm in allegiance to the British Crown throughout the conflict, a reservoir of manpower potentially important to England's successful prosecution of the war. By 1780 an estimated fifty thousand Loyalists were engaged in the conflict. Yet of that number barely ten thousand men were actually enrolled in organized provincial elements of the King's troops; the remainder were engaged in local mob violence and fratricidal, sanguinary guerrilla warfare having but little effect upon actual military operations.

In all, sixty-nine Tory regiments or corps were on the British army lists, but only twenty-one of them appear to have had actual substance.

This anomalous situation was a result of the blundering short-sightedness of the British government at home and the arrogant attitude of the British regulars in the field toward the provincial troops.

The principal Tory elements in the British Army in America included:

Queen's Rangers. Infantry.

Originally organized in Boston in 1776 by Robert Rogers of "Rogers's Rangers" fame. At Brandywine, under Captain James Weyness, it did good service. Later, under Colonel John Graves Simcoe, English regular officer, it operated with the traitor Benedict Arnold in Virginia (a detachment served with Ferguson at King's Mountain); later engaged at Yorktown and there surrendered.

Royal Greens. Infantry.

Raised in upper New York state by Tory Colonel Sir John Johnson. Participated in all the bloody engagements in that area.

Butler's Rangers. Infantry.

Also raised through the efforts of the influential Johnson family of northern New York. Commanded by Colonel John Butler. Engaged only in that area. Took part in the ravaging of the Mohawk Valley.

Royal Highlanders. Infantry.

Also known as the Royal Highland Emigrant Infantry. Organized in Canada and commanded by Colonel Allan MacLean, British regular. Took part in defense of Canada against invasion by Montgomery and Arnold. Later fought in the Carolinas. Apparently incorporated in its ranks were a number of North Carolina Highlanders loyal to the Crown.

De Lancey's New York Volunteers. Infantry.

A 1,500-man brigade. Organized by Oliver De Lancey, head of the New York Tory family of that name. One battalion operated in the New York area; the other two in the southern campaigns.

Queen's Own Loyal Virginians. Infantry.

Organized by Lord Dunmore, Royalist governor of Virginia. Operated locally. Later incorporated in the Queen's Rangers (see above).

East Florida Rangers. Infantry.

Guerrillas, organized and commanded by David Fanning. Operated in the Carolinas. Later incorporated in the King's American Regiment (see below).

Loyal American Rangers. Infantry.

Raised in New York by Beverley Robinson, prominent Tory. Took part in Clinton's up-Hudson campaign, capturing Fort Montgomery. Later garrisoned Stony Point and was there captured by Wayne.

Loyal Guides and Gunners.

Also organized by Beverley Robinson. Operated in New York area.

Royal Gunners and Pioneers.

With Howe at the Brandywine and in Philadelphia.

1st Pennsylvania Loyalists. Infantry.

Organized in Philadelphia, served with Clinton during his retreat from that city.

Volunteers of Ireland.

Commanded by Lord Rawdon, a British officer. Organized in Philadelphia; served with Clinton during his retreat. Later in the Carolinas.

Maryland Loyalists. Infantry.

Organized in Philadelphia and served with Clinton during his retreat.

Florida Rangers. Infantry.

Commanded by Tory guerrilla leader Thomas Brown. Active in operations with Prevost's forces in the Carolinas and in Georgia against Greene.

King's (4th) American Regiment. Infantry.

Originally organized and commanded by Lieutenant Colonel Abraham De Peyster, New York Tory. Known also as the New Jersey Volunteers. Operated in New York area and then in the Carolinas. A detachment formed part of Ferguson's command at King's Mountain.

Ferguson's Rangers. Infantry.

This corps was originally organized at Halifax by Patrick Ferguson (see p. 259), Scottish officer in the British Army and at that time a captain in the 70th Foot. The corps led von Knyphausen's command into the Battle of the Brandywine. It was later disbanded by Howe, but Clinton, knowing Ferguson's penchant for partisan warfare, later reconstituted it, and it served in the Charleston campaign. After some service with Tarleton, Ferguson was detached to raise a Tory aggregation bearing the same name. This was the principal increment of Ferguson's command at King's Mountain, where he was killed and his corps dissolved.

British Legion. Infantry and dragoons.

Known originally as Cathcart's Legion, or Caledonian Volunteers. Later made famous as Tarleton's Legion. Served first in the New York area, then with Cornwallis in the Carolinas, under command of Major Banastre Tarleton (see p. 289), English officer in the 16th Light Dragoons. Tarleton and the Legion left a bloody trail behind them throughout the campaign until he and his command were crushed at the Cowpens. However, the reconstituted Legion formed part of Cornwallis's force at Yorktown. The Legion was composed of a battalion of infantry and three troops of cavalry. A troop of the 17th Light Dragoons was for a time attached to the command, but the English troopers, who refused to doff their uniform for the Legion's green coats, apparently had little stomach for Tarleton's savagery. In 1778 the British Legion became a part of the regular British Army establishment in North America when Tarleton assumed command.

52

The French Army in North America

France's overt military participation in support of the Patriot cause brought more than sixteen thousand of her regular troops to the North American mainland. Rochambeau's expeditionary force of all arms, 5,270 strong, landed at Newport, R. I., in 1780, direct from France. Before the war's end, this force had been augmented by some 2,500 replacements. Rochambeau's troops took part in a number of minor engagements in the southern New England-New York area before marching overland to Yorktown as part of Washington's army.

But prior to Rochambeau's arrival, d'Estaing's fleet in 1779 had landed more than 4,000 French regulars, from the West Indies, to take part in the abortive siege of Savannah. A third increment was Saint Simon's force, 6,074 strong, brought up from the West Indies in 1781 by de Grasse and landed inside the Delaware Capes to reinforce Rochambeau's wing at Yorktown. Saint Simon's force included troops who had previously fought at Savannah.

The following French army units took part in the American mainland campaigns:

French Regiments

Régiment d'Agénois. Savannah, 1779; Yorktown, 1781.

Régiment d'Auxonne (2d Battalion only). Yorktown, 1781.

Régiment de Belzance (detachment only). Savannah, 1779.

Régiment Bourbonnais. Yorktown, 1781.

Régiment de Champagne (detachments only). Savannah, 1779; Yorktown, 1781.

Régiment Dillon (one of the famous units of France's Irish Brigade of Catholic expatriates). Savannah, 1779. (One battalion with original Rochambeau force, another with Saint Simon.) Yorktown, 1781.

Régiment de Foix. Savannah, 1779.

Légion de Fontanges (blacks from Santo Domingo). Savannah, 1779.

Régiment Gâtinais (offshoot of Régiment d'Auvergne). Savannah, 1779; Yorktown, 1781.

Régiment Royal Deux-Ponts (originally raised in the Palatinate; its officer roster contains an amazing number of Germanic names). Yorktown, 1781.

Régiment Saintonge. Yorktown, 1781.

Régiment Soissonais (one battalion only). Yorktown, 1781.

Régiment de Touraine. Yorktown, 1781.
Régiment Walsh (Irish Brigade). Savannah, 1779.

Cavalry

Légion de Lauzun (one squadron each of hussars, lancers, grenadiers, and chasseurs). Yorktown, 1781.

Artillery and Engineers

Régiment de Metz (six companies only). Manned both field and siege artillery; one additional company of engineers. All with Rochambeau's original force. Yorktown, 1781.

These French troops were well disciplined, well clothed, and well equipped. Their spick-and-span alignments brought admiration from American spectators and envy from the ragged, motley-uniformed Continentals and militia. Their march order was excellent and, being unencumbered by the hordes of camp followers accompanying both the British and the American armies, they moved rapidly (see p. 178). The French infantry hand arm was the Charleville musket, similar to but probably inferior to Britain's Tower musket, "Brown Bess." The field artillery pieces were of the then new de Gribeauval model. The French infantry regiment was normally of two-battalion strength, numbering approximately 1,200 men in ten companies, twice the size of the average British regular regiment. True to European custom, the flank companies consisted of grenadiers and chasseurs (light infantry).

53

The Navies

Before scanning the birth and operations of the Continental Navy and its successor, the United States Navy, one must examine briefly the principles and practice of war at sea during that period. Naval warfare of the eighteenth century followed rigid hammer-and-tongs procedure carried out in wind-driven ships of wood, whose cannon were ranged along their sides. The application of this firepower depended on the ability of the gunner to maneuver this practically rigid line of broadside guns so that they would bear upon the opponent. Hence, steering the vessel was a component factor in naval gunnery, and was no small task in craft dependent upon wind and weather for steerage way. Your man-o-warsman must be a navigator, a practical seaman, and a gunner.

Carried to its end, single-ship conflict in its final stage found the opposing vessels side by side—sometimes lashed together—in close-range cannonade until one gave up. The *coup de grâce* sometimes was the boarding party, men pouring across the bulwarks to engage in hand-to-hand conflict with cutlass, boarding pike, and musket.

In squadron or fleet actions, a rigid code was prescribed; each fleet in "line ahead"—a single file—engaging opposite ships in a succession of single-ship exchanges. Not until Britain's George Rodney, casting custom and King's Regulations to the winds, sailed into and broke up the French formation at the Battle of the Saints, did this somewhat silly custom go by the board.*

* Rodney met de Grasse on April 12, 1782, in West Indian waters; their respective fleets were moving on opposing courses, each in single file. Taking

The close of the Seven Years' War in 1763 found England mistress of the seas, with the most powerful navy in the world. The fleets of her enemies, France and Spain, were in ruin. By 1775 this situation had changed. The natural lethargy following victory in a great struggle, plus the fact that the British treasury had been sorely impoverished, brought about an austerity program threatening the efficiency of the Royal Navy. By 1775 its ships were twelve years older, for new construction had practically ended. They were tired; skimped in essential maintenance; dockyard stores at low ebb.

Worse yet, the rebellion of the thirteen colonies cut off the supply of timber, masts, and spars garnered in the past from the virgin forests of North America, as well as the considerable manpower furnished by the colonies to man the fleet. Yet the Royal Navy must now transport and victual a transatlantic expeditionary force to crush the insurrection, and at the same time maintain a blockading force along the American east coast.

Meanwhile, as the Admiralty well knew, both France and Spain had been assiduously building fleets of new warships in preparation for the day of revenge so earnestly hoped for.

A bleak situation, this. It would become bleaker by 1778, when the war spread and England stood alone; when her fleets kept the seas in a flurry of extemporizations, when brittle spars snapped, decayed timbers sprang, and rotting cordage failed. An outstanding example of deterioration was the case of the *Royal George* (100) in 1782. Careened in Portsmouth harbor for emergency repairs, her decayed frames gave way, the entire bottom dropped out of the ship, and she went down, taking to death Admiral Kempenfelt, his crew of 750 men, and some 200 visitors, mainly women and children.

Statistically, England entered the war with 131 ships of the line

---

advantage of a change of wind that slightly disarranged the French line, Rodney signaled his ships to turn into the enemy line, in three places. Rodney's ships closed on the four disorganized clumps of French ships in close combat, their carronades doing fearful execution at close range. Six French ships, including de Grasse's own flagship, the great 120-gun *Ville de Paris,* were captured; the remaining twenty-five fled.

and 139 frigates, sloops, and smaller craft. At once old ships were recommissioned and new vessels built, but it was a slow process. Meanwhile the commitments of the Royal Navy became too extensive, and the combined fleets of France and Spain too large. Naval pre-eminence began to slip from English hands.

It would have slipped even faster had it not been for the newly invented carronade, with which most English ships were now armed. This pudgy, short-ranged cannon, throwing a 36-pound shot, ripped oaken timbers to shreds in close combat, and close combat was what England's sailors sought. But the French, recognizing this, endeavored to open battle at a distance, closing only after they had weakened their British opponents by long-range pounding.

Even the oaken blockade cloaking the American Atlantic coast showed grievous rents during the middle years of the war. French squadrons and troop convoys bound for North America passed through it. The Gulf coast of Britain's Florida colonies gaped wide. Spain's Gálvez, from his New Orleans base, gained control of Florida's coastal waters, drove the British Army out of West Florida, and opened the broad Mississippi mouth to American merchantmen. Across the world, France's Admiral Pierre André de Suffren, lacking both bases and reinforcements, dominated the Indian Ocean, after thwarting England's attempt to seize the Cape of Good Hope, halfway station between Europe and Asia.

However, during these years there were some bright spots on the Royal Navy's escutcheon. Thrice—under Rodney, Derby, and Howe in succession—English squadrons broke through the eight-year Franco-Spanish blockade to revictual Gibraltar's beleaguered garrison. But in the long give-and-take of great fleets in West Indian waters, though tactical victories fell in the main to England's ships, they were unable to check de Grasse's great application of sea power off the Virginia Capes which doomed Cornwallis at Yorktown. All too late to influence the outcome in North America was Rodney's great victory over de Grasse in the Battle of the Saints a short time later. However, that victory did restore maritime pre-eminence to Britain. By 1783 the Royal Navy mustered a total of 468 vessels of all classes, and was once more mistress of the seas.

Let's look now at the situation of the colonies in 1775. They constituted in effect a maritime nation, with a thriving merchant fleet. Shipyards were many, designers were capable. Excellent sailors were in quantity, seafarers familiar with the seaways of the world. But they had no warships; the Royal Navy had up to that time afforded protection to Yankee world trade. So, while the Continental Congress extemporized by converting merchantmen to warships, and also began construction of warships, letters of marque were issued, beginning March 19, 1775, authorizing private American ships to prey on British shipping as privateers. Before the war ended, 1,697 of these letters had been issued and American privateers are credited with having captured as much as $18 million worth of prizes.

The privateersman combined business with patriotism. He was a legitimate cargo carrier, but he also was armed, and while plying his trade was entitled to capture any enemy ships he could and pocket the proceeds of his prowess. Profits were divided among the crews. It was risky business, but profitable. It was also disadvantageous to the Continental Army and Navy, for realistic Yankee sailormen naturally preferred profit to patriotism. As a result, privateer crews were always plentiful, while Continental Navy ships and Continental Army units were always short of men.

Most Yankee privateer cruises were individual affairs. However, in 1782 four Massachusetts skippers acted in concert to assault the prosperous fortified town of Lunenburg, Nova Scotia, batter and storm its defenses, and exact a ransom of £1,000 from the terrified townsfolk. Occasionally privateers took on King's ships, in true naval style.

Several of the thirteen states had their own navies. One of the great naval exploits of the war was performed by Captain Joshua Barney in the Pennsylvania State ship *Haidar Ally* (16). Convoying thirteen outbound merchantmen through the Delaware River estuary, then infested by British privateers, Barney attacked and captured in turn HM sloop of war *General Monk* (20) and privateer *Fair American* (16) within sight of a Royal Navy frigate. Barney, whose career in the Revolution comprised both naval service and privateering, entered French service later, but returned to the U.S. Navy in the War of 1812, where he and his Navy shore party shone gallantly in the otherwise disgraceful rout of the Americans at the Battle of Bladensburg.

The Continental Navy, both the converted merchantmen and the vessels later constructed by Congressional order, was minuscule in comparison to England's naval might. Perforce, after Esek Hopkins's Bahamas cruise in 1776, the usually blockaded Continental ships could attempt only daring individual cruises for commerce destruction. These small frigates and sloops of war succumbed, one by one, to Royal Navy blockaders, to storms, and in some cases to self-destruction in avoidance of capture.

But if England's Drake could boast in the sixteenth century of "singeing" the King of Spain's beard, the least one can say of the Continental warships was that they knocked King George's wig askew, for they carried the war to the fringes of the British Isles. The cruises of Lambert Wickes in *Reprisal* (16), of Gustavus Conyngham in *Surprise* (10) and *Revenge* (14), and of John Paul Jones in *Ranger* (18) and *Bonhomme Richard* (40) brought consternation to British coastal waters and sent English marine insurance rates soaring. Jones's victory over Pearson's *Serapis* (44) in plain view of English spectators on Flamborough cliffs was epic.

But war's attrition had almost erased the Continental Navy at the close of the war. Alone, the fast frigate *Alliance* (36), launched in 1777, remained afloat under Captain John Barry, crisscrossing the Atlantic, bearing diplomatic passengers, and capturing enemy ships, throughout her charmed life.

54

Women Camp Followers

Women have followed their men to war from time immemorial, wedded wives and courtesans, honest women and drabs. By the eighteenth century their presence in the armies of Europe had been legitimized to the extent that soldiers' wives—in small quotas, so many to each unit—were carried on official muster rolls. These women washed and cooked and attended to their men, and helped with the sick and wounded. They drew rations but received no pay. Some bold individuals among them occasionally took places on the firing line. On the march, their place was with the baggage.

Officers' wives accompanying the troops were, of course, the responsibilities of their husbands. Inevitably, there were other women, too—women of high and low birth—whose liaisons were sometimes winked at, sometimes frowned upon.

It is not surprising, then, that female camp followers accompanied both the British and the Patriot armies during the War of the Revolution. What is surprising is their number. This was particularly true of the British forces. Complete returns do not exist, but it would appear that at least five thousand women and probably an equal number of children traipsed through North America with King George's armies.*

Who were these women? Aside from officers' wives, they were a mixed bag of "baggage" indeed: a great many came over with the troops—from Whitechapel's cesspool and the stews of Dublin and

* Blumenthal, *Women Camp Followers of the American Revolution*, pp. 43, 44.

Edinburgh. Others were flaxen-haired German girls following the Hessians. Some were honest wedded wives, others prostitutes plying their trade, which included theft and illicit rum selling. In America, their ranks were swelled by local girls. Most of the horde would live, suffer, and die in anonymity; a few, both rankers' and officers' women, lent their names to history. Not infrequently, children were born along the wayside; many of them survived, many did not.

"Gentleman Johnny" Burgoyne's army came up Lake Champlain in the summer of 1777 in caravan fashion, carrying with it an estimated two thousand women and children. The queen bee was Burgoyne's own mistress, Hannah Foye, wife of his accommodating commissary officer, Captain Edward Foye.

"It would seem," comments one British historian of Burgoyne's expedition,* "as if all warriors of the correct model went on campaign with a sword in one hand, a lass on the disengaged arm, and a bottle knocking up against his cartridge box rearwards."

By the time that Burgoyne had poked his way as far as Fort Edward, four very gallant ladies determined to accompany their officer husbands had also joined up. One was Baroness Frederica Charlotte Louisa von Riedesel, wife of Burgoyne's Brunswick second-in-command, General Baron Adolph von Riedesel. She brought with her their three little girls (two more additions would come to this Teutonic family before their *via dolorosa* ended). "Red 'Azel" the cockney redcoats in admiration called the auburn-tressed Baroness.

There were also Major John Dyke Ackland's wife, Lady Harriet; Major Henry Harnage's wife; and Anne Reynals, the bride of a lieutenant, and two or three maidservants.

As it turned out, these women would together share the horrors of the end at Saratoga, crowded in a cellar under fire together with a horde of terrified soldiers, women and children. Shortly before she arrived in this refuge, the Baroness had comforted the last moments of mortally wounded British General Fraser. Now she

---

* Henry Belcher, *"The First American Civil War,* vol. 2, p. 280.

took charge. She ordered the rabble to clean out the befouled cellar, found pallets for wounded officers brought in, and comforted her own frightened children.

To the improvised shelter came wounded Major Harnage, to be succored by his wife. There, too, came young Reynals, to die in the arms of his bride. Lady Ackland, learning that her own wounded husband was a prisoner, took a canoe downriver to enter the American camp and nurse him. Indomitable "Red 'Azel" rustled food for her refugees and for the wounded, while praying for her husband's safety.

The crying necessity in that chamber of horrors was for water; the one spring in the vicinity was polluted, and hardy souls who attempted to carry water from the nearby Hudson were killed or wounded by American marksmen from across the river. Then came bold Jane Crumer, a sergeant's wife, pail in hand, to dare the sharpshooters. Time and again she made the trip unharmed, the Americans chivalrously holding their fire.

Burgoyne's surrender brought no relief to the horde of camp followers, who for the next three years streamed behind the dwindling columns of the captive "Convention Army." They froze and starved and sweltered with the seasons on the long trail that led first to Cambridge, Massachusetts, then south to Charlottesville in Virginia. Back to Pennsylvania they went in 1781. Thanks to Washington's compassion, some of the time the unfortunate women and children of the rank and file rode in wagons; the remainder of the time they trudged—many of them barefoot—in unhappy procession. In the end the "Convention Army" and its camp followers just melted away, swallowed in America's melting pot.

But the Brunswick regimental colors came home. While still at Cambridge, Riedesel confided to his wife that he had them hidden in his effects, but feared that in the coming long march down to Virginia they might be discovered. What to do? Gallant "Red 'Azel" had the answer. Sitting up all night with a trustworthy regimental tailor, she manufactured a mattress into which the colors were carefully sewn. Passed off as part of the baggage of one of the general's aides, the mattress and its precious contents finally returned to sleepy Wolfenbüttel on the Oder.

In the central and southern areas of the colonies, the British woman problem was also an enormous one. Daniel Wier, British Army Commissary General in America, plaintively noted in 1777 that the women and children carried on official rolls were "very numerous, beyond every idea of imagination." His figures were 2,778 women and 1,904 children, this in comparison to a male strength of 23,601.

Wier voiced an opinion common in the higher commands, that some plan should be adopted to control to some degree "this enormous expence." But nothing was done, despite the flood of injunctions and admonitions flowing continuously from various field headquarters.*

Be it noted that Wier's report did not include General Howe's pampered mistress, the notorious blue-eyed Mrs. Elizabeth Loring, wife of his complaisant—and also notorious—commissary officer, Captain Joshua Loring. She was immortalized in Francis Hopkinson's satire "The Battle of the Kegs," written during Howe's stay in Philadelphia:

> Sir William he, as snug as a flea,
> Lay all this time asnoring,
> Nor dreamed of harm as he lay warm,
> In bed with Mrs. Loring.†

Probably the largest collection of British camp followers accompanied Clinton's retreat northward from Philadelphia in 1778, swollen by the presence of Tory refugees. One estimate of the sad procession puts the number at 1,500 women and as many children. This is probably an understatement, for an abstract of women and children actually "on the ration" in Clinton's Philadelphia force gives—as of December 13, 1777—1,648 women and 539 children.‡

* Blumenthal, p. 18.
† Recalling that Burgoyne's mistress was also the wife of that commander's commissary officer, one might speculate if, in the British Army of that day, this was coincidence or custom.
‡ Blumenthal, p. 95.

In Patriot ranks the woman problem also loomed from the very beginning, when General Artemas Ward, at Cambridge in 1775, noted and decried the presence in his camp of a number of "lewd women."

Arnold's march to Quebec in 1776—one of the most extraordinary accomplishments of the war—was shared by a few stalwart women. On that march Aaron Burr was accompanied from Swan Island to the Kennebec River by his Indian mistress.

Later George Washington was frequently concerned by the number of camp followers. He accepted the necessity for permitting women to be carried legitimately "on the ration," but refused to establish any fixed quotas. Such restrictions, he asserted, would work unnecessary hardships on soldiers burdened by homeless families. He feared that otherwise the Continental Army (and the militia) might "lose by Desertion, perhaps to the Enemy, some of the oldest and best soldiers in the Service."*

Official returns were spotty, but it can be assumed that the number of American female followers never reached the proportions of those in the Royal forces. Some indication of the difference may be garnered from a strength return of the Continental Army at Newburgh and New Windsor of June 1781: "137 women." Again, a return from Newburgh for December 31, 1782, reports 405 women "on the ration." In the Pennsylvania Line in 1780, with a strength of some 1,700 men, about one hundred women and children were huddled with the troops.

Women were certainly on Washington's mind in the summer of 1777, as he was hurrying south from New Jersey to meet Howe's threat to Philadelphia. His march order of August 4, 1777, included strong admonition:

. . . In the present marching state of the army, every incumbrance proves greatly prejudicial to the service; the multitude of women in particular, especially those who are pregnant or have children, are a clog upon every movement. The Commander-in-Chief therefore earnestly recommends it to the officers commanding brigades and

---

* Fitzpatrick, *Writings of George Washington,* vol. 26, p. 78.

corps to use every reasonable method in their power to get rid of all such as are not absolutely necessary and the admission or continuance of any who shall or may come to the army since its arrival in Pennsylvania is positively forbidden. . . .*

Ordering returns to be made of the numbers present, Washington ordered that "women are expressly forbid . . . to ride in the waggons" and reiterated that "Officers are earnestly called upon to permit no more than are absolutely necessary, and such as are actually useful, to follow the army."†

Wives of officers were not uncommon in the camps of the Continental Army, although few, if any, followed them in the field. Martha Washington several times joined her husband temporarily in winter quarters and Baylor's 3rd Continental Dragoons were proud of its sobriquet: "Lady Washington's Horse." At Valley Forge, Martha, Mrs. Knox, and the bride of Nathanael Greene were present and together with a number of other wives ministered not only to the needs of their own husbands, but several wrapped bandages and tried to comfort the soldiers in their misery. They were present also at the Newburgh encampment and at West Point. Nor can we forget that Peggy Shippen, vivacious Philadelphia Tory, wooed and won by Benedict Arnold while commanding there, accompanied him to West Point and his treason; many authorities believe she persuaded him to desert his nation's cause.

On several occasions during the war, sturdy soldiers' wives proved themselves to be Amazons. Margaret Corbin, when her husband was killed at Fort Washington, New York, in 1776, took up his musket and place in the line. In 1779, Congress, recognizing her heroism, granted her half-pay for life. Margaret's body rests today in West Point's cemetery.

Molly Pitcher (Mary Ludwig) at Fort Clinton on the Hudson assisted her husband, artilleryman John Hays, in serving his field-piece, and actually fired the last cannon shot prior to the fort's fall in 1777. Again, at Monmouth in 1778, when Hays was killed,

* Fitzpatrick, vol. 9, p. 17.
† Ibid., p. 139.

Molly took his place as gun pointer. For that deed Washington made her a sergeant and put her on half-pay for life.

Another Amazon was Deborah Sampson, said to have been descended in family line from both Miles Standish and John Alden. Deborah enlisted in a Massachusetts regiment in 1781 as "Robert Shurtleff," successfully concealing her sex until she was wounded at Tarrytown, New York. Once again George Washington paid tribute, giving her a purse in reward, and Congress later voted her a pension.*

Not all the rag, tag, and bobtail American women camp followers were heroines, of course. Following the battle of Bemis Heights (Second Saratoga) harpies from the American camp were accused of stripping bare the dead of both sides.†

Remarkably enough, there appear to have been few female camp followers among the French forces operating in America during the Revolution, among either Rochambeau's troops, who moved directly from France, or the other units brought over with the fleets of de Grasse and d'Estaing from the West Indies.

Since the French army of that day, like all European armies, carried small quotas of women "on the ration" (the maximum limit during the reign of Louis XIII was four women per one hundred men), some doubtless were among the troops, but certainly nothing like the hordes who followed the British, Hessian, and our own Continental forces. And when the French left in 1783, they carried few back with them. Returns of Rochambeau's departing troops show only twenty women and six children on board. One regiment, the Royal Deux-Ponts, accounted for nine of these individuals: six women and three children.

What a lonely voyage it must have been for the rest of the French contingent.

* Blumenthal, p. 70.
† Blumenthal, p. 84.

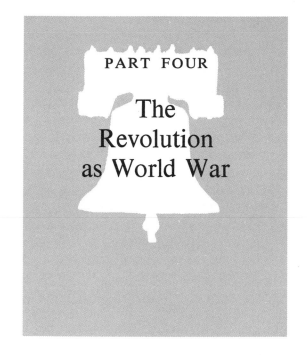

PART FOUR

The
Revolution
as World War

Geographically, the thirteen colonies lay athwart the conflicting interests of France, Spain, the Netherlands, and Britain, each engaged in selfish and sometimes sanguinary exploitation of the vast resources of Asia, Africa, and the New World.

How this situation was turned to the advantage of American independence is a story of diplomatic intrigue, the details of which are far beyond the scope of this book. Suffice it to say that the extraordinary acumen of Benjamin Franklin, John Jay, and others of a small group—the Committee of Secret Correspondence created by the Continental Congress in 1775—successfully played upon international rivalry in Europe to bring, in succession, France, Spain, and the Netherlands into open conflict with Britain.

It must not be forgotten, however, that this active warfare broke out only because of the ability of the revolting colonies to maintain an army in being in the field. The international stakes were high, and European statesmen played only for keeps. Had not one man—George Washington—kept the fragile flame of freedom glowing on land in North America, the "shot heard round the world" would have had as much effect as a popgun in a revival meeting.

The temperature of overt European involvement rose and fell in direct proportion to the success of Washington and his ragged Continentals. Ineluctably, then, the relatively small revolt which flared in the Massachusetts Bay Colony in 1775 blossomed within the space of four years into a world war, with England pitted worldwide against the three other predators. Unaligned European nations, pinched, as neutrals always are, by the resultant strangulation of commerce, were drawn into the turmoil vocally if not physically. The resultant free-for-all—out of which emerged a new nation, the United States of America—included among Britain's enemies tens of thousands of participants ignorant of or entirely out of sympathy with the basic issue: the independence of the Thirteen United Colonies.

Let's glance, then, at the initial situation and motivations of the major European participants.

Britain at Bay

As already noted, the tide of military preparedness in Britain reached low ebb in the years following the end of the Seven Years' War. The government was practically bankrupt. Repressive "taxation without representation" in her North American colonies brought about rebellion. Yet the importance of these colonies to the British economy was so great that King George's government strove to repress it by spending more money. The Earl of Chatham, aging William Pitt, summed up the situation in November 1777, when he stated that the thirteen colonies were ". . . the fountain of our wealth, the nerve of our strength, the nursery and the basis of our naval power."*

Politically, the British people were far from united in support of King George's decision to retain his colonies by force of arms. The powerful Whig Party remained in violent opposition to the war policy of Lord North's Tory government. Statesmen, politicians, and military men of all political persuasions joined the chorus. Public opposition swelled in antiwar demonstrations, some of them riotous. Detailed discussion of the situation in the British Isles is far beyond the limitations of this book. Suffice it to say that Britain entered the Revolutionary War a nation divided and remained that way to the end.

* G. J. Marcus, *A Naval History of England,* vol. 1, p. 416.

France

France, shorn of the major part of her New World acquisitions by the Treaty of Paris in 1763, still had interest in what might happen on the northern and southern extremities of the thirteen colonies. On the north she retained the island group of Saint Pierre and Miquelon, and valuable fishing rights off the Newfoundland coast. To the south lay her "sugar islands" of Martinique, Guadeloupe, and half of Santo Domingo (Haiti).

But above and beyond that rankled the humiliation France had suffered at Britain's hands in the Seven Years' War. The loss of her fortifications in India had reduced her former colonizing role there to that of trader. At home, the fortifications of her great naval base of Dunkerque had been razed, and a British commissioner sat there on French soil to see that the demilitarization was permanent. France, as one historian has put it,* had become "a cipher in European international politics."

France wanted revenge. And two great French Ministers of State—Etienne François, Duc de Choiseul (from 1763 to 1770), and Charles Gravier, Comte de Vergennes (from 1774 to the end of the war), successively bent their energies to see that she would be prepared militarily and financially when opportunity rose.

Vergennes, in 1775, saw in the worsening relations between England's George III and his North American colonies a potential lever with which to rescue France from her ignominious situation. By early 1776 he had persuaded Louis XVI to adopt a policy including military preparations by both France and Spain for a future war against Britain (hidden, of course, by deceptively friendly assurances to King George's government) and the furnishing of secret assistance to the revolting colonies, "without making any convention with them until their independence be established and notorious."†

* Samuel Flagg Bemis, *The Diplomacy of the American Revolution*, p. 16.
† Bemis, p. 24.

King Louis had donated one million livres ($200,000), would donate more, and wheedled an equal sum from Charles III of Spain; the monies were to be expended for the purchase of munitions to be delivered in the West Indies to the colonies through a fictitious trading company—Rodrique Hortalez et Cie. Louis had also ordered the rebuilding of the French Navy and the re-equipment of his army. The first steps had been taken.

These munitions for the American rebels were purchased in Holland and shipped to the West Indies under neutral flag to the Netherlands' St. Eustatius and France's Martinique and Cap Haitien. There they were transferred to American ships running England's blockade; it was lucrative business for all concerned. Also *sub rosa,* Patriot warships and privateers began making use of French ports as their informal bases for the harrying of England's home waters.

The defeat and surrender of Burgoyne's army at Saratoga ripped to shreds the last vestiges of France's pseudo neutrality. All doubts as to the viability of the United States erased from French minds, treaties of alliance were signed, on February 6, 1778, by the plenipotentiaries of both nations. France's population, unashamedly hypnotized by the magnetic personality of Benjamin Franklin, hailed the event with joy, while the rejuvenated French Army and Navy soberly took up the job of fighting Britain the world over. Open hostilities began on June 17.

Spain

Spain's situation differed from that of France, although she, too, wanted revenge for the pummeling she had received at the hands of Britain in the Seven Years' War. Even greater was her unending effort to regain control of Spanish Gibraltar from Britain's clutches. Complications arose, however, due to the fact that neither Charles III nor his Ministers of State—Jeronimo Grimaldi, and his successor, José Moñimo y Redondo, Conde de Floridablanca—sympathized with the American revolt. To Spain, with her enormous colonial holdings, the very thought of republican liberty was anathema, whether in Europe or the Western Hemisphere. In addition, while Charles III and Louis XVI—Bourbons both— were allied by virtue of the so-called Family Compact pitting them against the Hapsburg dynasty, Charles took a dim view of his young nephew as a diplomat. Against such opinions remained the stark fact that France and Spain must combine their military powers to defeat Britain in the future. The result for Spain was acquiescence—perhaps lukewarm—in support of France, but adamant opposition to alliance with the republican government sprouting in North America.

In a horse-trader swap—one of the provisions in the Treaty of Paris of 1763—Spain had ceded Florida to Britain in exchange for the release of Cuba. Spain in 1775 also held all of France's former North American possessions west of the Mississippi River, as well as the "island" of New Orleans on the east bank. Thus she controlled—in theory—the growing trade on "Old Man River."

On the other hand, Spain's maritime artery for trade and treasure, from Acapulco to Cádiz, via Panama and Havana, as well as her half-interest in the island of Santo Domingo, would both be vulnerable to any British incursions from Floridian bases. The weakening of Britain's position in North America meant the reduction of that threat.

All in all, then, Spain rightfully had keen interest in hampering the effectiveness of King George's effort to bring his recalcitrant colonies to heel. Accordingly, Floridablanca, wily diplomat, played his hand cautiously in North America: impede the classic enemy but shun alliance with these upstart republicans whose doctrines might infect His Gracious Majesty's colonial vassals. The result was astounding.

Floridablanca had just the man for such a job, in the person of his newly appointed governor of Louisiana, Don Bernardo Gálvez. This thirty-year-old soldier hated England as much as he abhorred any thought of republican principles. Already he was chafing at the situation of his province. England possessed Florida, which extended to the east bank of the Mississippi north of New Orleans. The southern fringe of the North American colonial revolt was flaring north of Louisiana and along the Florida frontier. So, with Floridablanca's acquiescence, Gálvez cast aside his Castilian repugnance to American republicanism.

Through the Patriot resident agent in New Orleans, Arthur Pollock, Gálvez began extending covert assistance to the rebels. He also broke up British river traffic sneaking past his own customs barriers to reach their east-bank posts north of New Orleans. These actions greatly assisted George Rogers Clark's western campaign. Personally, Gálvez apparently kept up a voluminous correspondence with Patriot Colonel Daniel Morgan, commanding at Fort Pitt, the staging point for Pollock's traffic. In addition, Patriot exports to both French and Spanish ports began flowing freely down the Mississippi.

Gálvez, learning from Havana in late July 1779 that Spain had declared war against England, took the offensive immediately, to forestall any possible British move against New Orleans. His forces consisted of the one "fixed" regiment of Louisiana (regulars recruited within the province), a nebulous militia, one small frigate, four gunboats each mounting an 18-pounder, and a miscellaneous assortment of ten fieldpieces.

Stirring up the New Orleans population, he instituted an active recruiting campaign. French Canadians in the area, keen to gain revenge for their previous sufferings when brutally transported from their homes in Canada, flocked to the colors.

On August 27 Gálvez moved upriver with five hundred regulars (330 of them newly recruited) and four battalions of militia; he swept over the small British garrisons at Manchac and Natchez. Only at Baton Rouge did he meet real resistance. Its garrison of three hundred men of the 16th Foot (Bedfordshire) plus the grenadier company of the Waldeck Regiment (German mercenaries) were soon overwhelmed, thus opening the Mississippi for both Spain and the Patriots.

In 1780 the energetic Gálvez mounted an expedition eastward against Mobile, which was fairly well fortified and garrisoned. A sandbar at the mouth of Mobile Bay rendered navigation dangerous to vessels of any considerable size, while Fort Charlotte barred land access to the harbor.

Gálvez sailed from New Orleans on February 5, with two thousand men and his artillery. A heavy storm in the Gulf scattered his small convoy, but it was finally regrouped and landed on the eastern shore of Mobile Bay.*

Gálvez now faced a dilemma. The delay had permitted British warships to escape and reach Pensacola, some seventy-five miles to the east, where Major General John Campbell, commanding British forces in the Floridas, was with nine hundred men: detachments of the 16th and 60th Foot (Royal Americans). Should Campbell move with alacrity, the Spaniards—considerably reduced in number by the ravages of the hurricane—might be caught in a vise.

Boldly, Gálvez invested Fort Charlotte, and breached its wall by artillery fire. The garrison surrendered on March 14, marching out with the honors of war. Campbell, moving leisurely to relieve Mobile, found the Spanish in possession and marched as leisurely back to Pensacola.

Gálvez, promoted to a major generalcy as reward for his victories, now turned his attention to Pensacola. First he sailed to Havana and arranged for reinforcements and support from the Governor of Cuba. His first expeditionary force was dispersed by a storm in October, but after wearisome refitting, he finally left Havana on February 28, 1781.

Escorted by a Spanish squadron of one ship of the line and a frigate, commanded by Admiral Don José Cabro de Irazabal, Gálvez's transports, containing 1,400 infantry and some artillery, arrived off the entrance to Pensacola harbor on March 9, 1781, and began landing on the island of St. Rosé on the westerly side of the harbor entrance. Marching overland from Mobile to join this expedition came Gálvez's own Louisiana troops—approximately a thousand strong. They took position on the western side of the Perdido River above the settlement. Gálvez's little naval squadron from New Orleans also arrived.

* Charles Gayaré, *History of Louisiana,* vol. 7, p. 135.

Gálvez demanded that the squadron from Cuba cross the bar, reconnaissance having determined that the channel was deep enough to carry its largest ship. Admiral Irazabal demurred; he would not risk his ships to the fire of British 24-pounders commanding a narrow channel. Boarding his own armed brig, Gálvez sailed through the gap, daring the fire of Campbell's guns on Fort George, and shamed Irazabal into following.

All this time Campbell had made no attempt to drive the invaders off the beach, although his forces consisted of seven companies of the 16th Foot, two battalions of the Royal Americans, a battalion of the German Waldeck regiment, and two battalions of local Tory militia, over 1,500 men in all. He contented himself with a series of negotiations under flag of truce, proposing that the settlement become neutral ground, in which case he would defend Fort George against investment. Gálvez agreed, but when the British fired some dwellings outside the fort he considered the agreement broken and commenced siege operations. But Fort George's walls were strong; its guns drove the Spanish squadron to the east side of the bay, out of range. Occasionally the Spanish warships sailed close for a brief bombardment, then returned to their anchorage.

The stalemate broke on May 8, when a Spanish shell struck the fort's principal magazine, blowing it up. A redoubt was demolished, and over one hundred British soldiers died in the debacle. Gálvez at once massed for an assault through the breach and Campbell threw in the towel. Gálvez having granted the British the honors of war, 1,113 officers and men marched out to lay down their arms. Some 300 others fled north to Georgia, and another 56 had already deserted.

Bernardo Gálvez, last of the *conquistadores,* had broken England's hold on West Florida and the Gulf of Mexico.

The Netherlands

When the American Revolution broke out, the Dutch people were sympathetic to the cause of liberty in England's rebellious colonies. The ruling assemblage of the Netherlands, however, could not afford to base the policies of a trading nation on popular emotions. Theoretically, at least, the Netherlands was allied to Britain, but the government quickly rejected an abortive attempt by Lord North's government to obtain Dutch troops for service in the colonies, forcing the British to turn to the German principalities for mercenary military manpower.

The principal concern of the Netherlands government, so far as the Revolution was concerned, was that the conflict should not interfere with the thriving trade of the Dutch colonies in the West Indies, in northern South America, with the thirteen colonies, or with Europe. It soon became evident that popular sympathy with the rebel cause could be combined profitably with trading expediency.

The clink of French gold, placed surreptitiously at the disposal of the Secret Committee of the Continental Congress, was heard clearly by the thrifty Dutch burghers of Amsterdam and the West Indies Netherlands colonies. They gleefully entered into the business of clandestine munitions supply to the American rebels. The sleepy little island of St. Eustatius in the Dutch West Indies became a roaring emporium, the major staging area for munitions and other supplies destined for King George's rebellious colonies. Its acres of warehouses were crammed with purchases made in the Netherlands, carried overseas in neutral bottoms, and funneled into North America by tough Yankee skippers who dared England's blockade of their coast.

Financed by the original surreptitious grants of Louis XVI of France and Charles III of Spain, one million livres each, the contraband was purchased by a totally fictitious trading firm, Rodrique Hortalez et Cie. (actually P. A. Caron de Beaumarchais, a French dramatist who was also a secret political agent of Louis XVI).*

The operations of Hortalez et Cie. extended also to the French

---

* For details of this extraordinary enterprise, in which were involved Benjamin Franklin, Silas Deane, Arthur Lee, and others of the Continental Congress's Committee of Secret Correspondence, see Bemis, pp. 27–39.

West Indian ports of Martinique and Cap François (now Cap Haitien), where great depots also rose.

Britain's remonstrances and threats of reprisal for these operations made little impression at first upon the Dutch, who relied upon the then current European rule of thumb concerning neutrals: "free ships, free cargoes." The same attitude was held by other European nations interested in any munitions activities in the Western Hemisphere. Later, however, when France and Spain entered the war, the unaligned nations were aroused by the danger to their own respective munitions traffic.

In July 1780 Russia's Catherine II led Sweden, Denmark, Prussia, Portugal, and Austria to join a so-called Neutrality Agreement, subscribing in principle: neutral vessels could engage in coastal trade with individual belligerents; property of belligerents —save for arms, equipment, and munitions of war—carried in neutral bottoms could not be seized; that blockade, to be binding, must include adequate naval force stationed in close proximity to the blockaded port. Britain, naturally, scoffed at such niceties and when the States General of the Netherlands, presumably still an ally of England, on December 17 also subscribed to the agreement, King George's government declared war against Holland three days later.

The bottom quickly dropped out of the thrifty Dutch burghers' dream. An English squadron swept into St. Eustatius harbor, seized a vast quantity of stores awaiting transport to America, and effectually snuffed out the Dutch trade with the colonies. Furthermore, the Netherlands with its relatively small naval strength, twenty ships of the line, at once felt the effect of British sea power throughout her widespread colonial possessions. The Dutch Navy, bottled up by Britain's geographic location, was unable to join the other allied forces. Except for one bitterly contested but tactically inconclusive contest in the North Sea it played no part in further operations. On August 5, 1781, Vice Admiral Sir Hyde Parker's British squadron, protecting a Baltic convoy, met a Dutch squadron off the Dogger Bank; they exchanged fire for several hours before the engagement was broken off.

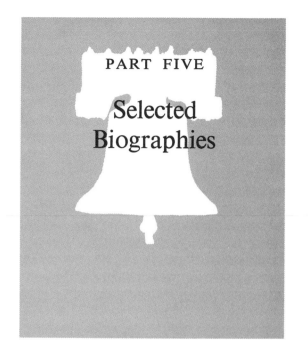

PART FIVE

Selected
Biographies

ALEXANDER, WILLIAM. *See* Stirling, William Alexander, Lord.

ALLEN, ETHAN. 1738–1790. Continental officer (Brevet Col.), militia officer (Maj. Gen.).

Born in Litchfield, Conn.; settled as a farmer in New Hampshire Grants (now Vermont), about 1769; organized (1770) and commanded the Green Mountain Boys, partisan fighters against New York claimants to the Grants; led his men, as a Patriot unit, in the capture of Fort Ticonderoga, May 10, 1775; lost the election as commander to Seth Warner when the Green Mountain Boys became a Continental unit; then volunteered for Maj. Gen. Philip Schuyler's Canadian expedition; was captured in a foolhardy small-unit assault on Montreal, October 24, 1775; was exchanged, May 6, 1778, breveted a Continental colonel, May 14, and became a major general commanding the Vermont militia, 1779; author of a number of books and pamphlets, most of them dealing with Vermont's rights.

ANDRÉ, JOHN. 1751–1780. British officer (Maj.).

Son of a Swiss merchant who had settled in London; aide-de-camp to General Henry Clinton, British commander-in-chief in North America; corresponded with and received intelligence information from Maj. Gen. Benedict Arnold in connection with Arnold's offer to turn the American fortress at West Point over to the British; was captured September 13, 1780 with incriminating papers that revealed the plot; was tried and executed as a spy in 1780 by the Americans; body was later interred as a national hero in Westminster Abbey in London.

ARBUTHNOT, MARRIOT. 1711–1794. British naval officer (Adm.).
Born in Weymouth (?), England; Commander-in-Chief on the American station, 1779; victorious, along with Gen. Henry Clinton, at Charleston, S.C., March–May 1780; temporarily superseded as commander-in-chief in 1780 by Admiral George Rodney; succeeded by Admiral Thomas Graves in 1781.

ARMAND, CHARLES. (Charles-Armand Tuffin Marquis de la Rouerie). Continental officer (Brig. Gen.).
French volunteer; commended for defense at Short Hills, N.J., June 26, 1777; took over command of the Pulaski Legion (October 11, 1779) after Pulaski's death, and led it at Camden; commanded Legion (renamed Armand's Partisan Corps) in Virginia operations and, after Yorktown, in South Carolina; during the French Revolution, fought as a Royalist, leading an uprising in Brittany.

ARMSTRONG, JOHN. 1717–1795. American statesman, Continental officer (Brig. Gen.).
Born in Brookbor, County Fermanagh, Ireland. A resident of Pennsylvania, was a civil engineer before the Revolution; brigadier general, 1776–1777; delegate to the Continental Congress, Pennsylvania, 1778–1780, 1787–1788.

ARMSTRONG, JOHN, JR. 1755–1843. Continental officer (Maj.), American statesman.
Born in Carlisle, Cumberland Co., Pa.; author of the Newburgh Addresses, March 10 and 12, 1783; son of General John Armstrong.

ARNOLD, BENEDICT. 1741–1801. Continental officer (Maj. Gen.), British officer (Brig. Gen.).

Connecticut resident; druggist, merchant, before Revolution. Accompanied Ethan Allen at the capture of Fort Ticonderoga, May 10, 1775; captured, then abandoned, Saint-Jean, Quebec, May 1775; led expedition, notable for its boldness and hardships, through wilderness to Quebec, September 13–November 9, 1775; wounded in unsuccessful attack on Quebec, December 31, 1775; promoted to brigadier general June 10, 1776; directed building of flotilla on Lake Champlain and commanded it in the Battle of Valcour Island, October 11, 1776; was defeated, but prevented British from attacking down the Hudson in 1776; promoted to major general, February 17, 1777; relieved Fort Stanwix, August 1777; played important role in defeat of Burgoyne at Saratoga, September 19 and October 7, 1777, despite hostility of General Gates, his superior; commanded Continental forces at Philadelphia, 1778–1779; court-martialed in 1779 for alleged, relatively minor, fiscal irregularities, and reprimanded; soon after began a plot to turn over to the British the strategic American fort at West Point, N.Y., of which he was commander; arranged plot through Major John André of the British army with the assistance of Mrs. Arnold and Loyalists Joshua Hett Smith and Joseph Stansbury; was revealed as traitor with the capture of André, September 23, 1780; fled to the British army and was made a brigadier general; sent to Virginia, December 1780, and conducted successful raids there; in 1781 went to Britain and spent the rest of his life in poverty and disgrace.

BARNEY, JOSHUA. 1759–1818. Privateer, Continental naval officer (Capt., Commodore).

Born in Baltimore Co., Md. Captured three times by the British and escaped three times; served with distinction in War of 1812, particularly at the Battle of Bladensburg, where few other Americans distinguished themselves.

BARRAS, LOUIS DE (or Jacques-Melchoir Saint-Laurent, Comte de Barras). d. c. 1800. French Naval officer (Adm.).

French commander at Newport, 1781; commanded French squadron under de Grasse in Yorktown campaign, 1781.

BARRY, JOHN. 1745–1803. Continental naval officer (Capt.).
Born in Ireland. Seaman, shipmaster, and shipowner before the Revolution. Called "Father of the United States Navy"; made the first capture in actual battle of a British warship (sloop *Edward*) by a regularly commissioned American cruiser, the USS *Lexington,* April 17, 1776; commanded USS *Alliance* in a well-conducted engagement against HMS *Sybil* and two other warships in January 1783, the last important naval encounter of the war.

BAUM, FRIEDRICH. d. 1777. German (Brunswick) officer (Lt. Col.).
Commander of the Brunswick Dragoons; commanded British forces at the Battle of Bennington, Vt., where he was defeated and mortally wounded.

BIDDLE, NICHOLAS. 1750–1778. Continental naval officer (Capt.).
One of the first four captains of the Continental Navy; killed in action, March 7, 1778, in West Indies. Pennsylvania resident.

BISSELL, DANIEL. d. 1824. Continental soldier (Sgt.).
Sergeant, Second Connecticut Regiment, Continental Line; received Badge of Military Merit (later, Purple Heart) from Washington for espionage work in British-held New York City; one of only three men known to have received this award during Revolutionary War.

BLAND, THEODORICK. 1742–1828. American statesman, Continental officer (Col.), physician.
Born in Cawsons, near Petersburg, Va. Colonel, Cavalry, Continental Army, 1776–1780; delegate to the Continental Congress, Virginia, 1776–1780; his inept reconnaissance con-

tributed to the American defeat at Brandywine; nephew of Richard Bland.

BRANT, JOSEPH. 1742–1807. Mohawk Indian leader (half-breed), Loyalist officer (Col.).

Known also as Thayendanegea; well educated; traveled to Britain; converted to the Anglican faith; served as secretary to his brother-in-law, Sir William Johnson, when latter was superintendent of Indian affairs; commissioned a colonel by the British; saw action at the Oriskany, N.Y., ambush, August 6, 1777, which he set up, and the Cherry Valley raid and massacre, November 11, 1778; was defeated at Battle of the Chemung River (Newton), N.Y., August 29, 1779.

BREYMANN, HEINRICH CHRISTOPH. d. 1777. German (Brunswick) officer (Lt. Col.).

Commanded a relief column to support Colonel Baum's command during the Bennington raid, August 15, 1777; was defeated and forced to retreat; commanded a redoubt at Stillwater (second Battle of Saratoga); killed in action.

BRODHEAD, DANIEL. 1736–1809. Continental officer (Brevet Brig. Gen.), surveyor.

Born in Albany, N.Y. Pennsylvania resident; surveyor before the Revolution; commanded Fort Pitt; destroyed Indian villages in Allegheny Valley expedition, September 11–14, 1779.

BUFORD, ABRAHAM. 1749–1833. Continental officer (Col.).

Born in Culpeper Co., Va. Served from 1775 throughout the war; was defeated by Banastre Tarleton at Waxhaws Creek, S.C., May 29, 1780, in a battle whose circumstances have led to accusations against Tarleton of treachery and inhumanity; settled in Kentucky after the war.

BURGOYNE, JOHN ("Gentleman Johnny"). 1722–1792. British officer (Lt. Gen.), member of Parliament, 1761–1792.

Came to America, May 25, 1775, as assistant to General Gage at Boston; returned to England; commanded relief expedition to Canada, 1776; returned to England again; chosen to lead the northern offensive, known as Burgoyne's offensive, an invasion of New York, June–October 1777 (which also included St. Leger's expedition); captured Fort Ticonderoga, July 2–5, 1777; fought an undecisive action at Freeman's Farm against Continental forces under General Horatio Gates (first Battle of Saratoga), September 19, 1777; was defeated in Battle of Bemis Heights (second Battle of Saratoga), October 7, 1777; surrendered to Gates at Saratoga (now Stillwater), October 17, 1777, a major turning point in the war; an enlightened commander who showed considerably more respect for his men than was the eighteenth-century custom; attributed his defeat to his being undersupplied and undersupported; actually his rashness was a great contributor.

BURR, AARON. 1756–1836. Continental officer (Lt. Col.), lawyer, statesman.

Born in Newark, N.J. Served in the Continental Army, 1774–1779, reaching the rank of lieutenant colonel as a favorite staff officer of General Gates; subsequent career was one of the most controversial of American history.

BUSHNELL, DAVID. c. 1742–1824.

Born in Saybrook, Conn. Invented the first submarine used in actual operations, the *Turtle*.

BUTLER, JOHN. 1723–1796. Loyalist officer (Col.).

Born in New London, Conn. Served as assistant to Sir Guy Johnson, superintendent of Indian affairs; led Tories at Wyoming Valley, Pa., July 3–4, 1778; was defeated at Newtown, N.Y., August 29, 1779, in the only pitched battle of Sullivan's expedition; father of Walter Butler.

BUTLER, RICHARD. 1743–1791. Continental officer (Col.).
Born in Ireland. Pennsylvania resident; Indian trader and agent before Revolution; became major, 1776, and Continental lieutenant colonel in Morgan's Rifles, 1777; fought at Saratoga and at Stony Point, N.Y., July 16, 1779; helped suppress mutiny of Pennsylvania Line, 1781; helped negotiate important treaties with Indians after the war; served as major general and second-in-command to Gen. Arthur St. Clair in Indian campaign of 1791; mortally wounded in battle.

BUTLER, WALTER. 1752(?)–1781. Loyalist militia leader, farmer.
Born in Johnstown, N.Y. Active in Loyalist activities in the Mohawk Valley, 1775–1778; most notorious operation was the Cherry Valley "Massacre" which he led, along with Joseph Brant, November 11, 1778; was defeated at Chemung River (Battle of Newtown), N.Y., August 29, 1779; killed in action at Jerseyfield, N.Y., October 30, 1781; son of John Butler.

CADWALADER, JOHN. 1742–1786. Militia officer (Brig. Gen.).
Born in Philadelphia, Pa.; Philadelphia resident and businessman. Failed to make planned crossing of Delaware with 2,000 men Christmas night 1776 in coordination with Washington's crossing; made unauthorized crossing December 27; fought at Princeton, Brandywine, and Germantown; supported Washington in Conway Cabal and wounded General Conway in a duel.

CAMPBELL, ARCHIBALD. 1739–1791. British officer (Lt. Col.), member of Parliament, 1774–1780.
Born in Inverness, Scotland. Occupied Savannah, Ga., December 29, 1778; occupied Augusta, Ga., January 29, 1779; commander of the 2nd Battalion of the new Fraser Highlanders (71st Regiment).

CAMPBELL, JOHN. d. 1806. British officer (Brig. Gen.).
Commander on Staten Island, 1777–1778; successfully de-

fended Staten Island from Sullivan's raid, August 22, 1777; sent to take command in West Florida, November 1778; ordered to capture New Orleans when Spain entered the war, but never had adequate forces; surrendered at Pensacola, May 9, 1781, to the Spanish.

CAMPBELL, WILLIAM. 1745–1781. Militia officer (Brig. Gen.), frontiersman.

Born in Aspenvale, near Abingdon, Va. Brigadier general of Virginia militia; was elected overall American leader at the Battle of King's Mountain.

CARLETON, SIR GUY. 1724–1808. British officer (General, local rank).

Born in Strahane, Ireland. Responsible for the drafting of the Quebec Act, May 20, 1774; governor of Quebec, 1775; independent commander of the British forces in Canada, 1775; carried out remarkable defense of the province of Quebec, 1776; after a feud with Lord Germain, asked to be recalled to England, 1777; commander-in-chief in America, 1782–1783; halted hostilities while the peace was being negotiated; governor of Quebec, 1786–1796.

CHURCH, BENJAMIN. 1734–1777. Physician, patriot, Continental Army officer, later Loyalist.

Born in Newport, R.I. Prominent in revolutionary politics in Massachusetts, 1770–1775; first surgeon general of the Continental Army; in 1775 was an informer to General Gage about American intentions at Bunker's Hill; tried and found guilty of treason, October 1775; imprisoned, then allowed to go to the West Indies in exile, but was lost at sea, 1777.

CLARK, GEORGE ROGERS. 1752–1818. Militia officer (Brig. Gen.), frontiersman.

Born Charlottesville, Va.; frontiersman, surveyor, landowner before the Revolution. As lieutenant colonel in the Virginia militia, commanded an expeditionary force in the Northwest Territory, 1778–1779; seized Kaskaskia (Illinois), 1778, and Fort Vincennes (Indiana), 1779, capturing the commander, Lt. Col. Henry Hamilton, February 25, 1779; fought the British and Indians in the northwest, 1779–1783, and is credited with saving this territory for the Americans; treated shamefully after the war (see p. 135).

CLEVELAND, BENJAMIN. 1738–1806. Militia officer (Col.), frontiersman, scout.

Born in Virginia. A Patriot leader at the Battle of King's Mountain; North Carolina resident.

CLINTON, GEORGE. 1739–1812. Continental officer (Brig. Gen.).

Born in Little Britain, N.Y.; New York resident, was a seaman, clerk, and businessman before the Revolution. Delegate to the Continental Congress, New York, 1775–1777; brigadier general, Continental Army, 1777–1783; participated in the efforts to stop Gen. Henry Clinton's expedition to the Hudson Highlands, October 1777; first governor of New York State, 1777; served six terms, until 1795, and again was elected in 1800; strongly opposed ratification of the Federal Constitution and preferred to see New York in a more independent role; coined the nickname "Empire State" to accentuate the independence of his state; in 1804, elected Vice President for second term of Thomas Jefferson; re-elected to serve under James Madison.

CLINTON, SIR HENRY. 1738(?)–1795. British officer (Lt. Gen.; General, local rank); member of Parliament, 1772–1784.

Born in Newfoundland, Canada. Was second-in-command to General William Howe at Boston 1775–1776; commanded the Charleston, S.C., expedition of 1776; commanded expedition to the Hudson Highlands in October 1777; commander-in-chief of British forces in North America, 1778–1782; commanded at Monmouth Courthouse, 1778; commanded

Charleston expedition of 1780; succeeded as commander-in-chief by Sir Guy Carleton, May 5, 1782.

CLINTON, JAMES. 1733–1812. Continental officer (Brig. Gen.).
Brigadier general, 1776–1783; leader at Battle of Chemung River (Battle of Newton), N.Y., August 29, 1779; father of DeWitt Clinton (1769–1828).

CONWAY, THOMAS. 1733–1800? Continental officer (Maj. Gen.).
Born in Ireland. Veteran of thirty years' service in French army; involved in the Conway Cabal of 1777–1778, an attempt to discredit Washington; brigadier general, Continental Army, 1777; major general, 1777–1778; dismissed by Congress, 1778.

CONYNGHAM, GUSTAVUS. 1744–1819. Continental Navy officer; privateer captain.
Born in Ireland; emigrated to Philadelphia, 1763; was apprenticed to a merchant relative; went to sea, and was a shipmaster in early 1770s. Stranded in Holland by British blockade, early 1776; given command of the armed lugger *Surprise* (10) at Dunkirk by American commissioners in Paris, captured several prizes; arrested by French after British complaint; released, sailed again as captain of cutter *Revenge* (14), July 1776; cruised North and Irish seas; took many prizes, 1777; cruised with much success in Atlantic and Mediterranean out of Spanish ports; sailed to West Indies, captured two British privateers off St. Eustatius, 1778; arrived Philadelphia February 21, 1779, having taken sixty prizes in eighteen months; was captured by British frigate off New York, April 27; sent to England in irons, July 1779; accused of piracy; mistreated in prison, escaped to Holland, November 1779; recaptured en route to America, March 1780; was exchanged after a year; returned to France, was at Nantes preparing for another cruise when ordered to stop because of peace negotiations; after the

war, returned to Philadelphia and again became a merchant sea captain.

CORNWALLIS, CHARLES (second Earl Cornwallis). 1738–1805. British officer (Lt. Gen.), statesman.

Born in London; a Whig member of the House of Lords (from 1762); consistently opposed both Parliament's efforts to tax the American colonies and the later coercive measures. Served with distinction under General Howe, 1776–1778, notably as corps commander at Long Island, White Plains, Brandywine, etc.; second-in-command to Sir Henry Clinton, 1778–1780; and in command of British forces in the South, 1780–1781; defeated Horatio Gates at Camden, August 16, 1780; won costly victory over Greene at Guilford Courthouse, March 1781; was defeated and forced to surrender to Washington at Yorktown, October 19, 1781. After the war, served with distinction as governor-general of India (1786–1794) and viceroy of Ireland (1798–1801).

DAWES, WILLIAM. 1745–1799. Patriot, tanner, grocer.

Born at Boston, Mass. Co-rider with Paul Revere, April 18–19, 1775.

DAYTON, ELIAS. 1737-1807. Continental officer (Brig. Gen.).

Born at Elizabethtown (now Elizabeth), N.J.; mechanic, storekeeper; French and Indian War veteran. Continental colonel, 1776; fought in actions throughout war, including Brandywine, Germantown, Monmouth, Sullivan's expedition of 1779, and Yorktown; also headed an important spy network; brigadier general, January 1783; member, Continental Congress from New Jersey, 1787–1788.

DEANE, SILAS. 1737-1789. American statesman, diplomat, lawyer.

Born at Groton, Conn. Delegate to the Continental Congress from Connecticut, 1774–1776; went to Paris, as a commissioner, to obtain French assistance for the American cause and possible recognition of independence; his efforts resulted in establishment of Rodrique Hortalez et Cie., a secret company to give munitions to the Americans; with Benjamin Franklin and Arthur Lee, aided in negotiating alliance with France and the recognition of American independence, 1778; apparently had later misgivings about the American cause, and favored an accommodation with the British, 1781; his dealings with a British agent were probably treasonous.

DE LANCEY, JAMES. 1746–1804. Loyalist leader.
Born Westchester Co., N.Y. Sheriff of Westchester County, N.Y., 1770–1776; led Westchester Light Horse Brigade, the "Cowboys" of the "Cowboys and Skinners," marauding Tory bands operating in New York; nephew of Oliver De Lancey, the elder; moved to Nova Scotia after the Revolution.

DE LANCEY, OLIVER, THE ELDER. 1718–1785. Loyalist officer (Brig. Gen.), landowner, merchant.
Born in Westchester Co., N.Y.; New York political leader before the Revolution. In America raised the 1,500-man brigade known as "De Lancey's Battalions," or "De Lancey's New York Volunteers," which served with distinction throughout the South as well as in Queens County, N.Y.; father of Oliver De Lancey, the younger, and uncle of James De Lancey; went to England after the war.

DE LANCEY, OLIVER, THE YOUNGER. 1749–1822. British officer (Lt. Col.), Loyalist.
Born at New York, N.Y. Adjutant general to General Clinton, 1780–1781; adjutant general of the British Army in America, 1781–1783; had a distinguished post-Revolution British Army career; promoted to full general in 1812; member of Parliament.

DEMONT, WILLIAM. American soldier, deserter.
Regimental adjutant, 5th Pennsylvania Battalion; deserted to

camp of General Hugh Percy, and gave the British the plans for Fort Washington, N.Y., November 2, 1776; his treason aided in the successful assault and capture of the fortress, November 16, 1776.

DENISON (DENNISON), NATHAN. Militia officer (Col.).
Born at New London, Conn. Leading member of the community of Connecticut settlers in Wyoming Valley, Pa.; commanded troops in the Battle (or "Massacre") of Wyoming Valley, July 3–4, 1778.

DE PEYSTER, ABRAHAM. 1753–1799. Loyalist officer (Lt. Col.).
Became commander of the King's American Rangers, after the Battle of King's Mountain, succeeding Patrick Ferguson, October 7, 1780; New York resident.

DE PEYSTER, ARENT SCHUYLER. 1736–1832. Loyalist officer (Col.).
Born in New York. Commanded posts at Detroit and Mackinac, helped keep the Indians loyal to British cause; uncle of Abraham De Peyster.

DESTOUCHES, CHARLES-RENÉ-DOMINIQUE SOCHET, CHEVALIER. French naval officer (Commodore).
Commander of the French squadron at Newport, R.I., 1780–1781.

DEUX-PONTS, GUILLAMME, COMTE. French officer (Col.).
Captured Redoubt No. 9 outside Yorktown, October 14, 1781.

DONOP, CARL EMIL KURT VON. c. 1740–1777. Hessian officer (Col.).
Commanded Hessian division on British left in New Jersey, late 1776, holding Mount Holly, Burlington, and Bordentown; withdrew to Princeton, N.J., after the Battle of Trenton; mor-

tally wounded at Fort Mercer (Red Bank), N.J., October 22, 1777.

DUNMORE, JOHN MURRAY, 4TH EARL OF. 1732–1809. Royal governor.

Royal governor of New York, 1770–1771; of Virginia, 1771–1776. Called up three thousand militiamen to suppress Shawnee uprising, 1774; ensuing fighting was known as Lord Dunmore's War; dissolved House of Burgesses because of its protests against Boston Port Act, May 1774; seized colony's store of powder, April 1775; declared Virginia under martial law, November 7, 1775; established Loyalist base at Norfolk; led successful action at Kemp's Landing, Va., November 14, 1775, but was defeated at Great Bridge, Va., December 9; fled to British warships; bombarded and set fire to Norfolk, January 1, 1776.

DUPORTAIL, LOUIS LE BEQUE DE PRESLE, CHEVALIER. 1743–1802. French volunteer (Continental Army officer, Maj. Gen.).

Born in Pithiviers, France. One of four officers specifically chosen by French government in response to Benjamin Franklin's 1776 request that trained military engineers be made available to the new nation; assigned by Congress to the Continental Army as Colonel of Engineers, February 13, 1777; on the basis of performance and Washington's recommendation, Congress gave him seniority over all engineers previously appointed, July 22, 1777; in Brandywine-Philadelphia campaign worked primarily on strengthening Delaware River fortifications; promoted to brigadier general and appointed Chief of Engineers, November 17, 1777; was at Valley Forge; participated in Monmouth campaign; sent by Washington to help Lincoln at Charleston, he arrived too late to play a significant role, and became a prisoner of war, May 12, 1780; exchanged, October 25, 1780; rejoined Washington in time to play a vital role in the siege operations at Yorktown; promoted to major general, 1781; one of a handful of foreign volunteers who contributed significantly to American independence.

ESTAING, JEAN-BAPTISTE CHARLES HENRI HECTOR THEODAT, COMTE D'. 1729–1794. French naval officer (Adm.).

Born in Auvergne, France. Commanded the French fleet dispatched to fight the British fleet in American waters, 1778; missed opportunity to bottle up British fleet in Chesapeake Bay, 1778; missed another in the West Indies, when with superior forces he retreated instead of pursuing the British under Byron, July 1779; captured Grenada and won some minor successes in West Indies, 1779; his failure at Savannah capped a generally unsuccessful tour of duty, October 9, 1779; returned to France, 1780.

FERGUSON, PATRICK. 1744–1780. British officer (Maj.), partisan leader, inventor.

Born in Scotland. Commanded King's American Rangers; led British forces in the successful raid on Little Egg Harbor (Mincock Island), N.J., October 14–15, 1778; was defeated and killed at King's Mountain, S.C., October 7, 1780; inventor of the Ferguson breech-loading rifle.

FERMOY, MATTHIAS ALEXIS DE ROCHE, CHEVALIER. b. c. 1737.

Born in Martinique. French volunteer; brigadier general, Continental Army, 1776–1778; performed poorly at Trenton and in the preliminaries to Princeton, 1776–1777; bungled his mission at Ticonderoga, July 1777; resigned, early 1778.

FLEURY, FRANÇOIS LOUIS TEISSEDRE DE. *See* Teissedre.

FORMAN, DAVID. 1745–1797. Militia officer (Brig. Gen.), Continental officer (Col.).

Born in Monmouth Co., N.J. Suppressed Loyalist uprising in Monmouth Co., N.J., November 1776; made Continental colonel, 1776 or early 1777; commissioned brigadier general of New Jersey militia, 1777; commanded New Jersey militia at Germantown; major activity in war was harassment and suppression of Loyalists in Monmouth County; called "Devil David" by Loyalists for his alleged cruelty; also directed intelligence group that observed British ship movements and that included spies on Staten Island, 1777–1782; served as county judge after the Revolution.

FRASER, SIMON; MASTER OF LOVATT. 1729–1777. British officer (Brig. Gen.).

Born in Scotland. Occupied Crown Point, N.Y., June 16, 1776; distinguished himself at Hubbardton, Vt., July 1777; mortally wounded at second battle of Saratoga.

GAGE, THOMAS. 1719?–1787. British officer (Lt. Gen.).

Born in Sussex, England. Commander-in-chief in America, 1772–1775; governor of Massachusetts, 1774–1775; sent troops to destroy military supplies at Concord, April 19, 1775, thus triggering the Revolutionary War; resigned his command, August 1775, under some pressure; was regarded as lacking the initiative and vigor needed for the job at hand.

GÁLVEZ, BERNARDO DE. 1746–1786. Spanish officer and government official.

Governor of Louisiana (and later Florida), 1777; worked covertly and effectively to weaken the British position in lower Mississippi Valley, 1777–1779; after Spanish declaration of war, 1779, took the British river posts of Manchac, Baton Rouge, and Natchez; sent expeditions to attack British posts in upper Mississippi Valley; seized the post of Mobile from the British, March 1780; forced British surrender of Pensacola, May 9, 1781; his victories ended British control of West Florida, resulting in Spanish acquisition of both Floridas (and control of the mouth of the Mississippi) under the peace settlement of 1783; was made captain-general of Louisiana and the Floridas, and played a prominent role in early Spanish diplomatic negotiations with the United States; became viceroy of New Spain, 1785, succeeding his father, but died the following year.

GANSEVOORT, PETER. 1749–1812. Continental officer (Col.).
Born in Albany, N.Y. Distinguished himself in many campaigns in New York state, notably the long defense of Fort Stanwix against St. Leger's expedition, June–September 1777.

GATES, HORATIO. 1728–1806. Continental officer (Maj. Gen.).
Born in England; served in America in French and Indian War; settled in Virginia. Appointed adjutant general to General Washington with rank of brigadier general, June 1775; served effectively; promoted to major general and sent to the northern department to serve under General Philip Schuyler as field army commander, 1776; continually attempted to undermine Schuyler's position; in spring 1777 Congress initially upheld Schuyler, despite Gates's protests on the floor of Congress, April 1777; after the fall of Ticonderoga, was finally named commander of the Northern Department to replace Schuyler, August 1777; defeated General John Burgoyne at Saratoga, N.Y., September 19 and October 7, 1777 (with assistance of Burgoyne's errors and the aggressive leadership of Gates's subordinate, Benedict Arnold); involved in the Conway Cabal against Washington while serving as president of the Board of War (an organization devised by Congress partly to remove some power from Washington), 1777–1778; appointed by Congress, despite Washington's recommendations of Greene, commander of the Southern Department, June 1780; defeated at Camden, August 16, 1780, and fled, abandoning his army; retired to his farm; cleared of wrongdoing by a congressional inquiry, 1782; rejoined the army at Newburgh near the end of the war.

GIRTY, SIMON. 1741–1818. Loyalist partisan, scout, interpreter.

Born near Harrisburg, Pa.; captured as boy by Seneca Indians and lived among them. Scout and interpreter for the Americans, 1774–1778; deserted to the British, 1778; ambushed Colonel David Rogers on the Ohio River and captured 600,000 Spanish dollars and other valuable supplies; took part in William Crawford's defeat, June 4–5, 1782; was present at the torture of Crawford; participated in the raid at Blue Licks, Ky., August 1782; closely involved with the Delaware Indians.

GIST, MORDECAI. 1743–1792. Continental officer (Brig. Gen.).

Born in Maryland. A planter before the Revolution. Major in Smallwood's Maryland Regiment, 1776; led it with distinction at Long Island; fought as colonel at Germantown; brigadier general, 1779, commanding 2d Maryland Brigade; fought well at Camden, August 16, 1780; settled in South Carolina after the war.

GLOVER, JOHN. 1732–1797. Militia officer, Continental officer (Brig. Gen.).

Born in Salem, Mass. A merchant and shipowner before the Revolution. Raised and commanded regiment from Marblehead, Mass., 1775; responsible for boats effectively transporting troops in retreat from Long Island, August 1776; fought well at Kips Bay, N.Y., September 15, 1776, Pell's Point, N.Y., October 18, 1776, and White Plains; he and his Marblehead regiment handled the boats for Delaware crossing, December 1776; brigadier general, 1777–1782.

GRANT, JAMES. 1720–1806. British officer (Lt. Gen.).

Born Ballindolloch, Banffshire, Scotland. Governor of the Floridas, 1764–1771; strongly anti-American; commanded two brigades at Long Island; commanded British outposts in New Jersey, 1776; his underrating of the Americans was a factor in the American victories at Trenton and Princeton, 1776–1777; unsuccessful at Barren Hill, Pa., May 20, 1778;

captured and successfully defended the West Indies island of St. Lucia, December 18–28, 1778; member of Parliament before and after the war.

GRASSE, FRANÇOIS JOSEPH PAUL, DE. 1722–1788. French naval officer (Admiral).
Born at Bar, Alpes-Maritimes. Defeated Rear Adm. Samuel Hood and captured Tobago, 1781; successfully commanded French naval force in the Battle of the Capes, defeating British Rear Adm. Thomas Graves and assuring Allied victory at Yorktown, September 5–10, 1781; defeated by Adm. George Rodney at the Battle of the Saints and taken prisoner, April 1782; released on parole, August 1782; court-martialed for his defeat but acquitted, 1784.

GRAVES, THOMAS. 1725?–1802. British naval officer (Rear Adm.).
Second-in-command to Admiral Arbuthnot on the American Station, 1780; took part in inconclusive battle off mouth of Chesapeake Bay, March 16, 1781; commanded British naval force at Battle of the Capes, September 5–10, 1781, where he was defeated by Admiral de Grasse; sailed to New York after this battle and returned with a larger fleet, too late to influence events at Yorktown.

GREENE, NATHANAEL. 1742–1786. Continental officer (Maj. Gen.).
Born Potowomut (Warwick), R.I.; Rhode Island resident; forge owner before Revolution. Brigadier general, 1775; major general, 1776; responsible for the loss of Fort Washington, N.Y., November 16, 1776; after that disaster, distinguished himself at Trenton, December 26, 1776; commanded a division at the Brandywine; led the column making the main effort at Germantown; Washington's most trusted subordinate; Quartermaster General, 1778–1780; commanded the Southern Department, 1780–1783, where his reputation was built on driving the British out of the Carolinas and Georgia in a strategically successful campaign devoid of tactical victories;

turned what seemed to be a retreat into victory by forcing the British to chase him into Virginia in the race to the Dan River, with subsequent battles at Guilford Courthouse, N.C., March 16, 1781; Hobkirk's Hill, S.C., April 25, 1781; the siege of Ninety-six, May 22–June 18, 1781; and Eutaw Springs, S.C., September 8, 1781; returned to besiege Charleston, S.C., the only remaining British stronghold in the South; generally considered most distinguished American commander of the war, after Washington.

GREY, CHARLES ("No Flint"). 1729–1807. British officer (Lt. Gen.).
Born in Howick, Northumberland, England. At Paoli, Pa., in a night attack, to prevent any premature firing that would ruin his planned surprise, ordered his men to remove the flints from their weapons (hence his nickname), defeated Wayne, September 21, 1777; fought commendably at Germantown, October 4, 1777; made raids on Bedford, Mass., September 6, 1778, Martha's Vineyard, c. September 8, 1778, and was particularly successful at Tappan, N.Y., September 28, 1779. Fought in the War of the First Coalition against France, became a full general in 1794, and became Viscount Howick and Earl Grey in 1806.

HALE, NATHAN. 1755–1776. Continental officer (Capt.), teacher.
Born in Coventry, Conn. Captured by the British and executed as a spy, September 22, 1776; his last statement reportedly closed with the words "I only regret that I have but one life to lose for my country."

HAMILTON, ALEXANDER. c. 1755–1804. American statesman, lawyer, Continental officer (Lt. Col.).
Born in Nevis, British West Indies; entered King's College (Columbia), New York City, in 1773. Active as a student in Patriot activities; spoke against British coercion at the "Meeting in the Fields," July 6, 1774; wrote a widely circulated

series of pamphlets supporting nonimportation, nonconsumption, and nonexportation, 1774–1775; commissioned captain of the New York Company of Provisional Artillery,* March 14, 1776; commanded his guns at Long Island, Harlem Heights, and White Plains, 1776; distinguished himself in a delaying action at Trenton, January 2, 1777, and in capture of Princeton next day; served as secretary, aide-de-camp, and adviser to Washington, March 1777–July 1781; crowned his Revolutionary career by commanding a battalion at Yorktown, where he led a successful assault on Redoubt No. 10, October 14, 1781; delegate to the Continental Congress, 1782–1783, 1787–1788, from New York. Subsequent career was one of the most distinguished, though in many respects controversial, of American history; one of America's Founding Fathers.

HAMILTON, HENRY ("the Hair Buyer"). d. 1796. British officer.
Commandant at Detroit, and Lieutenant Governor of Canada, 1775–1779; his task was to defend the West and to organize the Indians for attacks on the frontiers; his nickname came from his supposed practice of offering money for scalps; opposed George Rogers Clark in his western operations; was defeated and captured at Vincennes, February 25, 1779.

HAND, EDWARD. 1744–1802. Continental officer (Brig. Gen.), physician, statesman.
Born in Ireland; came to America as surgeon's mate with 18th Royal Irish Regiment, 1767; resigned to practice medicine. Served as lieutenant colonel at siege of Boston, 1775; appointed colonel, March 7, 1776; commanded regiment effectively at Long Island, White Plains, and Princeton; promoted to brigadier general, April 1, 1777; led unsuccessful western expedition, 1778; commander at Albany, 1777–1781; played important role in Sullivan's western New York expedition,

---

* Now Battery D, Fifth Field Artillery, oldest unit in the U.S. Regular Army, and the only unit of the regular armed services that can trace its history without break to the American Revolution.

1779; Adjutant General, 1781–1783. Delegate to the Continental Congress, Pennsylvania, 1784–1785; Federalist.

HAYS, MARY LUDWIG. 1754–1832. Patriot heroine.

Known as "Molly Pitcher"; heroine at Fort Clinton, 1777, and at the battle of Monmouth, 1778; appointed sergeant by General Washington, and pensioned by Congress. Pennsylvania resident.

HAZEN, MOSES. 1733–1803. Continental officer (Brevet Brig. Gen.), farmer.

Born at Haverhill, Mass.; served with distinction in French and Indian War. Appointed colonel of the 2d Canadian Regiment, 1776; brevet brigadier general, 1781–1783.

HEATH, WILLIAM. 1737–1814. Militia officer (Maj. Gen.), Continental officer (Maj. Gen.).

Born in Roxbury, Mass.; a farmer before the Revolution. Brigadier general of Massachusetts militia, February 1775; in command during militia harassment of British returning from Concord and during first dispositions for siege of Boston; appointed militia major general and then Continental brigadier general, June 1775; commanded a division in New York operations, 1776; major general, 1776–1783; attempted to capture Fort Independence, near King's Bridge, N.Y. and failed ignominiously, January 11–29, 1777; commanded Eastern Department (New England), 1777–1779; commanded in Hudson Highlands, to east of river, 1779–1783; served as judge and state senator after the war.

HEISTER, LEOPOLD VON (OR DE). 1707–1777. Hessian officer (General).

Commander-in-chief of German forces in America; commanded the center of the British line at the Battle of Long Island; led the Germans at White Plains; recalled, 1777, after German disaster at Trenton; died soon afterward.

HERKIMER, NICHOLAS. 1728–1777. Militia officer (Brig. Gen.).
Born near present-day Herkimer, N.Y. A farmer and Patriot leader in Mohawk Valley, where Tory sentiment was strong; led a force of eight hundred to relieve besieged Fort Stanwix, N.Y.; ambushed at Oriskany, August 6, 1777; directed successful defense but died of wounds.

HOPKINS, ESEK. 1718–1802. Continental naval officer (Commodore), seaman.
Born in Scituate, R.I.; sea captain in pre-Revolutionary period; privateer during French and Indian War. Brother of Continental Congress Delegate Stephen Hopkins; put in command of Rhode Island state militia, October 1775; made first commander-in-chief of the Continental Navy, December 1775; commanded successful expedition to Bahamas, February 1776, but was censured for disobedience of orders; British blockade prevented further fleet activities; dismissed January 1778.

HOWE, RICHARD ("Black Dick"), LORD (Viscount Howe). 1726–1799. British naval officer (Adm.).
Born in London, England. Went to America as naval commander-in-chief on the American Station, and also, at his insistence, as peace commissioner, a mission which his brother William shared, 1776; Howe brothers' powers to take action for peace were narrowly limited, partly because of official suspicions of their pro-American sentiments; provided naval support for the New York campaign, 1776; defended New York harbor against the French, 1778; broke up Franco-American operations against Newport, R.I., August 1778; resigned and returned to England, late 1778. Later had a brilliant naval career in the wars of the First and Second Coalitions against republican France.

HOWE, ROBERT. Continental officer (Maj. Gen.).
Born near the Cape Fear River, N.C.; a planter before the

Revolution. Brigadier general, 1776–1777; major general, 1777–1783; performed with distinction in Georgia, 1778–1779; played a major role in suppressing Pompton and Suffren mutinies, 1781.

HOWE, SIR WILLIAM. 1729–1814. British officer (Lt. Gen.), member of Parliament.

Served with distinction in the French and Indian War; sympathetic toward the Americans during the pre-Revolutionary period. Planned and led the British attack at Bunker's Hill (Breed's Hill); succeeded General Gage; served as commander-in-chief of British forces in North America, 1775–1778; held, with his brother, Lord Richard Howe, limited authority as peace commissioner, 1776; won brilliant victory at Long Island, August 1776; failed to pursue aggressively or to seize opportunities to destroy Washington's vulnerable forces in subsequent operations around New York; underestimated Washington and his army in the New Jersey campaign of 1776–1777; his forces suffered the significant defeats of Trenton and Princeton; outmaneuvered and twice defeated Washington (Brandywine and Germantown) in the Philadelphia campaign of 1777, but failed to win decisive victory; despite criticisms of slowness and lack of decisiveness, his performance was good by eighteenth-century standards of war-making.

HUGER, ISAAC. 1743–1797. Continental officer (Brig. Gen.).

Born in South Carolina; a planter before the Revolution. Brigadier general, January 9, 1779; commanded Georgia and South Carolina militia at Savannah, Ga., October 9, 1779; defeated by Tarleton at Monck's Corner, S.C., October 16, 1781; led one wing of Greene's army at Guilford Courthouse, and was seriously wounded; commanded the right wing at Hobkirk's Hill, S.C., April 25, 1781.

JOHNSON, GUY. c. 1740–1788. Loyalist, Indian agent.

Born in Ireland. A leading Loyalist in New York state; superintendent of Indian affairs, 1774–1782; succeeded in winning support of four tribes of the Iroquois nation to the Loyalist cause; may have been nephew of Sir William Johnson.

JOHNSON, SIR JOHN. 1742–1830. Loyalist, British government official.

Born at Johnstown, N.Y. Superintendent of Indian affairs, 1782; led Indian and Tory raid at Johnstown, N.Y., May 22–23, 1780; son of Sir William Johnson (1715–1774).

JONES, JOHN PAUL. 1747–1792. Continental naval officer (Commodore).

Born in Kirkcudbrightshire, Scotland; a seaman from the age of twelve, became a Virginia resident. Commissioned a lieutenant in 1775; served on the *Alfred* in the Bahamas expedition; commander of the *Providence* in 1776, brought in sixteen prizes in one cruise; commanding the *Ranger* (18) with the rank of captain, he terrorized British shipping in the English Channel and Irish Sea, successfully raided the port of Whitehaven, England, April 22–23, 1778; defeated HMS *Drake* (20) on April 24, 1778; as captain of converted merchant ship, which he renamed *Bonhomme Richard* (40), led a small squadron in a dramatic cruise around the British Isles, August–September, 1779; in one of the most hard-fought single-ship battles in history, he defeated HMS *Serapis* (44) by superior seamanship and determination, although his own ship was sunk, September 23, 1779; disbandment of the American navy after the war led him to volunteer for service in the Russian Navy, where he served with comparable distinction.

KALB, JOHANN ("Baron de Kalb"). 1721–1780. Continental officer (Maj. Gen.), French agent.

Born in Huttendorf, Germany, of peasant stock; became a soldier of fortune, took an assumed title, and thus gained the success in the French Army to which his talents and courage entitled him. Served as an agent to America for French Foreign

Minister Choiseul, 1768; when the Revolution broke out, volunteered for service in America, 1776; became a major general in the Continental Army, 1777–1780; was second-in-command to Lafayette for the proposed Canada invasion, 1778; serving in the southern campaigns of 1780, fought with especial skill and gallantry at Camden, where he was mortally wounded, August 16, 1780.

KIRKWOOD, ROBERT. 1730–1791. Continental officer, farmer.
Born at New Castle Co., Del. Commanded a Delaware company throughout the war; distinguished himself in the southern campaigns of General Greene; settled in Ohio after the war; killed in St. Clair's defeat by Indians, November 4, 1781.

KNOWLTON, THOMAS. 1740–1776. Militia officer (Capt.), Continental officer (Lt. Col.), farmer.
Born in West Boxford, Mass. Distinguished himself at Bunker's Hill; carried out daring raid on Charlestown, Mass., January 8, 1776; leader of a body of Connecticut Rangers at Harlem Heights, N.Y., September 16, 1776, where he was killed.

KNOX, HENRY. 1750–1806. Continental officer (Maj. Gen.).
Born in Boston, Mass.; a bookstore proprietor before the Revolution. Chief of artillery for the Continental Army; responsible for the "noble train of artillery," brought from Ticonderoga to Boston, January 1776, which forced the British to evacuate the city; brigadier general, 1776; played important role in Delaware crossing December 26, 1776 and at battles of Princeton, Brandywine, Germantown, Monmouth, and Yorktown; major general, 1781; commanded at West Point, 1782; generally considered one of Washington's abler subordinates. After the Revolution became Secretary at War under the Articles of Confederation and the Continental Congress; was the first Secretary of War under President Washington, 1789–1795.

KNYPHAUSEN, WILHELM, BARON VON. 1716–1800. German officer (Lt. Gen.).

Born in Prussia. Came to America as commander of Hesse-Cassel contingent, 1776; an extremely able soldier; commander-in-chief of German troops in America, 1777–1782; played a major role in battles of Brandywine, Monmouth, and Springfield (June 23, 1780); commanded New York garrison in absence of Clinton, 1779–1780. After return to Germany became the military governor of Cassel.

KOSCIUSKO, THADDEUS. 1746–1817. Polish patriot, Continental officer (Brevet Brig. Gen.).

Born in Lithuania. Volunteered his service to America, 1776; fortified Saratoga battlefield; served at West Point, N.Y., 1778–1780, where he planned and supervised construction of the defenses; chief engineer of the Southern Department under General Gates. After the Revolution, worked and fought for Polish independence the rest of his life.

LAFAYETTE, MARQUIS DE (MARIE JOSEPH PAUL YVES ROCH GILBERT DU MOTIER). 1757–1834. French officer, Continental officer (Maj. Gen.).

Born in Chevaniac Château, Auvergne; an extremely wealthy nobleman. Resigned from French Army, and became a volunteer in the Continental Army, serving at his own expense, 1776; commissioned a major general by the Continental Congress, July 1, 1777; became an intimate of Washington's; fought well at Brandywine and in operations near Valley Forge, Pa., 1777–1778; appointed commander of a proposed, but never enacted, Canada invasion, 1778; figured prominently in the Monmouth campaign and at Newport, R.I., July–August 1778. Returned to France, 1779; urged greater support of the Americans; his plan for an invasion of England was not approved, but he laid the groundwork for the expeditionary force sent to America under Rochambeau, 1780; returned to America, early 1781; was sent by Washington to command in

Virginia, where he proved himself to be a competent strategist and tactician; he distinguished himself at Green Springs, Va., July 6, 1781, and at Yorktown. Returning to France in 1781, he assisted American Minister Thomas Jefferson in many political and economic matters; was a republican leader in the early stages of the French Revolution, 1789–1791, but was forced to flee because of suspicions of his aristocratic background.

LANDAIS, PIERRE. 1731–1820. French naval officer, Continental naval officer.

Born in Normandy. After an undistinguished French naval career, named a captain in the Continental Navy in 1777; commanded the *Alliance,* under John Paul Jones in his circumnavigation of Great Britain, 1779; was repeatedly insubordinate, and actually fired upon Jones's ship in the *Bonhomme Richard-Serapis* battle, 1779; relieved of command by Jones; regained control over the *Alliance* by trickery and sailed back to the United States, where he was immediately courtmartialed and dismissed from the service; later went back to France. Joined the French Republican Navy in 1789 or 1790; retired, 1793, and returned to New York, where he died.

LAURENS, JOHN. c. 1754–1782. Continental officer (Lt. Col.).

Born in South Carolina. Aide-de-camp to George Washington; fought at Brandywine, Germantown, Monmouth, Yorktown; represented the Americans in the surrender negotiations at Yorktown, October 17, 1781; killed at Combahee Ferry, S.C., August 27, 1782.

LEE, CHARLES. 1731–1782. Continental officer (Maj. Gen.).

Born in England; served as British Regular Army officer for over twenty years; emigrated to America, 1773. Was made Continental major general, June 17, 1775; served well in defense of Charleston, 1776; insubordinate to Washington in New Jersey retreat, November–December 1776; captured ingloriously, December 13, 1776; apparently acted treasonably while prisoner of war, 1776–1778; exchanged April 1778; dismissed as a result of disgraceful conduct during and after the Monmouth campaign, 1778.

LEE, HENRY ("Light-Horse Harry"). 1756–1818. Continental officer (Lt. Col.), statesman.

Born in "Leesylvania," Prince William Co., Va. Cavalry leader; commanded daring raid on Paulus Hook, N.J., August 19, 1779; commander of Lee's Legion, which he led with distinction in Greene's southern campaigns. After the war was delegate to the Continental Congress, 1785–1788; governor of Virginia, 1792–1795; member, U.S. House of Representatives, 1799–1801; eulogized George Washington as "first in war, first in peace, and first in the hearts of his countrymen"; father of Robert E. Lee, cousin of Lee of "Stratford."

LESLIE, ALEXANDER. c. 1740–1794. British officer (Brig. Gen., local rank Lt. Gen.).

Commanded expedition to Salem, Mass., February 26, 1775, that almost became the first battle of the Revolution; served in Boston, 1775–1776; at Battle of Long Island; at Kips Bay, N.Y., September 15, 1776; and at Harlem Heights, N.Y., September 16, 1776; in Trenton-Princeton campaign; participated in southern campaign, 1781; fought at Cowan's Ford, N.C., February 1, 1781, and commanded the British right at Guilford Courthouse; succeeded Cornwallis as commander in the southern theater, October 1781; withdrew from Savannah, Ga., July 11, 1782, and Charleston, S.C., December 14, 1782.

LINCOLN, BENJAMIN. 1733–1810. Militia officer (Maj. Gen.), Continental officer (Maj. Gen.), local official.

Born in Massachusetts; was a farmer before the Revolution. Militia officer, 1755–1777; major general, Continental Army, 1777–1783; distinguished himself in organizing opposition to Bennington, Vt., raid, August 1777, and in supporting Gates at the battles of Saratoga; commanded the Southern Department, 1778–1780; commanded American troops in siege of Savannah, September–October 1779; was besieged and surrendered at Charleston, May 12, 1780; served at Yorktown, where he accepted British surrender as Washington's representative; Secretary at War, 1781–1783.

MCDOUGALL, ALEXANDER. 1732–1786. Continental officer (Maj. Gen.), statesman, privateer.

Born in Islay, Innes, Hebrides, Scotland; came to America as a child; commanded a privateer in the French and Indian War; was a prominent pre-Revolutionary radical leader in New York; wrote *A Son of Liberty to the Betrayed Inhabitants of the City and Colony of New York,* December 16, 1769; presided at the "Meeting in the Fields," July 6, 1774. Brigadier general, Continental Army, 1776–1777; major general, 1777–1783; commander at West Point, N.Y., 1780, succeeding Benedict Arnold; court-martialed in 1782 for insubordination to Maj. Gen. William Heath; delegate to the Continental Congress, New York, 1781–1782, 1784–1785.

MCLANE, ALLEN (or ALLAN). 1746–1829. Continental officer (Col.), partisan leader, merchant.

Born in Philadelphia, Pa. (probably). Participated in early actions in Virginia, 1774 and 1775; fought with Delaware militia at Long Island, N.Y., August 27, 1776, and White Plains, N.Y., October 28, 1776; distinguished himself at Princeton, January 3, 1777; immediately commissioned Continental captain; carried out numerous harassing, reconnaissance, and foraging missions; saved Lafayette from surprise attack at Barren Hill, Pa., May 20, 1778.

MARION, FRANCIS. c. 1732–1795. Continental officer (Lt. Col.), militia officer (Brig. Gen.), statesman.

Born in St. John's Parish (now Berkeley Co.), S.C.; a planter before the Revolution. Served as Continental officer at

Charleston and Savannah, 1775–1780; commanded South Carolina militia (also known as Marion's Brigade), 1780–1783; distinguished himself at Parker's Ferry, S.C., August 13, 1781, and Eutaw Springs, S.C., September 8, 1781; known as "the Swamp Fox," for his effective partisan hit-and-run tactics, especially in 1780–1781; elected to state senate, 1781, 1782, 1784.

MAWHOOD, CHARLES. d. 1780. British officer (Col.).
Led British forces at Battle of Princeton, January 3, 1777; also commanded at Quintain's Bridge, N.J., March 18, 1778, and Hancock's Bridge, N.J., March 21, 1778.

MAXWELL, WILLIAM. c. 1733–1796. Continental officer (Brig. Gen.), statesman.
Born in Ireland. As colonel, participated in Canada invasion of 1776; brigadier general, Continental Army, 1776–1780; commanded Maxwell's Light Infantry, 1777; fought at Cooch's Bridge, Del., September 3, 1777; commanded a division at Brandywine; after Germantown was charged with misconduct and excessive drinking, November 1777, but not convicted; served at Battle of Monmouth; retired 1780.

MERCER, HUGH. c. 1725–1777. Continental officer (Brig. Gen.), physician.
Born in Scotland; emigrated to America after defeat of Jacobites at Culloden; Virginia resident. Brigadier general, 1776–1777; reportedly suggested to Washington the strategy leading to the victory at Princeton, N.J., January 1777; mortally wounded in the battle.

MIFFLIN, THOMAS. 1744–1800. Continental officer (Maj. Gen.), statesman.
Born in Philadelphia, Pa. Quartermaster General, Continental Army, 1776–1777; brigadier general, 1776–1777; major general, 1777–1779; delegate to the Continental Congress, 1774–

1776, 1782–1784; implicated in Conway Cabal, 1777–1778; a poor (and possibly corrupt) Quartermaster General in 1777 and largely responsible for the suffering at Valley Forge, 1777–1778. Governor of Pennsylvania, 1790–1799; commanded Pennsylvania militia (reluctantly) during Whiskey Rebellion, 1794.

MONROE, JAMES. 1758–1831. Continental officer (Maj. or Lt. Col.), lawyer, statesman.

Born in Westmoreland Co., Va. Served with the 3rd Virginia Regiment at Harlem Heights, N.Y., September 16, 1776, and at White Plains and Trenton; appointed major and aide-de-camp to Maj. Gen. William Alexander in 1777; fought at Brandywine, Germantown, and Monmouth; resigned in 1778. Had a distinguished state and national legislative and diplomatic career after the war; Secretary of State during the War of 1812, and during part of the war was also Secretary of War; fifth President of the United States, 1817–1824.

MONTGOMERY, RICHARD. 1738–1775. Continental officer (Maj. Gen.).

Born in Ireland; fought as British officer in French and Indian War; settled as a farmer in New York, 1773. Continental brigadier general, 1775; major general, 1775; participated in the Canada invasion of 1775–1776; successfully besieged Saint-Jean, September 5–November 2, 1775; seized Montreal, November 13, 1775; killed in action at Quebec, December 31, 1775.

MORGAN, DANIEL. 1736–1802. Continental officer (Brig. Gen.).

Born in Bucks Co., Pa., or Hunterdon Co., N. J.; settled as a farmer in Shenandoah Valley of Virginia at seventeen. Raised a Continental rifle company, June 1775, and took it to Boston; led the van in Arnold's march to Quebec, September–November 1775; was captured in attack on Quebec, December 31; exchanged, 1776; played crucial part in Saratoga victories,

1777; resigned because of lack of recognition by Congress, despite Washington's recommendations for promotion to brigadier general; returned to duty after Gates's defeat at Camden, and promoted to brigadier general, 1780; served under Greene in South; most notable accomplishment was his classic double-envelopment victory over the British at the Battle of the Cowpens; retired soon afterward because of ill health. Served in U.S. House of Representatives, 1797–1799, from Virginia.

MOULTRIE, WILLIAM. 1739–1805. Continental officer (Maj. Gen.), statesman, military historian.

Born in Charleston, S.C. Commanded Fort Sullivan (later Fort Moultrie) in successful defense of Charleston, 1776; brigadier general, 1776–1782; major general, 1782–1783; successful at Beaufort, S.C., February 3, 1779; helped organize the defenses of Charleston, S.C., May 11–12, 1779. Governor of South Carolina, 1785–1787, 1794–1796.

NIXON, JOHN. 1727–1815. Militia officer (Col.), Continental officer (Brig. Gen.).

Born in Farmington, Mass.; veteran of French and Indian War. Fought at Concord and Bunker's Hill; Continental colonel, January 1776; brigadier general, 1776–1780; played a prominent role in the battle at Harlem Heights, N.Y., September 16, 1776; his brigade had relatively minor part in Saratoga battles, but led the ensuing pursuit; resigned, 1780, apparently because his vision and hearing had been impaired by a near-miss cannonball at Saratoga.

NOAILLES, LOUIS MARIE, VICOMTE DE. 1756–1804. French officer (Col.).

Member of aristocratic family; cousin of Lafayette's wife. Fought at Yorktown; represented French forces at the Yorktown surrender negotiations, October 17, 1781.

O'BRIEN, JEREMIAH. 1744–1818. American naval officer, privateer, customs collector.

Born in Kittery, Me. (then Massachusetts). Leader of the lumbermen who captured the British schooner *Margaretta* off Machias Bay, Me., June 12, 1775; commanded privateer *Resolution,* 1777, with which he captured the *Scarborough;* was captured along with his ship, *Hannibal,* 1780; escaped from Mill Prison, Plymouth, England; returned to America, 1781, and commanded privateers for remainder of war. Customs collector at Kittery, Me., 1811–1818.

O'HARA, CHARLES. 1740?–1802. British officer (Brig. Gen., local rank).

Served at Cowan's Ford, N.C., February 1, 1781; commanded the 2nd Battalion of Guards at Guilford Courthouse, and was instrumental in breaking the final resistance of Greene's army there; represented Cornwallis at the Yorktown surrender, October 17, 1781.

PARKER, SIR HYDE, JR. 1749–1807. British naval officer (Commodore, later Adm.).

Led raid to Tappan Sea (now Tappan Zee), July 12–18, 1776, and was knighted for it; saw action at Long Island; convoyed expedition and force that captured Savannah, Ga., December 29, 1778. His irresolution at Copenhagen and in the Baltic, 1801, were offset by Nelson's aggressiveness.

PARKER, JOHN. 1729–1775. Militia officer (Capt.), farmer, mechanic.

Born at Lexington, Mass. Captain of the local company of minutemen at Lexington common, April 19, 1775.

PARKER, SIR PETER. 1721–1811. British naval officer (Adm.).

Born in Ireland. Commanded naval contingent during Clinton's Charleston expedition of 1776; supported the New York campaign as a squadron commander, 1776; military commander at Jamaica, 1779–1781. Later succeeded Lord Howe as Admiral of the Fleet.

PARSONS, SAMUEL HOLDEN. 1737–1789. Continental officer (Maj. Gen.), lawyer, frontiersman.

Born at Lyme, Conn. Active pre-Revolution patriot; early advocate of intercolonial congress; brigadier general, 1776–1780; major general, 1780–1782; fought at Long Island; also at Kips Bay, September 15, 1776; conducted successful raid on Morrisania, N.Y., January 22–23, 1781. Went to Ohio after the war.

PATERSON (or PATTERSON), JAMES. British officer (Brig. Gen., local rank).

Adjutant general in America, 1776–1778; took Stony Point, N.Y., and Verplanck's Point, N.Y., June 1, 1779; participated in the Charleston expedition of 1780; wiped out an American force at Salkachatchie, S.C., March 8, 1780.

PEARSON, SIR RICHARD. 1731–1806. British naval officer.

Born in Lanton Hall, near Appleby, Westmoreland, England. Commanded the *Serapis* in its encounter with the *Bonhomme Richard* under John Paul Jones, September 23, 1779, off Flamborough Head; defeated in the hard-fought action.

PERCY, HUGH (also known as EARL PERCY). 1742–1817. British officer (Lt. Gen.).

Member of Parliament. Led the relief column that saved Col. Francis Smith's command after Lexington and Concord; division commander in the Battle of Long Island; also at the attack on Fort Washington, N.Y., November 16, 1776; served with Clinton in the occupation of Rhode Island, December 1776; assumed command of the Rhode Island post, 1777; became the Duke of Northumberland, 1778.

PHILLIPS, WILLIAM. 1731?–1781. British officer (Maj. Gen.).

Commander at Saint-Jean, Canada, July–December 1776; second-in-command to General Burgoyne at Montreal, December 1776, and in Burgoyne's offensive, 1777; distinguished himself at the capture of Ticonderoga, July 2–5, 1777, and at the first Battle of Saratoga; senior officer in the Convention Army (that surrendered at Saratoga); exchanged, October 13, 1780; commander in Virginia, March–May 1781; died at Petersburg, Va.

PICKENS, ANDREW. 1739–1817. Militia officer (Brig. Gen.), justice of the peace.

Born in Paxtang, Pa; settled with parents in South Carolina as a boy; a farmer before the Revolution. Fought at Ninety-six, S.C., November 1775; defeated Loyalists at the Battle of Kettle Creek, S.C., February 14, 1779; distinguished himself at the Cowpens, and received a sword from Congress for this action. Member, U.S. House of Representatives, South Carolina, 1793–1795.

PIGOT, SIR GEORGE. 1720–1796. British officer (Lt. Gen.).

Born in Patshull, Staffordshire, England. Lieutenant colonel of the 38th Foot, 1774; distinguished himself at Bunker's Hill in leading his regiment against the redoubt; commander in Rhode Island, 1777–1779; successfully defended Newport, July 29–August 31, 1778; became major general, 1777, and lieutenant general, 1782.

PINCKNEY, THOMAS. 1750–1828. Continental officer (Maj.), lawyer, statesman.

Born at Charleston, S.C.; member of distinguished South Carolina family. Served in various southern campaigns, 1774–1781. Governor of South Carolina, 1787–1789; minister to Great Britain, 1792–1796; negotiated "Pinckney's Treaty" of October 27, 1795 with Spain.

PITCAIRN, JOHN. 1722–1775. British officer (Capt. Royal Marines; local rank of major).

Born in Scotland. Second-in-command at Lexington and Concord; killed in action at Bunker's Hill.

PLESSIS, MADUIT DU, CHEVALIER DE. d. 1791. Continental officer (Lt. Col.).
French volunteer; artillery officer; distinguished himself at the battles of Brandywine, Germantown, and Fort Mercer (Red Bank), N.J., October 22, 1777; won the thanks of Congress for his performance.

PRESCOTT, WILLIAM. 1725–1795. Militia officer (Col.).
Born in Groton, Mass. A farmer, and minuteman commander before the Revolution; commanded the redoubt on the hill (Breed's Hill) at the battle of Bunker's Hill.

PREVOST, AUGUSTINE. 1723–1786. British officer (Maj. Gen.).
Born Geneva, Switzerland. Commanded British forces in East Florida, 1775; commanded all British forces in the South, 1778; performed outstandingly at Briar Creek, Ga., March 3, 1779, and in the defense of Savannah, Ga., October 9, 1779.

PREVOST, JAMES MARK (or MARC). British officer (Lt. Col.).
Distinguished himself at Briar Creek, Ga., March 3, 1779, where his brother, Maj. Gen. Augustine Prevost, commanded; appointed lieutenant governor of Georgia, March 1779, by British military authorities and served until July 1779.

PULASKI, CASIMIR, COUNT. c. 1748–1779. Continental officer (Brig. Gen.).
Born in Poland. Volunteer aide-de-camp to Washington at Brandywine; "Commander of the Horse," commanding the Continental dragoons, 1777–1778; organized Pulaski's Legion, 1778–1779; not a very effective commander; mortally wounded in a gallant but misguided cavalry charge at Savannah, Ga., October 9, 1779.

PUTNAM, ISRAEL. 1718–1790. Militia officer (Brig. Gen.), Continental officer (Maj. Gen.).

Born in Salem, Mass.; farmer and tavernkeeper before the Revolution; moved to Connecticut about 1740; won his military reputation in French and Indian War and Pontiac's War. Member, Sons of Liberty; present as a volunteer, shared command at Bunker's Hill with William Prescott; major general, 1775–1783; participated in the New York campaign of 1776; commanded the forces defeated at the Battle of Long Island; a fiery personality and inspiring symbol, but inept commander.

PUTNAM, RUFUS. 1738–1824. Militia officer (Lt. Col.), Continental officer (Brig. Gen.), engineer, surveyor, farmer, pioneer.

Born at Sutton, Mass. Worked on military engineering at siege of Boston; acting Chief Engineer of the army, 1776; worked on West Point defenses; brigadier general, January 1783; drew up Newburgh Petition of officer grievances, June 1783. Superintendent of the Ohio Company, 1788; first Surveyor General of the United States, 1796–1803; cousin of Israel Putnam.

RALL, JOHANN GOTTLEIB. c. 1720–1776. Hessian officer (Col.).

Born Hesse-Cassel. Fought well at White Plains and at Fort Washington, N.Y., November 16, 1776; commander of the outpost at Trenton, N.J., overrun by Washington, December 26, 1776; mortally wounded in the battle.

RAWDON-HASTINGS, FRANCIS (LORD RAWDON). 1754–1826. British officer (Lt. Col., Brigadier General, local rank).

Served at Bunker's Hill; aide-de-camp to General Clinton, 1778; adjutant general to Clinton, 1778–1779; distinguished himself in the Camden campaign, July–August 1780; was in command in South Carolina and Georgia, 1781; successful at Hobkirk's Hill, S.C., April 25, 1781, and Ninety-six, S.C., May–June 1781, but outmaneuvered by Greene; turned over his command to Col. Paston Gould, July 1781.

REED, JOSEPH. 1741–1785. American statesman, lawyer, Continental officer (Col.).

Born in Trenton, N.J. Continental officer, 1775–1777; Adjutant General in Washington's army, 1775–1777; declined appointment as brigadier general in 1777; delegate to the Continental Congress, 1777–1778; exposed attempt of George Johnstone (of Carlisle's peace commission) to bribe him and others in Congress, 1778; president of the Supreme Executive Council of Pennsylvania, 1778–1781; kept Washington informed of affairs in Continental Congress, 1777–1781; played a key role in settling the mutiny of the Pennsylvania Line, January 1781.

REVERE, PAUL. 1735–1818. Militia officer (Lt. Col.), silversmith.

Born in Boston, Mass.; noted silversmith. Made the famous "midnight ride" on the night of April 18–19, 1775, to warn of the British advance on Lexington and Concord; courier to Continental Congress for Massachusetts Provincial Assembly; served in the Penobscot (Me.) expedition, July–August 1779; acquitted by court-martial of alleged misconduct in that expedition.

RIEDESEL, BARON FRIEDRICH ADOLPH VON. 1738–1800. German officer (Lt. Gen., local rank).

Commander of the Brunswick contingent of German troops; took part in Burgoyne's offensive, 1777; distinguished himself at Hubbardton, Vt., July 7, 1777; and in both of the battles of Saratoga, N.Y., October 17, 1777; exchanged, October 13, 1780.

RIEDESEL, BARONESS FREDERICA VON. German writer.

Wife of Baron Friedrich Riedesel; accompanied her husband, with three young daughters, during his six years in America; wrote valuable memoirs of the experience.

ROCHAMBEAU, JEAN BAPTISTE DONATIEN DE VIMEUR, COMTE DE. 1725–1807. French officer (Lt. Gen.).

Born in Vendôme; distinguished himself during the Seven Years' War in the capture of Port Mahon, Minorca, 1745; at Crefeld, June 1758; and in saving the French from surprise attack at Clostercamp, October 1760; brigadier general, 1761, and also Inspector of Cavalry, in which post he carried out reforms in discipline, tactics, and troop welfare. Promoted to lieutenant general and made commander of the French Expeditionary Force in America, 1780; played important role as diplomat and strategist; assisted Washington in planning Yorktown campaign; marched four regiments from vicinity of New York to Yorktown; commanded French wing at siege of Yorktown. Became a Marshal of France, 1791; arrested during the Reign of Terror and narrowly escaped execution.

ROGERS, ROBERT. 1732–1795. Frontiersman, ranger leader, Loyalist officer.

Born in Methuen, Mass.; hero of French and Indian War; leader of Rogers's Rangers. Imprisoned on orders from General Washington, 1776, on suspicion of being a spy; escaped and was commissioned by the British to raise the Queen's American Rangers, 1776; led his men in a skirmish at Mamaroneck, N.Y. (near White Plains), October 22, 1776; no military duty after 1776.

ST. CLAIR, ARTHUR. 1737–1818. Continental officer (Maj. Gen.), landowner, statesman.

Born in Scotland; fought in French and Indian War; settled in Boston, 1762; moved to Pennsylvania frontier before the Revolution. Brigadier general, 1776–1777; commanded a brigade in Canadian expedition, 1775–1776; major general, 1777–1783; became commander on Lake Champlain, 1777; was forced to abandon Ticonderoga, July 5, 1777; held no further important commands during the Revolution. Delegate to the Continental Congress, Pennsylvania, 1785–1787; president of the Continental Congress, 1787; first governor of the Northwest Territory, 1789–1802; as major general commanding the U.S. Army, suffered disastrous defeat by Miami Indians, November 4, 1791.

ST. LEGER, BARRY. 1737–1789. British officer (Col.).
Famed for establishment of the St. Leger, English horseracing classic, 1776. Led expedition, June–September 1777, down the Mohawk Valley of New York as part of Burgoyne's offensive; principal engagements were those connected with the siege of Fort Stanwix, August 2–23, 1777, and the Oriskany ambush, August 6, 1777.

SALTONSTALL, DUDLEY. 1738–1796. Continental naval officer (Commodore).
Born in New London, Conn.; before the Revolution was a merchant and sea captain. A leader in the ill-fated Penobscot (Me.) expedition, July 22–August 14, 1779; court-martialed and dismissed from the Navy for his poor leadership at Penobscot Bay; later a successful privateer.

SCHUYLER, PHILIP JOHN. 1733–1804. Continental officer (Maj. Gen.).
Born in Albany, N.Y.; was a wealthy landowner. Commander of the Northern Department, 1775–1777; directed but did not personally participate in the Canada invasion of 1775–1776; relieved of command, after a bitter feud with Maj. Gen. Horatio Gates, August 4, 1777; delegate to the Continental Congress, New York, 1775–1777, 1778–1781.

SEVIER, JOHN. 1745–1815. Militia officer (Col.), statesman, farmer, trader, surveyor.
Born in New Market, Va. Colonel in the North Carolina militia; one of the leaders at the Battle of King's Mountain; led frontier militia in victory over the Tories and Indians at Lookout Mountain, Tenn., September 20, 1782. Member, U.S.

House of Representatives, North Carolina, 1789–1791, Tennessee, 1811–1815; first governor of Tennessee, 1796–1801.

SIMCOE, JOHN G. 1752–1806. British officer (Col.).

Born at Cotterstock, Northamptonshire, England. British commander of the Queen's Rangers, a Tory regiment; took part in the engagements at Quintain's Bridge, N.J., and Hancock's Bridge, N.J., March 1778, and at Stony Point, N.Y., June–July 1779; routed the militia defenders of Richmond, Va., January 1781. Became lieutenant governor of Upper Canada, 1791; lieutenant general, 1798.

SKINNER, JOHN. d. 1827. Loyalist, British officer.

New Jersey resident; joined the British Army, 1772. Served in the South during the Revolution; commanded a troop of Tarleton's British Legion ("Skinner's Horse") in the battles of Blackstocks, S.C., November 20, 1780, the Cowpens, and Guilford Courthouse; remained in the British Army and eventually became a general.

SMALLWOOD, WILLIAM. 1732–1792. Continental officer (Maj. Gen.), statesman.

Born in Charles Co., Md.; fought in French and Indian War; delegate to Maryland Assembly, 1761. Raised (1776) and commanded Smallwood's Maryland Battalion; wounded in effectively leading his men at White Plains; became brigadier general, October 23, 1776; sent south with de Kalb, 1780; did not distinguish himself at Camden, but succeeded to command of the remnants of de Kalb's Continental division after the battle; major general, 1780–1783. Governor of Maryland for three terms beginning in 1785.

SMITH, FRANCIS. 1723–1791. British officer (Maj. Gen.).

Lieutenant colonel and senior officer in Boston garrison in early 1775; commanded the expedition to Lexington and

Concord, April 19, 1775; major general, 1779; lieutenant general, 1787.

STARK, JOHN. 1728–1822. Militia officer (Col.), Continental officer (Brig. Gen.).

Born in New Hampshire; a farmer before the Revolution; fought in French and Indian War. Commanded militia regiment with distinction at Bunker's Hill; victor of the Battle of Bennington, August 16, 1777; cut off Burgoyne's last escape route, making certain complete American success at Saratoga, October 1777.

STEPHEN, ADAM. c. 1730–1791. Continental officer (Maj. Gen.).

Resident of Virginia; veteran of French and Indian War; brigadier general, 1776–1777; major general, 1777; endangered Washington's Trenton operations by sending unauthorized patrol across the Delaware, December 25, 1776; defeated at Piscataway, N.J., May 10, 1777, in an attempt to surprise the 42d Highlanders; dismissed, November 20, 1777, after being convicted of misconduct at the Battle of Germantown.

STEUBEN, FRIEDRICH WILHELM AUGUSTUS VON. 1730–1794. Continental officer (Maj. Gen.).

Born in Magdeburg, Prussia. Foreign volunteer, major general, 1778–1784; Inspector General of the Continental Army, 1778–1783; adapting his Prussian training and indoctrination to American circumstances, developed and carried out highly successful training program for Washington's army at Valley Forge, early 1778; took part in Virginia operations of 1781; settled in New York after the war.

STEVENS, EDWARD. 1745–1820. Militia officer (Maj. Gen.).

Born in Culpeper Co., Va. Commanded a brigade of Virginia militiamen at Camden; served with greater distinction in command of a different militia force at Guilford Courthouse; commanded a Virginia brigade under Lafayette at Yorktown.

STIRLING, WILLIAM ALEXANDER, LORD. 1726–1783. Continental
officer (Maj. Gen.), merchant.

Born in New York, N.Y.; a merchant before the Revolution.
Served in French and Indian War; failed to gain official British
recognition for his claim to the Scottish earldom of Stirling, but
was known as Lord Stirling in America. Brigadier general,
1776–1777; fought with distinction in the battles of Long
Island, Trenton, Brandywine, Monmouth; major general,
1777–1783; presided over the court-martial of Maj. Gen.
Charles Lee, July 4–August 12, 1778.

SUFFREN DE SAINT TROPEZ, PIERRE ANDRÉ DE. 1729–1788.
French naval officer (Adm.).

Distinguished himself at Newport, R.I., August 1778; later
defeated a British squadron at Porto Prayo, Azores, April 16,
1781, en route to a successful naval campaign in the Indian
Ocean; one of France's greatest admirals.

SULLIVAN, JOHN. 1740–1795. Continental officer (Maj. Gen.),
lawyer, statesman.

Born in Somersworth, N.H., or Maine. A leader of a group of
Patriot volunteers that took Fort William and Mary, Portsmouth, N.H., December 14, 1774; brigadier general, 1775–
1776; sent to reinforce the army invading Canada, 1776; and
took command upon the death of Maj. Gen. John Thomas;
defeated at Trois Rivières, June 8, 1776, and replaced by Maj.
Gen. Horatio Gates; major general, 1776–1779; was captured
at Long Island, August 27, 1776, but immediately exchanged;
played a significant role in the New Jersey campaign of 1776–
1777, especially at Trenton; led unsuccessful assault on Staten
Island, N.Y., August 22, 1777; fought at Brandywine and
Germantown; was commander in Rhode Island, 1778, during
unsuccessful Franco-American attack on Newport, July 29–
August 31, 1778; led expedition in upper New York State
against the Iroquois Indians, May–November 1779; delegate

to the Continental Congress, New Hampshire, 1774–1775, 1780–1781. Governor of New Hampshire, 1785–1790.

SUMTER, THOMAS. 1734–1832. Continental officer (Col.), militia officer (Brig. Gen.), statesman.

Born near Charlottesville, Va.; settled in South Carolina, 1765; was a storekeeper before the Revolution. Fought as Continental officer in Georgia and Florida, resigning in 1778; became partisan commander, 1780; noted for victories at Williamson's Plantation, S.C., July 12, 1780, and Hanging Rock, S.C., August 6, 1780; defeated by Tarleton at Fishing Creek, S.C., August 18, 1780. Member, U.S. House of Representatives, 1789–1793, 1797–1801; member, U.S. Senate, 1801–1810; last surviving general of the Revolution.

TARLETON, BANASTRE. 1754–1833. British officer (Lt. Col.), statesman.

Born in Liverpool, England. Commander of the British Legion, a Tory unit of dragoons and light infantry; won victories in South Carolina in 1780 at Monck's Corner, April 14, Lenund's Ferry, May 6, and Waxhaws, May 29; defeated Thomas Sumter at Fishing Creek, N.C., August 18, 1780; was defeated by Daniel Morgan at the Cowpens; conducted a raid on Charlottesville, Va., June 4, 1781, and another Virginia raid, July 9–24, 1781; was victor at Tarrant's Tavern, N.C., February 1, 1781; was probably the British officer most hated by patriot Americans. After the war was member of Parliament, 1790–1806, 1807–1812; was made a full general, 1812, and created baronet, 1815.

TEISSEDRE DE FLEURY, FRANÇOIS LOUIS. b. 1749. Continental officer.

Born in Provence, France. French volunteer; distinguished himself at Brandywine and at Stony Point, N.Y., July 1779; awarded one of eight medals presented by Congress during war.

TERNAY, CHARLES LOUIS D'ARSAC, CHEVALIER DE. 1722–1780.
French naval officer (Adm.).

Commanded fleet that accompanied Rochambeau's expeditionary force to America, 1780; died at Newport, December 12,
1780.

THOMAS, JOHN. 1724–1776. Continental officer (Maj. Gen.).

Born in Marshfield, Mass.; trained as a surgeon, practiced
medicine before the Revolution. Brigadier general, 1775–
1776; major general, 1776; in charge of the operation at
Dorchester Heights, Mass., March 2–27, 1776; sent to take
command of disaster-ridden Quebec expedition, March 1776;
died of smallpox after withdrawal to Sorel, June 2, 1776.

THOMPSON, WILLIAM. 1736–1781. Continental officer (Brig.
Gen.).

Born in Ireland; settled near Carlisle, Pa.; fought in French
and Indian War. Served on local committees of correspondence and safety; raised and commanded Thompson's Rifle
Battalion (later 1st Continental Infantry), 1775–1776; commanded American counterattack on Lechmere Point, Mass.,
November 9, 1775; commanded disastrous attack at Trois
Rivières, Canada, June 8, 1776.

TRONSON DE COUDRAY, PHILLIPPE CHARLES JEAN BAPTISTE. 1738–
1777. French officer (Chef de Brigade), Continental officer (Maj.
Gen.).

Born in Reims, France. As French officer, assembled French
matériel and advisers for American use before the alliance; as
a foreign volunteer, commissioned major general, Continental
Army, 1777; appointment brought resentment and threats of
resignation from senior American officers who had been passed
over; drowned accidentally, 1777.

TRYON, WILLIAM. 1725 or 1729–1788. British government official,
British officer (Lieut. Gen., local rank).

Born at Norbury Park, Surrey, England. Royal Lieutenant Governor of North Carolina, 1764–1765; royal Governor of North Carolina, 1765–1771; suppressed the Regulator movement, ultimately defeating the Regulators at the Battle of Alamance, May 16, 1771; royal governor of New York, 1771–1775; served in Revolution as British officer commanding Loyalist troops; as colonel, led the Danbury (Conn.) raid, April 1777; destroyed the patriot camp and supply depot called Continental Village, near Peekskill, N.Y., October 1777; led the Connecticut coast raid, July 1779; major general, 1778; lieutenant general, 1782.

VARNUM, JAMES M. 1748–1789. Continental officer (Brig. Gen.), militia officer (Maj. Gen.), lawyer, statesman.

Born in Dracut, Mass. Served as colonel at siege of Boston, 1775, and in battles of Long Island and White Plains; brigadier general, 1777–1779; responsible for defense of Fort Mercer, N.J., and Fort Mifflin, Pa., 1777, at time of their loss; took active part in Monmouth campaign; delegate to the Continental Congress, 1780–1782, 1786–1787.

WARD, ARTEMAS. 1727–1800. Continental officer (Maj. Gen.).

Born in Shewsbury, Mass.; was a jurist and militia officer before the Revolution. Major general, 1775–1776; commander-in-chief of troops in Massachusetts, 1775; commander, from his post at Cambridge, of patriot forces at the Battle of Bunker's Hill June 17, 1775; delegate to the Continental Congress, 1780–1781. Member, House of Representatives, 1791–1795.

WARNER, SETH. 1743–1784. Continental officer (Col.), militia officer (Brig. Gen.).

Born in Woodbury (now Roxbury), Conn. Moved to Bennington, Vt., 1763. A leader of the Green Mountain Boys, originally under Ethan Allen; aided in the capture of Fort Ticonderoga, N.Y., May 10, 1775; occupied Crown Point, N.Y.,

May 12, 1775; elected commander of the Green Mountain Boys when they became a Continental unit; led them in invasion of Canada, under Maj. Gen. Richard Montgomery, 1775; fought at Longueil, near Montreal, September 25, 1775; fought unsuccessful but commendable rearguard action at Hubbardton, Vt., July 7, 1777; played important role at Bennington, Vt., August 16, 1777; brigadier general in the Vermont militia, 1778.

WASHINGTON, GEORGE. 1732–1799. Continental general and commander-in-chief.

Born in Westmoreland Co., Va.; was a successful surveyor and landowner at twenty-one; commissioned major of Virginia militia in 1753; undertook a mission to the French commander at Fort Le Boeuf for Governor Dinwiddie of Virginia, 1753–1754; returned to alert the governor to French preparations for war (the French and Indian War); promoted to lieutenant colonel, was sent to reinforce frontier militiamen at the Forks of the Ohio (site of present-day Pittsburgh) but was forestalled by the French, who had established Fort Duquesne on the site; was overwhelmed by a much larger French force and surrendered Fort Necessity, the first important engagement of the French and Indian War; serving with General Edward Braddock on the disastrous expedition of 1755, helped to rally the survivors of the Battle of the Monongahela and to bring them back safely; promoted to colonel, made commander of all Virginia militia, and spent the rest of the French and Indian War protecting the Virginia frontier from Indian attack; a member of the House of Burgesses, 1759–1774; favored military preparations to protect colonists' rights. Delegate to the First and Second Continental Congresses, 1774, 1775. On June 15, 1775 was unanimously elected by Congress as "General and Commander-in-Chief of the army of the United Colonies"; forced the British to evacuate Boston, March 1776; ordered by Congress to hold New York (an impossible task); made serious errors in defending Long Island, August 1776;

skillfully managed the withdrawal to Manhattan after that defeat, and the long retreat, punctuated by battles, up Manhattan and through Westchester and New Jersey; particularly brilliant and daring were his strikes back across the Delaware River against Trenton, December 25–26, 1776, and Princeton, January 3, 1777, triumphs of tactics, logistics, and morale maintenance under overwhelming difficulties; recognizing vulnerability of Burgoyne's army, he transferred many of his best units and commanders to the northern theater, mid-1777; this decision, compounded by his own errors, led to defeat at Brandywine, September 11, 1777; he withdrew from Philadelphia, September 26, 1777; was defeated again at Germantown, October 4, 1777; withdrew to winter at nearby Valley Forge, Pa., where his men suffered severely but were effectively drilled by General von Steuben; meanwhile, thanks to his strategy and the reinforcements he sent to Gates's command in the North, Burgoyne was defeated at Saratoga by Gates and Arnold, assuring France's entry on the American side, and turning the tide of the Revolution; salvaged the Battle of Monmouth Courthouse, after Maj. Gen. Charles Lee's mismanagement had caused near-disaster; with the main action of the war then shifted to the South, he exercised overall strategic supervision, after Gates's defeat at Camden; he again saw strategic opportunity when French sea power briefly overbalanced that of Britain, and another British army appeared vulnerable in Virginia, August 1781; in coordination with Rochambeau, planned and executed a land and sea envelopment of General Cornwallis's British army at Yorktown, May–October 1781, the decisive action of the war; major credit for American victory in the Revolution is due to his skillful strategic management of a fundamentally defensive, delaying conflict, to his superb tactics on crucial occasions, and to his inspirational leadership. After the war Washington retired to Mount Vernon, his home near Alexandria, Va., but was soon forced out of retirement to preside over the federal Constitutional Convention (1787), and to become the first President of the United States.

WASHINGTON, WILLIAM. 1752–1810. Continental officer (Col.), statesman.

Born in Virginia. Wounded at Long Island; played significant role at Trenton; as a cavalry (dragoon) commander fought Tarleton in South Carolina, 1780; won impressive victories at Rugeley's Mill, S.C., December 4, 1780, and in his Hammond's Store (S.C.) raid, December 27–31, 1780; fought well at the Cowpens, Guilford Courthouse, and Hobkirk's Hill, S.C., April 25, 1781; wounded and captured at Eutaw Springs, S.C., September 8, 1781; a cousin of George Washington.

WAYNE, ANTHONY ("Mad Anthony"). 1745–1796. Continental officer (Brig. Gen.).

Born in Chester Co., Pa.; was a tanner and surveyor before the Revolution. Brigadier general, 1777–1783; commander of the Pennsylvania Line at Brandywine; was surprised at Paoli, Pa., September 21, 1777, by Maj. Gen. Charles Grey, but was acquitted of negligence; served prominently at Germantown; helped Washington salvage victory from defeat at Monmouth; won impressive victory at Stony Point, N.Y., July 16, 1779; handled mutiny of the Pennsylvania Line, January 1–10, 1781; won further distinction, despite defeat by overwhelming odds, at Jamestown Ford, Va., July 6, 1781; served at Yorktown. Member, U.S. House of Representatives from Georgia, 1791–1792; major general and commander-in-chief of the U.S. Army in the northwest, 1792–1796; victorious at the Battle of Fallen Timbers, August 20, 1794.

WICKES, LAMBERT. c. 1742–1777. Shipmaster, Continental naval officer (Capt.).

Born on Eastern Neck Island, Kent Co., Md. Given command of Continental brig *Reprisal* (16), 1776; took three prizes on his first cruise and defeated HMS *Shark* (16) off Saint Pierre, Martinique; conveyed Benjamin Franklin to France, October–November 1776, taking two prizes in the English Channel, January 1777; commanding three vessels, carried out successful raiding mission in Irish Sea, capturing eighteen small merchant vessels; by brilliant seamanship, escaped British ship of the line *Burford* (74) on return voyage to France; lost at sea off Newfoundland, October 1777.

WILKINSON, JAMES. 1757–1825. Continental officer (Brevet Brig. Gen.).

Born in Benedict, Md. Participated in Quebec expedition, 1775–1776; served as aide-de-camp to Brig. Gen. Benedict Arnold, 1776; served as aide-de-camp to Maj. Gen. Horatio Gates at the second Battle of Saratoga; brevet brigadier general, 1777–1778, a rank to which he was promoted solely because he carried to Congress Gates's dispatch reporting Burgoyne's surrender; resigned, 1778; Clothier General of the Continental Army, 1779; resigned again under a cloud because of financial irregularities. Brigadier general and second-in-command to Maj. Gen. Anthony Wayne in Indian fighting, 1792; succeeded Wayne as senior officer and nominal commander-in-chief, 1796; Governor of Louisiana, 1805; involved in Aaron Burr's conspiracy, but acquitted by a series of courts-martial; still Commanding General of the army at the outset of the War of 1812, he was promoted to major general, 1813; served with his customary lack of distinction; acquitted by a court of inquiry investigating charges of misconduct, 1815; honorably discharged, 1815; documents in Spanish archives later revealed he was an agent in the pay of the Spanish government during the time he commanded the United States Army; known as the general who "never won a battle and never lost a court-martial."

WILLETT, MARINUS. 1740–1830. Continental officer (Col.), merchant, landowner.

Born at New York, N.Y.; served in French and Indian War. Son of Liberty; helped foil a Tory plan to take arms from New York City, June 6, 1775; served under Maj. Gen. Richard

Montgomery in Canada invasion, 1775; led many campaigns in New York against Tories and Indians, 1776–1783.

WILLIAMS, OTHO HOLLAND. 1749–1794. Continental officer (Brig. Gen.).

Born in Prince Georges Co., Md. Served with distinction in southern campaigns under de Kalb, Gates, and Greene, 1780–1781; led Americans in skirmish with Cornwallis at Wetzell's (or Whitsall's) Mills, N.C., March 6, 1781; brigadier general, 1782–1783.

WOOLSEY, MELANCTHON LLOYD. d. 1819. Continental officer (Lt.).

Born at Middleburg, N.Y.; New York resident. Successfully repulsed 1,000 British, Tories, Hessians, and Indians, led by Joseph Brant and Sir John Johnson, October 15, 1780.

WOOSTER, DAVID. 1711–1777. Continental officer (Brig. Gen.), militia officer (Maj. Gen.), seaman.

Born at Stratford (now Huntington), Conn.; veteran of King George's War (1744–1745) and the French and Indian War. Brigadier general, 1775–1777; served in the Canada invasion, 1776; major general of Connecticut militia, 1776; killed in the Danbury, Conn., raid, May 2, 1777.

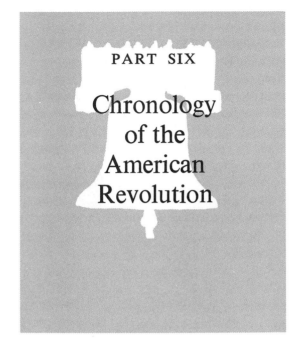

PART SIX

Chronology
of the
American
Revolution

1763
February 10   Treaty of Paris concludes Seven Years' War.
October 7   Proclamation of 1763.

1764
April 5   Parliament passes Sugar Act (or American Revenue Act).

1765
March 22   Stamp Act approved by Parliament.
March 24   Parliament's Quartering Act takes effect in North America.
May 29   Stamp Act Resolutions in Virginia.
October 7–25   Stamp Act Congress.

1766
March 18   Repeal of Stamp Act receives royal assent.
March 18   Declaratory Act approved by Parliament.

1767
June 29   Townshend Acts receive royal assent.

1768
February 11   Massachusetts resolution against Townshend Acts.
October 1   British troops land in Boston.

1769
May 16   Virginia Resolves against Townshend Acts.

1770
January 19   Battle of Golden Hill, New York City.

March 5	The Boston "Massacre."
April 12	Parliament repeals the Townshend Acts.
December 5	Boston Massacre soldiers acquitted, after defense by John Adams.

1771

May 16	Battle of Alamance Creek, N.C.

1772

June 9–10	*Gaspé* incident.
November 2	Committee of Correspondence organized in Boston by Samuel Adams and Joseph Warren.

1773

May 10	Parliament passes the Tea Act.
October 14	British cargo ship burned at Annapolis, Maryland.
October 16	Philadelphia citizens protest Tea Act.
November 27	New Yorkers organize to oppose tea shipments.
December 16	The Boston Tea Party.

1774

March 31	King George III signs the Boston Port Act, first "Coercive" or "Intolerable" Act.
May 13	General Gage arrives in Boston as military governor.
May 20	King George approves additional "Coercive" Acts.
May 24	Virginia protests Boston Port Act.
June 1	Boston Port Act goes into effect.
June 2	Parliament re-enacts Quartering Act; fourth "Coercive" or "Intolerable" Act.
June 10	Outbreak of Lord Dunmore's War.
June 22	Parliament passes Quebec Act; fifth "Intolerable" Act.
September 1	General Gage seizes colonists' powder at Charleston, Massachusetts.
September 5	First Continental Congress convenes in Philadelphia.
September 9	Suffolk Resolves.
October 14	First Continental Congress adopts a Declaration of Rights.
October 25	Congress approves Address to the King.
October 26	First Continental Congress adjourns.

1775

January 27	Gage authorized to use force to maintain royal authority in Massachusetts.
February 1	Parliament rejects William Pitt's "Plan for Conciliation with the Colonies."
March 22	Edmund Burke's Address on Conciliation with America in the House of Commons.
March 23	Patrick Henry delivers "Give me liberty or give me death" speech at Richmond, Virginia.
March 30	Royal assent given to New England Restraint Act.
April 18	General Gage orders expedition to Concord.
April 19	Battle of Lexington-Concord; siege of Boston begins after British retreat.
May 9–10	Capture of Fort Ticonderoga.
May 10	Second Continental Congress convenes at Philadelphia.
May 18	Capture of Saint-Jean, Quebec, by Benedict Arnold.
May 20	Mecklenburg (N.C.) Declaration of Independence.
May 24	John Hancock elected president of the Second Continental Congress.
June 11–12	Capture of HMS *Margaretta,* Machias, Maine.
June 12	General Gage proclaims martial law in Massachusetts.
June 15	Birth of the United States Army.
June 15	George Washington elected Commander-in-Chief of the Continental Army.
June 16	Washington accepts command at Philadelphia.
June 17	Battle of Bunker's Hill.
July 3	Washington on Cambridge Common assumes command of all Continental forces.
July 5	Congress adopts Olive Branch Petition.
July 25	Dr. Benjamin Church becomes the first surgeon general of Continental Army.
July 31	Congress rejects Lord North's plan for reconciliation.
August 8	Captain Daniel Morgan and his Virginia riflemen arrive in Cambridge.
August 23	Proclamation of Rebellion by George III.

September 1	Congress's Olive Branch Petition refused by the King.
September 2	General Washington commissions a naval force to interdict British supply vessels to Boston.
September 6	Siege of Saint-Jean, Canada, begins.
September 12	Start of Arnold's expedition to Quebec.
September 13	Brigadier General Richard Montgomery takes command of American besiegers of Saint-Jean.
September 18	Congress establishes the Secret Committee.
October 10	General Sir William Howe succeeds Gage as British commander in Boston.
October 13	Congress authorizes a navy.
October 19	New York Governor Tryon retires to HMS *Duchess of Gordon* in New York Harbor.
October 27	Surgeon General Dr. Benjamin Church tried and convicted of treason.
October 30	Congress authorizes two more ships for the Navy.
October 30	Naval committee appointed by Congress.
November 2	Capitulation of Saint-Jean, Canada, to General Montgomery.
November 5	Esek Hopkins appointed commodore of the Continental Navy squadron outfitting at Philadelphia.
November 8	Arnold's expedition reaches the St. Lawrence.
November 13	Americans under General Montgomery occupy Montreal.
November 15	Arnold occupies the Plains of Abraham.
December 3	General Montgomery with 300 men joins Arnold at Quebec.
December 3	First official American flag raised aboard Continental warship *Alfred*.
December 6	Congress answers the royal proclamation of rebellion of August 23.
December 8	Action at Edenton, North Carolina.
December 8–31	Siege of Quebec, Canada.
December 9	Battle of Great Bridge, Virginia.
December 23	Royal proclamation closes colonies to all commerce.
December 31	Battle of Quebec.

1776

January 1	George Washington hoists first national flag at Cambridge, Massachusetts.
January 5	New Hampshire adopts first written state constitution.
January 6	Founding of Alexander Hamilton's Provincial Company of Artillery of the Colony of New York.
January 9	Thomas Paine's *Common Sense* published in Philadelphia.
January 24	Colonel Henry Knox reaches Cambridge with 43 cannon and 16 mortars from Fort Ticonderoga.
February 17	First Continental Navy squadron puts to sea.
February 27	Battle of Moore's Creek Bridge.
March 3–4	Hopkins's raid on the Bahamas.
March 4–5	American occupation of Dorchester Heights, near Boston.
March 7	Action at Hutchinson's Island, Georgia.
March 9	Action at Nook's Hill, Massachusetts.
March 17	British evacuate Boston.
March 23	Congress authorizes privateering.
April 6	USS *Alfred* (24) vs HMS *Glasgow* (20).
April 6	Congress declares colonial ports open to all countries except Great Britain.
April 12	Halifax Resolves.
April 13	Washington and main army arrive in New York from Cambridge.
April 17	USS *Lexington* (16) vs HMS *Edward* (8).
May 1	Major General John Thomas takes over command of American forces at Quebec.
May 2	French clandestine support to colonials begins.
May 3	King George III appoints Admiral Lord Richard Howe and General Sir William Howe as peace commissioners.
May 4	Rhode Island declares independence from Britain.
May 6	Arrival of British reinforcements at Quebec; Americans driven away.
May 19	Action at the Cedars, Canada.

June 1	British expeditionary force appears off Charleston, South Carolina.
June 4	General Charles Lee arrives from New York to take command at Charleston, South Carolina.
June 7	Virginia delegate Richard Henry Lee introduces resolution for independence in Congress.
June 8	Battle of Trois Rivières, Canada.
June 11	Congress appoints a committee to draft a Declaration of Independence.
June 12–30	American retreat from Canada.
June 12	Congress creates a Board of War and Ordnance.
June 12	Virginia Convention adopts George Mason's Bill of Rights.
June 16	Action at Chambly, Canada.
June 20	General Assembly of Connecticut proclaims independence from Britain.
June 21	Discovery of Hickey "assassination plot" against Washington and others.
June 24	Action at Ile aux Noix, Canada.
June 25	British fleet arrives off Sandy Hook, New Jersey.
June 27	Thomas Hickey hanged as a traitor.
June 28	Battle of Sullivan's Island, South Carolina.
June 28	British joint expedition sails under Admiral Howe into New York Bay.
June 28	Thomas Jefferson presents his draft of the Declaration of Independence to Congress.
June 30	British occupy Staten Island, New York.
July 1	Congress, as a committee, approves Lee resolution on independence.
July 2	Congress votes for independence.
July 4	Declaration of Independence signed.
July 7	American withdrawal down Lake Champlain to Fort Ticonderoga.
July 9	New York City patriots pull down equestrian statue of George III in Bowling Green.
July 12	General Howe arrives from Halifax to join forces with his brother in New York harbor.
July 12–18	British warships sail up the Hudson.

July 12	Dickinson's Articles of Confederation and Perpetual Union presented to Congress.
July 15	Action at Rayborn Creek (Lyndley's Fort), South Carolina.
August 1	Sir Henry Clinton and his force arrive at Staten Island from Charleston.
August 22	British land on Long Island.
August 27	Battle of Long Island.
August 29–30	Washington evacuates Long Island.
September 6–7	First use of the submarine in war.
September 9	The name United States of America adopted by resolution of Congress.
September 11	Peace Conference on Staten Island.
September 15	Action at Kips Bay, New York.
September 16	Battle of Harlem Heights.
September 22	Nathan Hale executed by the British as an American spy.
September 23	Action at Montressor's (now Randall's) Island, New York.
October 11–12	Battle of Valcour Island, Lake Champlain.
October 12–13	Battle of Throg's Neck, New York.
October 14	Action at Crown Point, Lake Champlain, New York.
October 18	Action at Pell's Point (New Rochelle), New York.
October 18	Polish volunteer Thaddeus Kosciusko commissioned a colonel of engineers by Congress.
October 22	Action at Mamaroneck, New York.
October 23	Washington completes evacuation of Manhattan.
October 28	Battle of White Plains, New York.
November 3	British General Carleton abandons Crown Point, New York.
November 16	Battle of Fort Washington, New York.
November 19–20	British night crossing of Hudson River at Closter, New Jersey.
November 21	Washington begins retreat across New Jersey to the Delaware River.
November 28	British occupy Newark, New Jersey.
December 1	Action at Brunswick, New Jersey.

December 2	General Charles Lee crosses the Hudson into New Jersey at North Castle.
December 3	Washington arrives at Trenton, New Jersey.
December 7	Action at Tappan, New York.
December 8	British occupy Newport, Rhode Island.
December 13	British army goes into winter quarters in New York and New Jersey.
December 13	British patrol captures General Charles Lee.
December 17	Action at Springfield, New Jersey.
December 19	Publication of Thomas Paine's *American Crisis*.
December 26	Battle of Trenton.
December 27	Congress grants dictatorial power to General Washington, and resolves to raise sixteen regiments "at large."
December 29	Washington again crosses Delaware to occupy Trenton.

1777

January 1	Victory march in Philadelphia.
January 1	Cornwallis reaches Princeton in advance toward Trenton.
January 1	Benjamin Franklin appointed commissioner to France.
January 2	Action at Trenton.
January 3	Battle of Princeton.
January 6	Washington goes into winter quarters at Morristown, New Jersey.
January 16	New Hampshire Grants (present-day Vermont) declare independence.
January 17–29	Fiasco at Fort Independence, King's Bridge, New York.
January 28	General John Burgoyne in London submits a campaign plan for 1777; approved by Lord Germain.
February 2–4	Action at Fort McIntosh, Georgia.
March 3	Lord Germain approves General Howe's campaign plan for 1777.
March 13	Congress requests agents in Europe to recruit qualified foreign military experts.

March 16	Action at Peeksill, New York.
April 13	Action at Bound Brook, New Jersey.
April 19	Action at Woodbridge, New Jersey.
April 26	British raid Danbury, Connecticut.
May 6	General Burgoyne arrives in Quebec to command British forces in Canada.
May 10	Action at Piscataway, New Jersey.
May 23	American raid at Sag Harbor, Long Island, New York.
May 28	Washington advances from Morristown to Middlebrook Valley, to begin campaign of maneuver against Howe.
June 14	Stars and Stripes adopted by Congress as American flag.
June 14	John Paul Jones appointed captain of USS *Ranger*.
June 16	Burgoyne's advance guard occupies Crown Point, New York.
June 17	Action at Millstone (Somerset Courthouse), New Jersey.
June 17	Burgoyne's main body starts south, via Lake Champlain, from Saint-Jean, Quebec.
June 22	Action at Brunswick, New Jersey.
June 26	Action at Short Hills (Metuchen), New Jersey.
June 26	Lambert Wickes's *Reprisal* pursued by HMS *Burford*.
June 30	Burgoyne's army begins disembarking near Fort Ticonderoga.
June 30	General Howe withdraws British troops from New Jersey to New York City and Staten Island.
July 6	British occupy Fort Ticonderoga, New York.
July 7	Battle of Hubbardton, Vermont.
July 8	Vermont convention at Windsor adopts a written constitution as independent republic.
July 8	Action at Fort Anne, New York.
July 23	General Howe sails from New York with 15,000 troops.
July 25	Murder of Jane McCrea, near Fort Edward, New York.

July 25	Colonel Barry St. Leger advances from Oswego.
July 27	Arrival of Marquis de Lafayette and "Baron" Johann de Kalb at Philadelphia.
July 29	General Philip Schuyler evacuates Fort Edward, New York.
July 31	Congress commissions Lafayette a major general.
August 3	St. Leger invests Fort Stanwix, New York.
August 4	General Horatio Gates replaces General Schuyler as commander of the Continental Army of the North.
August 6	Battle of Oriskany, New York.
August 7	Colonel Peter Gansevoort rejects St. Leger's demand for surrender of Fort Stanwix.
August 10	Benedict Arnold leads relief expedition for Fort Stanwix from Stillwater.
August 16	Battle of Bennington, Vermont (fought entirely in New York).
August 21–22	American raid on Staten Island, New York.
August 22	St. Leger abandons siege of Fort Stanwix.
August 25	Howe's army disembarks at Head of Elk, Maryland.
September 1	Siege of Fort Henry (Wheeling), Virginia (present-day West Virginia).
September 3	Action at Iron Hill (Cooch's Bridge), Delaware.
September 11	Battle of the Brandywine, Pennsylvania.
September 13	Burgoyne crosses the Hudson.
September 14	Lambert Wickes begins his final cruise in the *Reprisal*.
September 15	Congress commissions de Kalb a major general.
September 16	Action at Admiral Warren Tavern (White Horse Tavern), near Malvern, Chester Co., Pennsylvania.
September 18	Congress adjourns at Philadelphia, flees westward as British approach.
September 18–24	American raid on Lake George area.
September 19	First Battle of Saratoga (or Freeman's Farm), New York.
September 20–21	Battle of Paoli, Pennsylvania ("Paoli Massacre").
September 23	Action at Diamond Island, New York.
September 26	British occupy Philadelphia.

September 30	Congress convenes at York, Pennsylvania; adjourns immediately.
October 3	Clinton leads a British expedition from New York up the Hudson.
October 4	Battle of Germantown, Pennsylvania.
October 6	Clinton captures Forts Clinton and Montgomery on the Hudson; turns back to New York.
October 7	Second Battle of Saratoga (or Bemis Heights), New York.
October 17	Burgoyne surrenders at Saratoga (now Schuylerville), New York.
October 22	British attack on Fort Mercer (Red Bank), New Jersey.
October 23	Battle of Fort Mifflin, Pennsylvania.
November 2	John Paul Jones commanding USS *Ranger* (18) sails from Portsmouth, New Hampshire.
November 3	Washington learns of the Conway Cabal.
November 15	Evacuation of Fort Mifflin, Pennsylvania.
November 15	Articles of Confederation and Perpetual Union adopted by Congress.
November 20–22	Battle of Fort Mercer (Red Bank), New Jersey.
November 27	Congress names Gates president of the Board of War.
November 28	John Adams appointed commissioner to France.
December 2	John Paul Jones and the USS *Ranger* reach Nantes, France.
December 5–8	British sortie from Philadelphia.
December 11	Washington leaves Whitemarsh for Valley Forge.
December 11	Action at Gulph's Mills, Pennsylvania (Matson's Ford).
December 19	Washington goes into winter quarters at Valley Forge, Pennsylvania.
1778	
January 5	The "Battle of the Kegs," Delaware River.
January 8	France decides to enter alliance with the United States.
January 27	American raid on Nassau, Bahamas.

February 6	Franco-American Treaty of Commerce and Treaty of Alliance signed in Paris.
February 9	End of the Conway Cabal.
February 17	Lord North presents a plan for conciliation with the colonies to Parliament.
February 23	Lieutenant General Baron Friedrich Wilhelm von Steuben arrives at Valley Forge.
March 7	Clinton ordered to relieve Howe as British commander-in-chief.
March 7	USS *Randolph* (32) vs HMS *Yarmouth* (64); death of Nicholas Biddle.
March 16	Lord North's plan for conciliation with the colonies is adopted.
March 20	King Louis XVI of France receives Franklin, Deane, and Lee.
March 21	Action at Hancock's Bridge, New Jersey.
April 17	Action at Bristol, Pennsylvania.
April 22–23	John Paul Jones's raid on Whitehaven, England.
April 24	USS *Ranger* (18) vs HMS *Drake* (20).
May 5	Von Steuben appointed Inspector General of the Continental Army.
May 8	Action at Bordentown, New Jersey.
May 11	General Clinton succeeds General Howe as British commander-in-chief.
May 20	Action at Barren Hill, Pennsylvania.
May 31	Action at Tiverton, Rhode Island.
June 6	British Peace Commission arrives in Philadelphia.
June 17	Outbreak of war between France and England.
June 18	British evacuate Philadelphia.
June 28	Battle of Monmouth Courthouse (Freehold), New Jersey.
June 30	Action at Alligator Bridge, Florida.
July 2	Congress convenes at Philadelphia.
July 3–4	Wyoming Valley "Massacre."
July 4–5	Colonel George Rogers Clark occupies Kaskaskia, Illinois.
July 8	Arrival of Comte d'Estaing's French fleet in Delaware Bay.

July 20	George Rogers Clark's troops occupy Vincennes, Indiana.
July 30	Washington blockades New York at White Plains.
August 8	Sullivan and d'Estaing begin joint operation against Newport, Rhode Island.
August 29	Battle of Newport (Tiverton, Quaker Hill), Rhode Island.
September 5–8	British amphibious raids on Massachusetts coast.
September 13	Indian and Tory raid at German Flats (now Herkimer), New York.
September 14	Congress elects Benjamin Franklin Minister to France.
September 16	Action at Saw Mill River (Westchester), New York.
September 26–28	Action at Fort Henry (Wheeling), Virginia (present-day West Virginia).
September 28	Tappan Massacre.
October 6–8	American raid on Indian town of Unadilla, New York.
October 15	British raid at Mincock Island (Egg Harbor), New Jersey.
November 11	Cherry Valley Massacre.
November 19	Action at Spencer's Hill (Bulltown Swamp), Georgia.
November 24	Action at Medway Church, Georgia.
November 27	British commissioners leave New York for England.
December 10	John Jay elected president of Congress.
December 11	Washington goes into winter quarters at Middlebrook, New Jersey.
December 17	British Colonel Hamilton recaptures Vincennes, Indiana.
December 20	Battle of Savannah; British occupy Savannah.

1779	
January 6–9	Actions at Fort Morris (Sunbury), Georgia.
January 29	Action at Augusta, Georgia.
February 3	Action at Beaufort, Port Royal Island, South Carolina.
February 4	John Paul Jones takes command of USS *Bonhomme Richard* (40).

February 10	Action at Car's Fort, Georgia.
February 14	Action at Cherokee Ford, South Carolina.
February 14	Battle of Kettle Creek, Georgia.
February 23–25	Clark retakes Vincennes, Indiana.
March 3	Battle of Briar Creek, Georgia.
April 3	Spanish ultimatum to Britain.
April 12	Convention of Aranjuez.
April 20	American raid on Onondaga Indians, New York.
May 9	British raid on Norfolk, Virginia.
May 11	British General Prevost advances from Savannah to threaten Charleston, South Carolina.
May 21	British raid on North Kingstown, Rhode Island.
June 1	Sir Henry Clinton starts offensive up the Hudson River, New York.
June 20	Battle of Stono Ferry, South Carolina.
June 21	Spain declares war against Great Britain.
June 28	Action at Hickory Hill, Georgia.
July 2	Actions at Bedford and Pound Ridge, New York.
July 5–11	British Connecticut coast raid.
July 15–16	Battle of Stony Point, New York.
July 21– August 20	Penobscot Expedition, Maine.
July 22	Battle of Minisink, New Jersey.
July 31– September 30	Sullivan's expedition in Genesee Valley, New York, area.
August 5	Action at Morrisania (now the Bronx), New York.
August 14	John Paul Jones and USS *Bonhomme Richard* sail from Lorient.
August 19	American raid on Paulus Hook (Jersey City), New Jersey.
August 27– September 21	Spanish expedition into British West Florida; Gálvez captures Manchac, Natchez, and Baton Rouge.
August 29	Battle of the Chemung River (Battle of Newton), New York.
August 30	Action at Tarrytown, New York.
September 5	American raid at Lloyd's Neck, Long Island, New York.
September 11–14	Brodhead's Allegheny Valley expedition.

September 14	American squadron destroyed in Penobscot Bay by British fleet.
September 16	Allied blockade of Savannah, Georgia.
September 23	Siege of Savannah begins.
September 23	USS *Bonhomme Richard* (40) vs HMS *Serapis* (44).
October 4	Indian ambush at Licking River, Kentucky.
October 9	British repulse allied assault on Savannah.
October 11–25	British evacuate Rhode Island.
October 20	Allies abandon siege of Savannah.
October 26	Action at Brunswick, New Jersey.
November 7	Action at Jefferd's Neck, New York.
December 1	Washington's army goes into winter quarters at Morristown, New Jersey.
December 26	General Clinton sails from New York with British expedition to South Carolina.
1780	
January 11	Mutiny of the Massachusetts Line at West Point, New York.
January 14–15	American raid on Staten Island.
January 18	Action at Eastchester, New York.
January 25	British raid on Newark and Elizabeth, New Jersey.
January 26	Court-martial directs reprimand of Maj. Gen. Benedict Arnold, commanding Philadelphia, for minor financial irregularities.
February 1	Clinton's expedition arrives off Charleston, South Carolina.
February 11	Clinton's expedition lands on Johns Island, near Charleston.
March 8	Action at Salkahatchie, South Carolina.
March 14	Spanish capture Mobile, British West Florida.
March 23	Action at Pon Pon, South Carolina.
March 27	Action at Rentowl, South Carolina.
April 6	Washington officially reprimands Arnold as result of court-martial verdict of January 26.
April 10	British siege of Charleston begins.
April 14	Action at Monck's Corner (Biggins's Bridge), South Carolina.

April 15	Action at New Bridge, New Jersey.
April 16	Action at Paramus, New Jersey.
May 6	Action at Lanneau's (Lenud's) Ferry, South Carolina.
May 7	Surrender of Fort Moultrie, South Carolina.
May 12	Surrender of Charleston to the British.
May 22	Tory and Indian raid at Caughnawaga, New York.
May 22–23	Tory and Indian raid at Johnstown, New York.
May 25	Mutiny of the Connecticut Line at Morristown, New Jersey.
May 26	Spanish repulse British expedition at St. Louis, Missouri.
May 29	Massacre of the Waxhaws, Waxhaws Creek, South Carolina.
June 6	Action at Elizabethtown (Elizabeth), New Jersey.
June 7–8	Action at Connecticut Farms (Union), New Jersey.
June 13	Gates appointed by Congress to command Southern Army.
June 20	Action at Ramsour's Mills, North Carolina.
June 23	Battle of Springfield, New Jersey.
July 10	Count de Rochambeau and 6,000 French troops arrive from France at Newport, Rhode Island.
July 14	Action at Pacolett River, North Carolina.
July 20	Action at Flat Rock, South Carolina.
July 25	Gates takes command of Southern Army at Coxe's Mill, North Carolina.
July 27	Gates advances south toward South Carolina.
July 30	Capture of Fort Anderson (Thicketty Fort), South Carolina.
August 1	Battle of Rocky Mount, South Carolina.
August 1	Action at Green Springs, South Carolina.
August 2	Indian and Tory raid on Fort Plain, New York.
August 5	Arnold assumes command at West Point.
August 6	Battle of Hanging Rock, South Carolina.
August 15	Action at Fort Carey (Wateree Ferry), South Carolina.
August 15–16	Action at Gum Swamp, South Carolina.
August 16	Battle of Camden, South Carolina.
August 18	Battle of Fishing Creek, South Carolina.

August 27	Action at Kingstree, South Carolina.
September 20–24	Washington-Rochambeau Conference at Hartford, Connecticut.
September 21	Arnold meets Major John André near Haverstraw, New York.
September 23	André's capture.
September 25	Arnold flees.
October 2	Major André hanged as spy at Tappan, New York.
October 7	Battle of King's Mountain, South Carolina.
October 11	Action at Fort George (Fort William Henry), New York.
October 14	Cornwallis withdraws to winter quarters at Sinnsborough, South Carolina.
October 14	Congress appoints Greene to command Southern Department, on Washington's recommendations.
October 17	British, Tory, and Indian raid on Schoharie, New York.
October 19	Battle at Fort Keyser (or Stone Arabia), New York.
October 19	Battle of Klock's Field, New York.
October 26	Action at Black River (Tearcoat Swamp), South Carolina.
October 29	Action at German Flats, New York.
November 4	Congress asks states for war support quotas.
November 15–16	Action at Georgetown, South Carolina.
November 20	Battle of Blackstocks (Tiger River), South Carolina.
November 30	Creation of Lee's Legion.
December 2	Greene assumes command of the Southern Department at Charlotte, North Carolina.
December 4	Action at Rugeley's Mill, South Carolina.
December 9	Action at Horseneck, Connecticut.
December 19	Greene advances into South Carolina.
December 20	Great Britain declares war on the Netherlands.
December 27–31	American raid at Williamson's Plantation, South Carolina.
December 30	British Brig. Gen. Benedict Arnold arrives at Hampton Roads with expedition to Virginia.

1781

January 1–10	Mutiny of the Pennsylvania Line.
January 3	Action at Hood's Point (James River), Virginia.
January 5–7	British raid on Richmond, Virginia.
January 8	British raid on Charles City Courthouse, Virginia.
January 17	Battle of the Cowpens, South Carolina.
January 19	Cornwallis advances north to get between Greene's and Morgan's armies.
January 19	Action in Georgetown County, South Carolina.
January 20	Mutiny of the New Jersey Line at Pompton, New Jersey.
January 22	American raid at Morrisania, New York.
January 24	Action at Georgetown, South Carolina.
January 30	Morgan and Greene join forces at the Catawba River, retreat north, pursued by Cornwallis.
February 1	Battle of the Catawba River (Cowan's Ford), North Carolina.
February 1	British occupy Wilmington, North Carolina.
February 1	Action at Torrence's (Tarrant's) Tavern, North of Charlotte, North Carolina.
February 14	Greene crosses the Dan River to escape Cornwallis.
February 18	Lee's Legion crosses Dan River, spearhead of Greene's return to North Carolina.
February 25	Battle of Haw River (Pyle's Defeat), North Carolina.
February 27	Action at Wright's Bluff, South Carolina.
March 1	Ratification of Articles of Confederation.
March 2	Action at Clapp's Mill, North Carolina.
March 6	Action at Wetzell's (or Whitsall's) Mill, North Carolina.
March 15	Battle of Guilford Courthouse, North Carolina.
March 16	First naval Battle of the Virginia Capes.
April 2	USS *Alliance* (36) vs HMS *Mars* (22) and HMS *Minerva* (10).
April 12	Action at Fort Balfour, South Carolina.
April 15–23	Siege of Fort Watson, South Carolina.
April 16–	Americans begin siege of Augusta, Georgia.
April 25	Battle of Hobkirk's Hill, South Carolina.
April 25	Action at Camden, South Carolina.

April 25	Cornwallis marches northward into Virginia from Wilmington with 1,500 men.
April 25	Action at Petersburg, Virginia.
April 25	Action at Hillsborough, North Carolina.
April 27	Lafayette with 1,200 Continentals reaches Richmond.
May 9	Spanish under Gálvez capture Pensacola.
May 10	British evacuate Camden, South Carolina.
May 10	British occupy Petersburg, Virginia.
May 14	Tory raid at Croton River, South Carolina.
May 14	Action at Nelson's Ferry, South Carolina.
May 20	Washington sends Wayne with 1,000 Continentals to join Lafayette in Virginia.
May 20	Cornwallis arrives at Petersburg, Virginia, assumes command.
May 21	Capture of Fort Galphin (Fort Dreadnought), Georgia.
May 21–24	Washington-Rochambeau conference at Wethersfield, Connecticut.
May 22–June 19	Greene's siege of Ninety-six, South Carolina.
May 29	USS *Alliance* (36) vs HMS *Atalanta* (16) and HMS *Trepassy* (14).
June 4	British raid on Charlottesville, Virginia.
June 5	Surrender of Augusta, Georgia, to Americans.
June 5	British raid at Point of Fork, Virginia.
June 10	Wayne and reinforcements join Lafayette in Virginia.
June 15	Congress appoints peace commission.
June 26	Action at Spencer's Tavern, Virginia.
July 3	Action at King's Bridge, New York.
July 5	Rochambeau's French army joins Washington's forces above New York.
July 6	Battle of Green Spring (Jamestown Ford), Virginia.
July 9	Tory and Indian raid at Currytown, New York.
July 15	Action at Tarrytown, New York.
July 17	Action at Quinby's Bridge, South Carolina.
August 5	Cornwallis occupies Yorktown and Gloucester Point on the York River, Virginia.
August 6	Defense of Shell's Bush, New York.

August 8	USS *Trumbull* (38) vs HMS *Iris* (32) and HMS *General Monk* (20).
August 13	Action at Parker's Ferry, South Carolina.
August 13	De Grasse's French fleet sails from Haiti for Chesapeake Bay.
August 25	Washington begins march south toward Virginia.
August 25	French squadron under Admiral de Barras sails from Newport, Rhode Island, for Chesapeake Bay.
August 25	Lochry's Defeat, Ohio River.
August 26	Comte de Grasse with French fleet arrives in Chesapeake Bay.
August 31	French troops land near Jamestown.
September 5–9	Battle of the Capes.
September 6	British raid New London, Connecticut.
September 7	Indian raid at Fort Plain, New York.
September 8	Battle of Eutaw Springs, South Carolina.
September 13	Tory raid on Hillsboro, North Carolina.
September 14–24	French fleet ferries allied armies down Chesapeake Bay.
September 17–18	Washington-de Grasse conference.
September 28	Allied advance on Yorktown.
September 30	Allied siege of Yorktown begins.
October 3	Action at Gloucester, Virginia.
October 10	American raid at Treadwell's Neck (Fort Slongo), New York.
October 16	Action at Monck's Corner, South Carolina.
October 16	British sortie from Yorktown.
October 16–17	British effort to evacuate Yorktown via Gloucester fails.
October 19	"The world turned upside down," Cornwallis's surrender at Yorktown.
October 20–30	British, Tory, and Indian raid in Mohawk Valley, New York.
October 25	Action at Johnson Hall (Johnstown), New York.
November 9	Action at Hayes's Station, South Carolina.
November 18	British evacuate Wilmington, North Carolina.

1782

March 4	Action at Morrisania, New York.

April 1	Washington establishes headquarters at Newburgh.
April 4	Sir Guy Carleton is appointed British commander-in-chief in America.
April 12	Peace talks begin in Paris.
April 24	Action at Dorchester, South Carolina.
May 9	Sir Guy Carleton arrives in New York to take command.
June 4–5	Action at Sandusky, Ohio (Crawford's defeat).
July 11	Savannah, Georgia, evacuated by British.
August 15	Indian and Tory raid on Bryan's Station, Kentucky.
August 19	Battle of Blue Licks, Kentucky.
September 11–12	Siege of Fort Henry, Virginia (present-day West Virginia).
September 20	Action at Lookout Mountain, Tennessee.
November 30	Provisional treaty of peace signed in Paris.
December 14	Charleston, South Carolina, evacuated by the British.

1783

January 20	Cessation of hostilities signed by British and U.S. commissioners.
January 20	Peace between Britain and France, and Britain and Spain.
February 4	Britain formally proclaims cessation of hostilities.
March 10	USS *Alliance* (36) vs HMS *Sybil* (32).
March 10	First Newburgh Address.
March 12	Second Newburgh Address.
March 15	Washington addresses the Continental officers at Newburgh.
April 11	Congress proclaims end of the war.
April 15	Congress ratifies provisional treaty of peace.
June 17	Mutinous soldiers threaten Congress.
September 3	Treaties of Paris and of Versailles.
November 2	Washington's "Farewell Address to the Army."
November 3	Army disbands by Congressional order.
November 25	British evacuation of New York City.
December 4	British complete evacuation of Staten Island and Long Island.

December 4   Washington bids farewell to his officers at Fraunces
                Tavern, New York.

December 23   Washington returns to civilian life. He resigns his
                commission as Commander-in-Chief before Con-
                gress at Annapolis.

Bibliography

Abbot, Willis J. *The Naval History of the United States.* New York, 1896.

Albion, Robert G. *Forests and Sea Power.* Cambridge, 1926.

Alden, John R. *The American Revolution.* New York, 1954.

Allen, G. W. *Naval History of the Revolution.* 2 vols. Boston, 1913.

American Revolution in New York, The. Albany: University Division of Archives and History of the State of New York, 1926.

Anburey, Thomas. *Travels Through the Interior Parts of America.* 2 vols. London, 1789.

Bakeless, John. *Turncoats, Traitors and Heroes.* Philadelphia, 1959.

Balch, Thomas. *The French in America.* Philadelphia, 1895.

Belcher, Henry. *The First American Civil War.* 2 vols. London, 1911.

Belloff, Max, ed. *The Debate on the American Revolution, 1761–1783.* New York, 1960.

Bemis, Samuel Flagg. *The Diplomacy of the American Revolution.* Bloomington, 1935.

Berg, Fred A. *Encyclopedia of Continental Army Units.* Harrisburg, 1972.

Blanchard, Claude. *The Journal of Claude Blanchard* (translation of William Duane). Albany, 1876.

Blumenthal, Walter Hart. *Women Camp Followers of the American Revolution.* Philadelphia, 1952.

Boatner, Mark M., III. *Encyclopedia of the American Revolution.* New York, 1966.

Bolton, Charles Knowles. *The Private Soldier under Washington.* New York, 1902.

Bonsal, Stephen. *When the French Were Here.* Garden City, 1945.

Bowen, Catherine. *The Miracle at Philadelphia.* Boston, 1966.

Bowman, Allen. *The Morale of the American Revolutionary Army*. Washington, D.C., 1943.

Burgoyne, John. *A State of the Expedition from Canada, as Laid Before the House of Commons*. London, 1780.

Callahan, North. *Royal Raiders: The Tories of the American Revolution*. New York, 1963.

Chapelle, Howard I. *The American Sailing Navy*. New York, 1949.

Clinton, Henry. *The American Rebellion* (William B. Willcox, ed.). New Haven, 1954.

Commager, Henry S. and Morris, Richard B., eds. *The Spirit of 'Seventy-Six*. 2 vols. Indianapolis, 1958.

Dupuy, R. Ernest. *Battle of Hubbardton* (monograph). Montpelier, 1960.

———. *The National Guard*. New York, 1971.

Dupuy, R. Ernest and Dupuy, Trevor N. *The Compact History of the Revolutionary War*. New York, 1963.

———. *Encyclopedia of Military History*. New York, 1970.

Dupuy, Trevor N. *The Military Life of George Washington*. New York, 1969.

Dupuy, Trevor N., and Hammerman, Gay M. *Revolutionary War Land Battles*. New York, 1970.

Dupuy, Trevor N., and Hayes, Grace P. *Revolutionary War Naval Battles*. New York, 1970.

Eelking, Max von, ed. *Memoirs, and Letters and Journals of Major General Riedesel* (translated by William L. Stone). 2 vols. Albany, 1868.

Esposito, Vincent J., ed. *The West Point Atlas of American Wars*. New York, 1959.

Farmer, J. S. *Regimental Records of the British Army*. London, 1901.

Fortesque, Sir John W. *A History of the British Army*. 13 vols. London, 1899–1930.

Fraser, Simon. "General Fraser's Account of Burgoyne's Campaign on Lake Champlain." *Proceedings*. Montpelier, 1898.

Freeman, Douglas S. *George Washington*. 6 vols. New York, 1948–1954.

Frost, Halloway H. *We Build a Navy*. New York, 1929.

Galvin, John R. *The Minute Men,* New York, 1967.

Gayaré, Charles. *History of Louisiana*. New York, 1854.

Heitman, Francis B. *Historical Register and Dictionary of the U.S. Army*. Washington, D.C., 1903.

Hough, Frank O. *Renown*. New York, 1938.

Klein, Randolph. Document 537, 50th Congress, First Session. Washington, D.C., 1907.

Knox, Dudley A. *A History of the U.S. Navy*. New York, 1936.

Lawrence, Archer, J. G. *The British Army*. London, 1888.

Lewis, Michael. *The Navy of Britain*. London, 1948.

Lossing, Benson J. *The Pictorial Field Book of the American Revolution*. New York, 1851.

————. *History of the American Revolution*. New York, 1865.

Lowell, Edward J. *The Hessians* (reprint of 1884 edition). Port Washington, 1965.

Mahan, Alfred T. *The Influence of Sea Power Upon History*. Boston, 1890.

Marcus, G. J. *A Naval History of England*. Vol. 1, *The Formative Centuries*. Boston, 1961.

Moore, Frank. *The Diary of the American Revolution, 1775–1781* (John A. Scott, ed.). New York, 1967.

Morison, Samuel Eliot. *John Paul Jones*. Boston. 1959.

————. *Sources and Documents Illustrating the American Revolution, 1764–1788*. Oxford, 1923.

Morris, Richard B. *The Peacemakers*. New York, 1965.

————. *The American Revolution, 1763–1783*. Columbia, S.C., 1970.

Morse, Jeddiah, ed. *Annals of the American Revolution*. Hartford, 1824.

Naval Records of the American Revolution, 1775–1788. Washington, D.C., 1906.

Nickerson, Hoffman. *The Turning Point of the Revolution*. Boston, 1928.

Scheer, George F. and Rankin, Hugh F. *Rebels and Redcoats*. New York, 1957.

Sparks, Jared. *The Writings of George Washington*. 12 vols. Boston, 1858.

Spaulding, Oliver L. *The U.S. Army in War and Peace*. New York, 1937.

Tharp, Louise H. *The Baroness and the General*. Boston, 1962.

Trevelyan, Sir George O. *The American Revolution*. 6 vols. London, 1909–1914.

Upton, Emory. *The Military Policy of the United States.* Washington, D.C., 1917.

U.S. Army. *The Army Lineage Book; Infantry.* Washington, D.C., 1953.

Varg, Paul A. *Foreign Policies of the Founding Fathers.* Baltimore, 1963.

Ward, Christopher. *The War of the Revolution.* 2 vols. New York, 1963.

Index

Ackland, Lady Harriet, 224–25
Adams, John, 37
Adams, Samuel, 4, 11, 20
Albany (N.Y.), 66, 77–78, 85, 89, 91, 99
Alexander, William (Lord Stirling), 49–50, 94, 96–97, 104–5
Allen, Ethan, 30–31, 245
André, John, 159–62, 245–46
Arbuthnot, Marriot, 150–52, 246
Armand, Charles (Armand-Charles Tuffin, Marquis de la Rouerie), 151, 156–57, 196, 246
arms and armament
  American, 191–92, 241–42
  British, 200
  French, 217
  German mercenaries, 206
  naval, 218
Armstrong, John, 94, 102, 106–7, 246
Armstrong, John, Jr., 246
Arnold, Benedict, 246–47
  as British officer, 175, 212
  Canada invasion, 30–33, 227
  Gates quarrel, 100–1, 108–9
  New York campaigns, 56, 58–59, 80, 87, 93, 99–101, 108–11
  treason of, 159–62, 199, 228
Arnold, Peggy Shippen, 161, 228
Articles of Confederation, 14
Austria, 242

Bahamas Expedition, 36–37, 222
Baltimore, Continental Congress flight to, 14, 45
Barney, Joshua, 221–22, 247
Barry, John, 222, 248

Barras, Louis de, 178, 181, 247
Baum, Friedrich, 89–90, 248
Beaumarchais, P. A. Caron de, 241
Bemis Heights (Second Saratoga) (N.Y.), 99, 101, 107–11, 229, 236
Bennington (Vt.), 84, 89–91
Biddle, Nicholas, 248
Bingham, William, 59–60
Bissell, Daniel, 248
Bland, Theodorick, 94–95, 248–49
Bonhomme Richard, cruise of, 141–46
Bordentown (N.J.), 71, 73
Boston, 19, 35–36, 39–40
  pre-Revolutionary, 4–6, 8, 11–12
  Massacre, 4
  siege of, 22, 26–28, 189
  Tea Party, 4, 11
  Tories, 28, 212
Brandywine (Pa. and Del.), 92–97, 198–99, 208, 212, 213–14
Brant, Joseph, 85–87, 249
Breymann, Heinrich C. von, 81, 90–91, 100, 110
British Army (*see also* names, engagements), 199–204
  mercenaries (*see also* Mercenaries [with British]; names of officers), 205–11
  Tories in, 211–15
  women camp followers, 223–26
British Navy, 218–22, 242
  colonies as supply sources, 8, 34, 139–41
  French and Indian War, 3
  Lake Champlain, 56–59, 81, 82

British Navy (*cont'd*)
New England coast, 19, 22–24, 35–36, 129–32, 139–41
New York (City) area, 44, 45, 47, 65, 92, 137
raids on England and, 114–17, 143–46
Southern campaigns, 38–42, 92, 151–52, 178–81, 185
West Indies, 60–61, 124
Brodhead, Daniel, 249
Brooklyn Heights (N.Y.), 47–50
Broughton, Nicholas, 35
Brown, Thomas, 214
Buford, Abraham, 153, 249
Bunker's (Breed's) Hill, 21–25
Burgoyne, John, 9, 77–78, 249–50
Canada, 32, 39, 205, 209
New York campaigns, 81–84, 86–87, 89–93, 97–101, 107–11, 209, 236
women camp followers, 224–25
Burr, Aaron, 227, 250
Bushnell, David, 42, 44, 250
Butler, John, 212, 250
Butler, Richard, 138, 251
Butler, Walter, 251

Cadwalader, John, 71, 73–75, 251
Cambridge (Mass.), 21, 227
Camden (N.C.), 153–59
camp followers, women, 223–29
Campbell, Archibald, 147, 251
Campbell, John, 239–40, 251–52
Campbell, William, 163, 252
Campbell, Lord William, 38–39
Canada, 12, 39, 77–78, 97, 99
contingents from, 94, 109, 196
French Canadians, 29, 31, 196, 238
invasion of, 29–33, 212, 227
Tories, 212
Carleton, Sir Guy, 31–32, 78, 252
casualties, total American (*see also* specific engagements), 192–93
mercenaries, German, 206–7
Catherine II, 242
Chad's Ford (Pa. and Del.), 94–97, 208
Charles III, 236–37, 241

Charleston (S.C.), 8, 40–42, 150–55, 184, 214
Charlestown (Mass.), 21–24, 26
Charlotte, Fort (Mobile Bay), 239
Chesapeake Bay area, 92, 94, 176–81
see also place names
Chew House, 104–5
Choiseul, Etienne François, Duc de, 235
chronology of American Revolution, 299–302
Church, Benjamin, 252
Clark, George Rogers, 132–35, 238, 252–53
Cleveland, Benjamin, 163, 253
Clinton, Fort, 228
Clinton, George, 54, 253
Clinton, Sir Henry, 159–60, 208, 213, 253–54
Northern campaigns, 38–42, 48–49, 92, 108, 123–28, 136–37, 176, 208, 213–14, 226
Southern campaigns, 147, 150–54, 164, 176–78, 184–85
Clinton, James, 254
Collier, Sir George, 140
colonies
boundary disputes, 7
deterioration of British relations, 4–6, 10–13, 233–34
economy, 7–8
government, 10–15
life style, 8–10
population, characteristics of, 6–7
see also names of persons, places
Committee of Secret Correspondence, 14, 233, 241
Committees of Correspondence, 4, 11–13
Committees of Safety, 5, 12, 13
Concord, 6, 12, 19–21
Congress of Confederation, 15
Congress, U.S., 15
Connecticut, 42
boundary dispute with Pennsylvania, 7
contingents (*see also* names of officers), 53–4, 99, 189–90, 193–94

Constitution, 15
Continental Army, 12, 45–46, 52,
    70–71, 74–75, 123, 125, 189–
    99
  ancestors of National Guard units,
    193–94
  casualties, 192–93
  commands, 13, 15, 25–26, 30, 39–
    40, 63, 155, 159, 164
  Conway Cabal, 14–15, 118–20,
    135, 198, 254
  firearms, 191–92
  mercenaries, foreign, 195–96
  volunteers, foreign, 196–99
  Von Steuben, training by, 121–
    23, 128
  women camp followers, 227–29
  see also engagements, state con-
    tingents, names of officers,
    specific subjects
Continental Congress, First, 5, 12
Continental Congress, Second, 12–
    15, 47, 60, 113
  Articles of Confederation, 14
  Burgoyne "Convention" re-
    pudiated, 111
  Continental Army and, 12–13,
    15, 25–26, 30, 39–40, 45–46,
    129, 139, 155, 159
  Continental Navy and, 14, 36–37,
    59, 111
  Conway Cabal, 118–20
  evaluation of, 15
  French Canadians appealed to by,
    29
  membership, 15
  mercenaries, use of commissioned
    by, 195
  Olive Branch Petition, 13–14
  recruiting, European, 197–98
Continental Navy, 14, 26, 34–36
  Bahamas Expedition, 36–37
  Bonhomme Richard cruise, 141–
    46
  casualties, 193n
  French ships (see also France,
    Navy), 117, 141–42
  hero, first, 59–61
  Lake Champlain, 56, 58–59
  Ranger cruise, 111–17
  Reprisal cruise, 59–61

Southern campaigns, 151
submarine, first, 42–44
"Convention Army," 9, 110–11, 225
  see also Burgoyne, John; engage-
    ments
Conway, Thomas, and Conway
    Cabal, 14–15, 118–20, 135, 198,
    254
Conyngham, Gustavus, 222, 254–55
Cooper River (S.C.), 151–52
Corbin, Margaret, 228
Cornwallis, Lord Charles, 208, 255
  Northern campaigns, 47, 49–50,
    53, 60–63, 67–68, 73–76, 95,
    97, 102, 106, 126–27
  Southern campaigns, 38, 150, 153–
    54, 156–59, 162–64, 166, 169–
    78, 182–88
Cowpens (N.C.), 164–68, 171
Crown Point (N.Y.), 33, 59, 81
Crumer, Jane, 225
Cuba, 237–40
culture, colonial, 6–10
Cunningham, John, 166

Davis, Isaac, 20
Dawes, William, 19, 255
Dayton, Elias, 255
Dayton, Fort (N.Y.), 85–87
Deane, Silas, 14, 113, 197, 241n,
    255–56
Dearborn, Henry, 99, 109
Declaration of Independence, 14
De Grasse, Count François J. P.,
    177–81, 185, 216, 218n, 220,
    229, 263
De Kalb, Johann, 154, 156–58, 198,
    269–70
De Lancey, James, 256
De Lancey, Oliver, the Elder, 212,
    256
De Lancey, Oliver, the Younger, 256
Delaware contingents (see also
    names of officers), 63, 157–58,
    165, 191
Delaware River, 70–71, 73–76, 94,
    102, 107, 196
Demont, William, 256
Denmark, 242
Denison (Dennison), Nathan, 257
De Peyster, Abraham, 214, 257

De Peyster, Arent Schuyler, 257
D'Estaing, Comte Charles H. T.,
  129–32, 148–49, 216, 229, 259
Destouches, C.-R.-D. Sochet,
  Chevalier, 257
Detroit (Mich.), 132–35
Deux-Ponts, Guillamme, Comte,
  183–84, 257
Dickinson, John, 13
Donop, Carl Emil Kurt von, 257–58
Dorchester Heights (Mass.), 26–28
Dunmore, John Murray, Lord, 36,
  213
Duportail, Louis le Beque de Presle,
  198, 258

East Florida, 220
  Loyalists in, 213
  see also Florida
economy, colonial, 7–8
education, colonial, 9–10
England
  deterioration of colonial relations,
    4–6, 10–13, 233–34
  France and, 3, 124, 129, 235
  impact of American Revolution
    on, 233–42 passim
  raids on, 113–17, 143, 222
  Seven Years' War, 3, 219, 235–37
  see also British Army; British
    Navy
Europe, impact of American Revolution on, 233–42
  see also names of countries
Eutaw Springs, 175

Family Compact, 237
Fanning, David, 213
Ferguson, Patrick, 152, 162–64,
  214–15, 259
Fermoy, Mathias A. de Roche, 81,
  82, 198, 259
Flamborough Head (England), 143–
  46, 222
Fleury, François Teissedre de, 138,
  198–99, 289
Florida, 220, 237–40
Floridablanca, José Moñimo y
  Redondo, Conde de, 236–37
Forman, David, 104, 106–7, 259–
  60

forts, see specific names
Fox, Charles James, 208
Foye, Hannah, 224
France, 60–61, 113–14, 117, 135
  alliance, 15, 111, 123–24, 133
  England and, 3, 124, 129
  impact of American Revolution
    on, 233–37
  Navy, 129–32, 141–43, 148–49,
    176–81, 216, 219–20, 229, 236
  officers, volunteers (see also
    names), 196–99
  Seven Years' War (French and
    Indian War), 3, 219
  troops in American forces, 148–
    49, 176–78, 182–85, 215–17
  West Indies, 59–61, 124, 235–
    36, 241–42
  women camp followers, 229
Francis, Ebenezer, 83–84
Franklin, Benjamin, 9, 10, 13, 141,
  194, 233
  France and, 14, 60, 113, 117,
    120, 236, 241n
Fraser, Simon, 81–84, 90, 99–100,
  108–10, 166–67, 224, 260
Frederick the Great, 208
Freeman, Douglas Southall, 198
Freeman's Farm (First Saratoga)
  (N.Y.), 97–101, 209
French and Indian War, 3, 29
French Canadians, 29, 31, 196, 238

Gadsden, Christopher, 4, 44
Gage, Thomas, 6, 19, 21, 22, 26,
  189, 260
Gálvez, Bernardo de, 134, 220, 237–
  40, 260–61
Gansevoort, Peter, 85–86, 261
Gates, Horatio, 13, 164, 261
  Arnold quarrel, 100–1, 108–9
  Conway Cabal, 14–15, 118–20
  Northern campaigns, 80, 87, 99–
    101, 107–11
  Southern campaigns, 155–59
George III, 3, 10, 12–14, 21, 77,
  205, 207, 234–35
George, Fort (Fla), 240
Georgia, 12, 13, 147–50, 195
  contingents, 165–68, 191
Germain, Lord George, 77–78

Germantown (Pa.), 102–7
Gibault, Father Pierre, 133–34
Girty, Simon, 262
Gist, Mordecai, 157–58, 262
Glover, John, 63, 71, 99, 110, 196, 262
government, colonial, 10–15
Grand Portage (N.Y.), 85
Grant, James, 48–49, 106, 262–63
Grasse, François Joseph Paul, de. See De Grasse, Count François
Graves, Sir Charles, 22, 24
Graves, Thomas, 178–81, 185, 263
Green Mountain Boys, 30–31, 83–84, 90–91, 192
Greene, Nathanael, 13, 161–62, 263–64
    Northern campaigns, 47–48, 63, 65–69, 71–72, 94–97, 104–6, 119, 121, 128
    Quartermaster General, 123
    Southern campaigns, 155, 159, 165, 169–75, 195, 197
Greene, Mrs. Nathanael, 228
Grey, Charles, 264
Grimaldi, Jeronimo, 236
guerrillas, 154–59
Guilford Courthouse (N.C.), 169–75

Hale, Nathan, 55, 264
Hale, Col. Nathan, 83–84
Halifax (N.S.), 45
Hamilton, Brig. Gen., 81, 100–1
Hamilton, Alexander, 72, 119, 121–22, 158, 161, 184, 192
Hamilton, Henry ("Hair-Buyer"), 132, 134–35, 245
Hampton (Va.), 8
Hancock, John, 12, 15
Hand, Edward, 62, 265–66
Harlem Heights (N.Y.), 52–55, 61
Harnage, Henry, 224–25
Haslet, John, 63–64
Hays, Mary Ludwig (Molly Pitcher), 128, 228–29
Hazen, Moses, 94–96, 196, 266
Heath, William, 13, 47, 63, 66, 266
Heister, Leopold von. See Von Heister, Leopold
Helm, Leonard, 133–34

Henry, Patrick, 11, 133
Herkimer, Nicholas, 85–87, 267
Hessians, see Mercenaries (with British); names of officers, engagements
Hobkirk's Hill, 175
Hood, Samuel, 179
Hopkins, Esek, 36–37, 111, 222, 267
Hopkins, Steven, 37
Hopkinson, Francis, 226
Hortalez (Rodrique), et Cie., 236, 241–42
Howard, John E., 165–67, 174
Howe, Richard, 45, 47–48, 50, 129–32, 220, 267
Howe, Robert, 147, 267–68
Howe, Lord Robert, 38
Howe, Sir William, 38, 77–78, 87, 125, 226, 268
    Chesapeake Bay area, 92, 94–96
    Massachusetts, 23–28
    New Jersey, 71, 73, 92
    New York area, 38, 42, 50, 53, 55, 61–67, 71, 97, 205, 208
    Pennsylvania, 102–5, 107, 117
Hubbardton (N.Y.), 82–84, 90–91
Hudson River Valley, 7
    campaigns, 65–69, 77–78, 91–93, 99–101, 107–8, 110, 136–39, 159–62
    see also place names
Huger, Isaac, 149, 151–52, 169, 268
Hutchinson, Thomas, 11

Illinois, 132–35
Indians, 81, 85–87, 89–90, 109, 132, 134–35
"Intolerable" or "Coercive" Acts, 5, 11
Ireland, 114, 117, 142
Irazabal, José Cabro de, 239–40

Jameson, James, 160–61
Jay, John, 233
Johnson, Guy, 268–69
Johnson, Capt. Henry, 60
Johnson, Lt. Col. Henry, 137–39
Johnson, Sir John, 85–88, 212, 269
Jones, John Paul, 37, 111–17, 141–46, 222, 269

Kalb, Johann. *See* De Kalb, Johann
Kaskaskia (on Mississippi), 132–33
Kentucky, 133
King's Mountain (N.C.), 162–64, 212, 214–15
Kips Bay (N.Y.), 52
Kirkwood, Robert, 270
Knowlton, Thomas, 53–54, 270
Knox, Henry, 26–27, 105, 161–62, 270
Knox, Mrs. Henry, 228
Knyphausen, Wilhelm, Baron von, 67–68, 72, 95, 97, 126–27, 150, 205, 208–9, 271
Kosciusko, Thaddeus, 80, 99, 198, 271

Lafayette, Marquis de, 119, 125, 127–28, 131–32, 161–62, 176–78, 179, 198, 271–72
Lake Champlain, fighting around, 29–30, 33, 56–59, 77, 80–83, 92
    see also names of persons, places
Lancaster (Pa.), Continental Congress in, 14
Landais, Pierre, 142, 145, 272
Laurens, John, 121–22, 272
Learned, Ebenezer, 99, 109–10
Lee, Arthur, 14, 113, 241*n*
Lee, Charles, 13, 39–41, 63–66, 124–29, 272–73
Lee, Ezra, 44
Lee, Fort (N.J.), 62–63, 66, 68
Lee, Henry ("Light-Horse Harry"), 171, 197, 273
Leslie, Alexander, 172–74, 273
letters of marque, 221
Lexington, 12, 20
Leitch, Andrew, 54
life-style, colonial, 8–10
Lincoln, Benjamin, 63, 93, 108–9, 147–55, 184, 273–74
Little Egg Harbor, 195
Livingston, James, 99
Long Island (N.Y.), 44–51, 196, 208
Loring, Elizabeth, 226
Loring, Joshua, 226
Lossberg, von, 72
Louis XVI, 235–37, 241

Louisiana Territory (Mississippi Valley) (Spanish), 132–35, 233–39
Lovell, Solomon, 140
Loyalists, 5
    see also Tories; names of persons and places
Lunenberg (Nova Scotia), 221

Machias (Me.), 34–35
MacLean, Allan, 212
MacLean, Francis, 140
Magaw, Robert, 65–69
Maine, 30, 34–36, 139–41
Maitland, John, 148
Marion, Francis, 154, 159, 194, 274–75
Martin, Josiah, 38–39
Maryland, 7
    contingents (*see also* names of officers), 49–50, 54, 104, 157–58, 165, 173–74, 189, 191, 194
    Tories, 214
Massachusetts, 10–11, 140, 233–34
    Committees of Correspondence, 11–12
    Committees of Safety, 13, 23
    contingents (*see also* names of officers), 19–28, 63, 71, 83, 85–86, 99, 108, 190, 193–94, 196, 229
    deterioration of British relations, 4–6, 10–12
    fighting in, 12, 19–28
    Loyalists or Tories, 5, 11, 28, 212
    "Patriots," 5
    privateers, 35, 221
    Provincial Congress, 12
    "Resolves" against Coercive Acts, 5
    see also Boston, names
Mathew, Edward, 62–68
Mawhood, Charles, 75–76, 275
Maxwell, William, 94–97, 105, 275
McCall, James, 166
McDougall, Alexander, 11, 13, 104, 274
McDowell, Charles, 162–63, 165–66
McLane, Allen, 274
medical science, colonial, 10

mercenaries (with Americans), 195–96

mercenaries (with British), 205–11, 241
  Florida, Spanish campaign in, 238–39
  New Jersey area campaigns, 71–74, 126–27
  New York and Hudson Valley campaigns, 45, 47–49, 53, 64, 67–69, 81–85, 89–91, 99–101, 108–11
  Pennsylvania area campaigns, 95, 97
  Southern campaigns, 148–49, 172–73
  women camp followers, 224–26
  see also names of officers

Mercer, Hugh, 72, 75–76, 275

Mifflin, Thomas, 275–76

Miles, Samuel, 48

militia and minuteman (*see also* names of officers, states; engagements), 5, 20–23, 189

Minute Men, The (Galvin), 189n

Mississippi Valley, 132–34, 237–39

Mobile Bay, 238–39

Mohawk Valley, 77, 85–87, 212

Molasses Act, 4

Monmouth Courthouse (N.J.), 123–29, 192, 228–29

Monroe, James, 276

Montgomery, Fort, 23

Montgomery, Richard, 13, 30–32, 276

Montreal, 30–33

Morgan, Daniel, 30–32, 93, 99–100, 109–10, 164–71, 194–95, 238, 276–77

Moultrie, William, 40–41, 148, 277

Murray, Earl John, 38

Musgrave, Thomas, 105

National Guard, Revolutionary War antecedents of, 193–94

naval action (*see also* British Navy; Continental (U.S.) Navy; France, Navy; Privateers), 218–22

Netherlands, 111, 236
  impact of American Revolution on, 233–34, 240–42

Neutrality Agreement, 242

New Brunswick (N.J.), 71, 76

New England
  contingents (*see also* names of officers, states), 53–54, 75, 80, 189–91
  culture and economy, colonial, 6–10
  see also place names

New Hampshire contingents (*see also* names of officers), 83–84, 90–91, 99–100, 108, 110, 131, 189, 191

New Hampshire Grants, 30, 84
  boundary disputes, 7
  contingents (*see also* names of officers), 21, 24, 30
  see also Vermont

New Jersey
  campaigns in (*see also* place names), 62–63, 66, 68–77, 92–93, 123–29, 190, 196, 208–9
  contingents (*see also* names of officers), 104, 191

New Orleans, 238–39

Newport (R.I.), 37, 129–32

New York (City) and area
  campaigns in and around, 45–55, 61–69, 89, 92, 108, 123, 125, 129–30, 136, 150, 176–79, 186, 208–9, 228
  fire in Manhattan, 55
  radicalism, 11
  submarine attempt on British fleet, 44
  Tories, 51, 212–13

New York (State)
  boundary dispute with Vermont, 7
  contingents (*see also* names of officers), 85–86, 99–100, 191–92
  fighting in, 93–94, 107–11, 136–39
  Tories, 85–86, 212–14
  see also Hudson River Valley; Lake Champlain; New York (City), place names

Nixon, John, 99, 277

Noailles, Louis Marie, Vicomte de, 277
North Carolina, 38–42, 153–57, 162–75, 214–15
  contingents (*see also* names of officers), 40, 151, 162–64, 165–68, 172, 191
  Tories, 212
North, Lord, 13, 205, 234, 241
Northwest Territory, 132–35
Nova Scotia, 3, 221

O'Brien, Jeremiah, 34–35, 278
O'Hare, Charles, 172–74, 278
Ohio Valley, 132–35
Olive Branch Petition, 13, 14
Oriskany (N.Y.), 85–87
Ottendorf, Barron, 195–96

Paris, Treaty of (1763), 235, 237
Parker, Sir Hyde, Jr., 147, 242, 278
Parker, John, 20, 192, 278
Parker, Sir Peter, 38, 41–42, 278–79
Parsons, Samuel Holden, 279
Paterson (Patterson), James, 279
Paterson, John, 81, 99, 110
Patriots, 5
  Continental Army (*see also* Continental Army; engagements, names), 189–99
  see also names
Pearson, Sir Richard, 143–45, 222, 279
Penn, Richard, 13
Pennsylvania, 94–97, 117–23
  boundary dispute with Connecticut, 7
  contingents (*see also* names of officers), 30, 33, 48, 62, 70, 76, 102, 189–90, 194, 196, 227
  navy, 221–22
  see also place names
Penobscot (Me.), 139–41
Percy, Lord Hugh, 19, 21, 67–68, 279
Philadelphia, 8, 65–66, 77, 89, 92–94, 123, 125, 226
  campaigns around, 14, 102–7, 226–28
  Continental Congress, 12, 14, 15
  contingents, 194

radicalism, 11
  Tories, 213–14, 226, 228
Phillips, William, 81, 108, 280
Pickens, Andrew, 154, 166–67, 280
Pigot, Sir George, 24–25, 280
Pinckney, Thomas, 280
Pitcairn, John, 20, 280–81
Pitcher, Molly (Mary Ludwig Hays), 128, 228–29
Pitt, Fort, 133, 192, 238
Pitt, William, 208, 234
Plessis, Maduit du, Chevalier de, 281
Pollock, Arthur, 238
Pollock, Oliver, 134
Pomeroy, Seth, 13
Poor's Brigade, 81, 99–100, 109–10
population, colonial, 6–7
Portugal, 242
Powell, Brig. Gen., 81
Prescott, Samuel, 19
Prescott, William, 23–25, 194, 281
Prevost, Augustine, 147–48, 214, 281
Prevost, James Mack, 281
Princeton (N.J.), 73–76, 190
Pringle, Thomas, 57–59
privateers, 34–35, 140, 196, 221–22, 236
Provincial Congress (Massachusetts), 12
Prussia, 242
Pulaski, Casimir, and Pulaski's Legion, 148–49, 195–96, 198, 281
Putnam, Israel, 13, 24, 46–49, 50, 52, 54, 63, 65, 282
Putnam, Rufus, 63, 282

Quebec, 29–33, 227

radicalism, colonial, 11–12
Rall, Johann Gottlieb von, 64, 72, 282
Randolph, Peyton, 12, 15
Ranger, cruise of, 111–17
Rawdon, Lord (Francis Rawdon-Hastings), 214, 282
Reed's New Hampshire regiment, 24–25
Reed, Joseph, 54, 283
regionalism, colonial, 7, 10
Reprisal, cruise of, 59–61

Revere, Paul, 19, 140–41, 283
Reynals, Anne, 224–25
Rhode Island, 37, 129–32
    contingents (*see also* names of
        officers), 21, 189, 191
Richelieu River Valley, 29–30
Riedesel, Baroness Frederica C. L.
    von, 224–26, 283
Riedesel, Friedrich Adolph von, 81–
    82, 90, 100–1, 108–10, 205,
    208–29, 283
Robinson, Beverley, 213
Rochambeau, Count Jean B. de,
    176–81, 199, 215–16, 229, 284
Rodney, George, 218, 220
Rogers, Robert, 212, 284
Rogers's Rangers, 113, 212
Ross, James, 95–96
Russia, 242
Rutledge brothers, 11
Rutledge, John, 40, 148, 151

Sackville, Fort (Ill.), 133–35
St. Clair, Arthur, 72, 81–84, 162,
    284–85
St. Eustatius (W.I.), 241–42
Saint-Jean (Can.), 30–31, 33, 57,
    78, 81
St. Lawrence Valley, 29–33, 38, 78
St. Leger, Barry, 78, 84–87, 89, 91,
    97, 285
Saint Simon, 216
Saltonstall, Dudley, 140–41, 285
Sampson, Deborah, 229
Santo Domingo, 235, 237
Saratoga (N.Y.)
    First (Freeman's Farm), 97–
        101, 209
    Second (Bemis Heights), 107–
        11, 229, 236
Savannah (Ga.), 147–50, 195,
    216–17
Schott, Paul, 196
Schyler, Hon Yost, 87
Schuyler, Philip John, 13, 30, 56,
    80, 86–87, 89, 285
Schuykill River (Pa.), 102–4, 117
Scotland, 114–17, 142–43
secret service, 160
Seven Years' War, 3, 219, 235–37
Sevier, John, 162–63, 285–86

Shelby, Isaac, 162–63
Shuldham, Molyneaux, 27
Simcoe, John Graves, 212, 286
Skene, Philip, 89
Skenesboro (N.Y.), 56, 82–84, 89
Skinner, John, 286
slave trade, 8
Smallwood, William, 49–50, 104,
    106–7, 157–58, 194, 286
Smith, Francis, 19–21, 286–87
Smith, William, 160
South Carolina, 148, 150–54, 162
    contingents (*see also* names of
        officers), 149, 166, 191
    fighting in (*see also* place
        names), 37–42
    Loyalists, 36–37
    radicalism, 11
Southern colonies, 7, 8–9, 11
    see also names
Spain, 111, 218, 220
    Florida, 220, 237–40
    impact of American Revolution
        on, 233–40
    Mississippi Valley, 132–35, 237–
        39
    Seven Years' War, 236
Specht, General von, 81, 100
Spencer, Joseph, 13, 46–47, 63
spies, 51, 55, 160
Stamp Act, 4
Stanwix, Fort (N.Y.), 85–87
Stark, John, 24–25, 90–91, 110, 287
Staten Island (N.Y.), 45, 47
Stephen, Adam, 72, 94, 96–97, 104,
    106, 287
Steuben, Friedrich Wilhelm Augus-
    tus von. *See* Von Steuben,
    Friedrich
Stevens, Edward, 157, 173, 287
Stirling, William Alexander, Lord,
    49–50, 94, 96–97, 104–5, 288
Stony Point (N.Y.), 136–39, 199,
    213
Stuart, Duncan, 173–74
submarine, 42–44
Suffolk (Mass.) "Resolves," 5
Suffren de Saint Tropez, Pierre
    Cendre de, 220, 288
Sugar Act, 4
Sugar Loaf (N.Y.), 80, 82

Sullivan, John, 13, 63, 75–76, 94–
  96, 104–6, 130–32, 288–89
  Canada invasion, 32–33
  Middle Atlantic campaigns, 46–
    49, 56
Sullivan's Island (S.C.), 38–42, 71–
  72
Sumter, Thomas, 154, 156, 159, 289
Sunbury, Fort (Ga.), 148–49
Sweden, 242

Tallmadge, Benjamin, 160
Tarleton, Banastre, 152–54, 156–59,
  163, 166–68, 214–15, 289
taxation issue, colonial, 3–5, 7, 11–
  12
Ternay, Charles Louis d'Arsac,
  Chevalier de, 290
Thomas, John, 13, 32, 290
Thompson, William, 32–33, 194, 290
Thomson, Charles, 11
Throg's Neck (N.Y.), 62–63
Ticonderoga, Fort (N.Y.), 26–27,
  30, 33, 56, 80–83, 99, 108, 198
Tories, 5, 11, 28, 37, 40, 51, 85–86,
  89–90, 211–15
Townshend Acts, 4
trade, colonial, 8
Trenton (N.J.), 69–73, 190, 196,
  208
Trois Rivières (Can.), 32–33
Tronson de Condray, Philippe
  C. J. B., 290
Turtle (submarine), 42–44
Tryon, William, 290–91

Valcour Island (N.Y.), 56–59
Valley Forge (Pa.), 14, 117–23,
  128, 228
Varnum, James M., 291
Vergennes, Charles Gravier, Comte
  de, 235
Vermont
  boundary dispute with New York,
    7
  contingents (*see also* names of
    officers), 30, 83–84, 90–91, 192
  see also New Hampshire Grants;
    place names
Vincennes (Ill.), 132–35

Virginia, 7, 36, 38, 133, 175–85
  Committees of Correspondence,
    11
  contingents (*see also* names of
    officers), 30–32, 40, 135, 151,
    157, 165–68, 171–74, 189–90,
    193, 197
  radicalism, 10–11
  Tories, 213
  see also place names
volunteers, pro-American, 197–99
  Canadian, 197
  French, 196–99
  Polish, 148–49, 151, 195–96, 198
  Prussian, 198
Von Bose, Col., 172
Von Heister, Leopold, 47–49, 205,
  208, 266
Von Steuben, Baron Friedrich W.A.,
  121–23, 162, 175–76, 192, 198–
  99, 298

Ward, Artemas, 13, 22–24, 227, 291
Warner, Seth, 83, 90–91, 192, 291–
  92
Warren, Joseph, 5
Washington, Fort (N.Y.), 62–69,
  228
Washington, George, 233, 292–93
  Arnold treason and, 161–62
  Boston siege, 26–28
  bodyguard, 194
  Canada invasion, 30
  Commander-in-Chief (*see also*
    specific campaigns, engage-
    ments), 13, 14–15, 26, 118–20,
    155, 189
  Conway Cabal and, 118–20
  evaluation of, 15
  Hessian conscripts, 209
  Middle Atlantic campaigns, 39,
    44–47, 49–55, 61–76, 92–97,
    102, 105–6, 124–28, 136–38
  navy, 35–36
  southern campaigns, 154–55, 175–
    78, 182–85
  volunteers, foreign and, 197–98
  women camp followers, 225, 227–
    29
Washington, Martha, 228

Washington, William, 153, 165–68, 173–74, 195, 294
Waxhaws, massacre of, 153–54, 163
Wayne, Anthony, 94–97, 104–6, 125, 127–28, 137–39, 175–76, 294
Webster, James, 172–74
Weedon, George, 54, 96
West, fighting in, 132–35
West Indies, 3, 235–42 *passim*
  Bahamas Expedition, 36–37
  Reprisal cruise, 55–61
  slave trade, 8
West Point (N.Y.), 159–61, 192
Weyness, James, 212
Whig Party (British), 234
Whitehaven (Scotland), 115–17
White Plains (N.Y.), 61–65

Wickes, Lambert, 59–61, 222, 294–95
Wilkinson, James, 135, 295
Willett, Marinus, 86, 295–96
Williams, Otho Holland, 156–58, 173, 296
women
  camp followers, 223–29
  education, colonial, 9–10
Woolsey, Melanthon Lloyd, 296
Wooster, David, 13, 32, 296

Yankee-Pennamite War, 7
York (Pa.), 14
Yorktown (Va.), 176–80, 182–85, 196, 199, 212, 215–17

Zenger, Peter, 11